The Survival Guide to DB2 Universal Database for Client/Server

Concepts,
Design,
Programming,
and Reference

V. Mitra Gopaul

UnityWorks.com
Newmarket, ON

The Survival Guide to DB2 Universal Database for Client/Server
    Concepts, Design, Programming, and Reference

Published by UnityWorks.com
    P.O. Box 21541
    17600 Yonge Street
    Newmarket, Ontario Canada L3Y 8J1

Printed in Canada

Products and services that are referred to in this book may be either trademarks and/or registered trademarks of their respective owners. The Publisher and Author make no claim to these trademarks.

While every precaution has been taken in the preparation of this book, the Publisher and the Author assume no responsibility for errors or omissions, or for damages resulting from the use of information contained herein. In no event shall the Publisher and the Author be liable for any loss of profit or any other commercial damage, including but not limited to special, incidental, consequential, or other damages.

Canadian Cataloguing in Publication Data

Gopaul, V. Mitra
    The Survival Guide to DB2 Universal Database for Client/Server
        concepts, design, programming and reference

Includes index.
ISBN 0-9682976-1-7

   1. IBM Database 2 (Computer file) 2. Database management. I. Title.

QA76.9.D3G66 1998   005.75'85
        C99-900024-1

Copy editor: Pat Verge

About the Author

V. Mitra Gopaul is an independent consultant based in Ontario, Canada, offering his expertise to such major international companies as Merrill Lynch, IBM, XEROX, and the Royal Bank of Canada. Active for more than 25 years in the data processing field, he currently specializes in software development and database administration. He has extensive experience in relational databases including DB2, Oracle, and Informix. He has also written many computer books including *DB2 2.1 for OS/2 Made Easy* and *IBM Mainframe Programmer's Desk Reference*.

By the same author

Personal Computers in the Bahá'í Faith
C Programming in The MVS Environment
IBM Mainframe Programmer's Desk Reference
Developing C/C++ Software in the OS/2 Environment
OS/2 Programmer's Desk Reference
DB2 2.1 for OS/2 Made Easy

Contents

Chapter 11: DB2 Command Line Process Commands 243

Preface

Man is the supreme Talisman... The Great Being saith: Regard
man as a mine rich in gems of inestimable value. Education can,
alone, cause it to reveal its treasures, and enable mankind to
benefit therefrom.

Bahá'u'lláh

DB2 is very powerful software to manage information in a relational database. It is widely used in many operating systems; it is made up of many members of IBM's family of relational database management systems (RDBMS); some of the members are DB2 for OS/2, DB2 for MVS running on the mainframe computers; DB2 for AIX (IBM's version of UNIX); DB2 for HP-UX; DB2 for Solaris; DB2 for Windows 95, Windows 98, and Windows NT; and DB2 for AS/400 (midsize computer).

DB2 uses some of the most advanced techniques of computing and database management. It comes with distributed database features that allow it to easily communicate with other members of DB2 regardless of local or remote connection. It harnesses the latest and most powerful hardware and software architectures, like parallel processing and disk arrays. But the most sought-after feature is that it can operate as a stand-alone RDBMS or it can function very comfortably as part of a client/server computing configuration.

After receiving a copy of DB2, you may want to install it on your computer and start playing with it immediately. Consider this: Before you can harness its power of data management, the first step is to understand the basics of a relational database, including the concepts of design and implementation of the database.

The Survival Guide to DB2 Universal Database for Client/Server, first, guides the reader in a step-by-step manner, illustrating through the basics of client/server architecture and the different pieces of software that are part of it. Next, it steps through many features of this powerful RDBMS — taking the reader through all the necessary tasks of designing, creating a sample database — all along showing how DB2 works. After covering the basics, this book explains in detail the concepts of distributed databases and how to write C, C++, COBOL, REXX, and JAVA programs in this complex environment.

■■■ About The DB2 Versions

Like any software, DB2 evolves with time and it has already gone through many changes of functions and names — from 1.0 through 6.0. The latest one is known as DB2 Universal Database. Also DB2 has gone through many versions; there are many improvements over older versions, but, as far as this book is concerned, the basic concepts apply to any version. In fact, this book is equally useful to users, developers, and administrators of any other members of the DB2 family.

■■■ About This Book

Most of the information found in this book can be found in manuals accompanying DB2 but scattered in many different places. When writing this book, I made an attempt to demystify two important concepts: client/server architecture and relational database management system (big words!). By presenting these two ideas in a simple form, you will not only derive the most out of DB2, but enjoy it too. And, this is precisely the objective of this book. If you are not too familiar with databases in a client/server environment, it can be oppressively frustrating to get started. Here, we try not to give you everything at once, which can lead to frustration and confusion. What we do is give you little by little all the information that you need on a particular aspect of DB2. In some situations, we visit the same topic more than once. It is not to bore you, rather to look at the same information — from a different angle — to acquire the understanding of a new concept.

■■■ How This Book is Organized

Chapters 1-2 describe the basic ideas of client/server that are applicable to a DB2 database. Chapter 3 is about how to run a DB2 client. Chapter 4 acquaints the reader with the basic concepts of a relational database management system. It describes the many different parts of DB2. Chapter 5 gets down to the interesting part of DB2: designing and creating a database. It covers the basic operations, such adding data to a database, changing existing records and purging the information you do not need, and finally viewing of the data in many different ways. Chapter 6 takes you through all the necessary steps of maintaining data in the database. In chapter 7, we discuss some of the advanced techniques of database management and queries.

Chapter 8 is about the middleware that is needed to run DB2 distributed databases. It covers three important standards: DRDA, ODBC, and JDBC.

Chapter 9 describes steps needed for C, C++, COBOL, REXX, and Java programs to work with a DB2 database. For embedded SQL programing, it discusses how to use cursors and dynamic SQL. Also, it gives information on how to precompile, compile, bind, and link such programs. A similar approach is taken for the development of REXX or Java applications. Chapter 10 discusses all the built-in functions of DB2. Finally, Chapter 11 is a reference of all the DB2 CLP (Command Line Process) commands.

■■■■ A Word on Style

In the general format of the commands and statements used in this book, a few symbols are not part of the syntax and must *not* be included when you code or issue a command to your program. These symbols and their meanings are as follows:

Symbol   Meaning

[ ]   The option enclosed by the brackets ([ ]) is not required but can be included, for example, [and] are not part of the following command,

```
db2 [-f filename]
```

< >   Only one of the alternatives enclosed by the angle brackets (< >) must be chosen, for example,

```
CONNECT [TO <server-name or host-variable>]
```

or   The alternatives enclosed by the brackets (< > or [ ]) are separated by "or", for example,

```
CONNECT  [RESET]    or
     [TO <server-name or host-variable>]
```

```
[IN [SHARE or EXCLUSIVE] MODE]
```

_____ The underlined word is the default value.

... The horizontal or vertical ellipses indicate that the preceding parameter(s) can be coded more than once. This applies to variables, filenames, options, keywords, and so on, that are enclosed in brackets.

All keywords of the command syntax are written in uppercase characters; they can be in either upper or lowercase.

All strings in italic lowercase characters are variables that can be changed to any other strings to suit your style. In your code they represent values that you supply to the commands.

▮▮▮ Conclusion

In the back of every author's mind, there is a lingering question: "How will this book be received by the readers?" One can only try their best and hope that it is worth the money you paid for it.

Chapter 1
Introducing Client/Server Architecture

At this time in human history, changes are happening at an unprecedented rate globally. Some of them are happening in the fields of medicine, global economy, telephones, television, telecommunication, world trade, space travel, and many more. Only one thing is clear: change is the only constant. The computer industry is no exception; it evolves through many stages of growth just like many other human concerns. One emerging trend, something that deeply interests us, is that computing is at the heart of many of the world's transformations.

Over the past decade, the computing industry has been going through another movement called client/server. Although relatively young, the forces of client/server have touched every aspect of computing. Now, let's look at some of the reasons warranting this change.

▮▮▮▮ The Jurassic Age

Once, the mainframes roamed the Earth; they were the rulers of the computing world. They were housed in air-conditioned rooms with raised floors. Only trained operators, analysts and programmers ever worked with them. Usually users revered them with awe.

This kind of computing is known as the hierarchical or master-slave model. Simply, it means all the computing is done at one huge place with massive CPU power, with farms of disk and tape drives. The users were hooked to the mainframe through character-based 'dumb' terminals in an octopus-like fashion as shown in Figure 1.1.

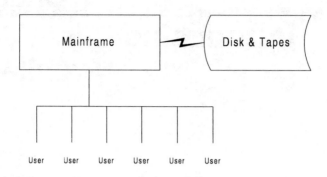

Figure 1.1 Mainframe Model.

As a DB2 user, developer or administrator, you didn't need be concerned with clients, servers, or distributed processing. In a way, life was much simpler. When problems occurred, all you had to do was call the vendor-supplied specialists who were usually on site. They would be busy resolving the problem and the users just raised their hands and said, "computer is down." All computing was temporarily suspended. Everyone was resigned to it; that's the way it was.

One main disadvantage of such a model is the centralized processing; the traditional IT (information technology) department dictated the needs of the users. As computing needs grew, the end-users got more frustrated because of long delays in software development and resolving problems, often compounded by cost over-runs.

▌▌▌▌ The Client/Server Era

In the 80s, PCs were introduced and within a short period, all kinds of user-friendly software were available for them. It made it easier to have computing on one's desk, rather than in a secluded place far away. Many software vendors, like Novell, Microsoft, Corel, Harvard Graphics, and Lotus, emerged as champions of desktop computing. Each passing year they brought to the market new, powerful software that dazzled the computing world. A new trend emerged as an alternative to mainframe computing.

Over a decade of usage, two kinds of hardware became prevalent: PC (Intel CPU-based) and Apple (MAC). In the software area, the driving force of the

PC revolution, hundreds of major companies sprung up and some, like Microsoft, Lotus, Novell, and WordPerfect, became major players.

In the meantime, desktop computing was proliferating at a phenomenal pace, which created many complexities and challenges. One was sharing resources like printers and disk space as departments could not justify giving every user all the equipment. It also meant sharing information from a central disk space. The next logical step in this evolution was LAN (local area network) with capabilities to share resources.

This gave birth to the client/server concept. A server is a software that manages the usage of a resource. In this LAN configuration, the client is the one requesting the service. Figure 1.2 gives a simple picture of a client/server architecture.

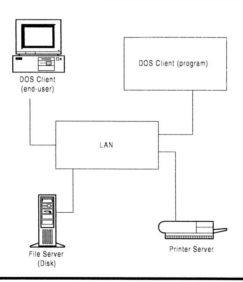

Figure 1.2 Clients, servers, and LAN

Here we have two servers: the printer server and file server. The printer server takes requests from an end-user, for example, to print a file using the DOS print command. Or, a program like WordPerfect requests to read or write to LAN disk files using the file server.

▉▉▉ Growing Up

In the client/server world, life can become very complicated; new kinds of servers are always being developed. Figure 1.3 shows seven servers, two of which are printer and file servers which we looked at earlier.

The database and transaction servers are of special interest to us. Here, we will briefly describe the purpose of each server.

File server. A file server processes requests from client (typically a PC) for file records over a network. File servers provide the facility to share disk space among network users. The files on the disk are shared repositories of documents, drawings, and other data objects.

Database server. A database server processes requests, issued by clients, to manage data in a database like DB2. The language of the client is SQL (structured query language, also called "sequel"), and upon processing a request, the server returns the result over the network. The DB2 clients are shrink-wrapped software or specialized programs that make such database requests.

Transaction server. A transaction server processes a request, issued by a client, to execute a remote procedure. The procedures always reside on the server that is connected to an SQL database engine that manages the information. The procedures are made of one or more SQL statements, and these grouped statements are called a transaction.

After executing the request, the server returns the result of the transaction through the network to the client. This is different from database server where the network exchange is made up of request/reply message for each SQL statement.

The transaction server is commonly used for online transaction processing, or OLTP. A typical transaction processing application consists of a client with a GUI (graphic user interface). The server component usually processes SQL transactions against a database.

Groupware server. Groupware server is another specialized server to manage information such as text, mail, bulletin, and work flow. The main purpose of this kind of client/server system is to allow people working together to be in direct contact with each other. Lotus Notes is an example of groupware software.

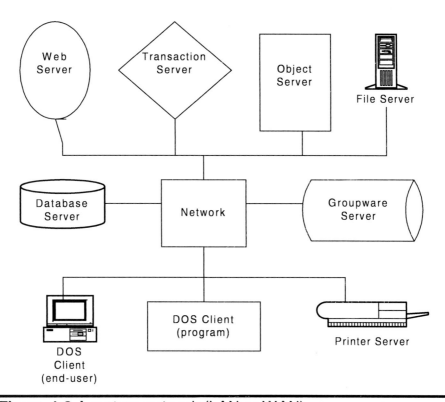

Figure 1.3 A mature network (LAN or WAN)

Object server. A set of communication objects is the backbone of the client/server application with object server. The client object exchanges information with the server object using the Object Request Broker (ORB). The client initiates a method or a piece of code on the server. The ORB has three main tasks: locate an instance of appropriate object server class, execute the requested method, and return the result to the client.

There are many implementations of ORB, such as Digital's Object Broker, IBM's SOM, and Sun's NEO. These and other vendors try to conform to the industry standard CORBA of Object Management Group.

Web server. The main task of a web server is to find documents requested by a client. The client, typically a web browser, communicates with the server using the HTTP protocol on top of TCP/IP.

■■■ Distributed Processing of Clients and Servers

Client/server computing emerged from the need to share resources by a group of people, namely, LAN users. To manage the resources, software is divided into two categories: clients and servers. In this environment, both kinds of software are equal, unlike the host-base computing model where a master-slave relationship exists among different components.

A server is defined as the one providing the service and a client is the requester of the service. The role of the application can be either or both — server and client — depending on its functionality. Clients and servers can reside on the same computer, but they can also be distributed among many computers across a network that could span a building or as wide as the whole globe. The distribution mainly depends on the computing requirement and throughput. For example, you can have a database server on one computer with a printer server. This depends on the configuration, computing power and hardware needs of a network.

The one thing obvious about client/server computing is that it can be distributed among clients and servers. In fact, not all clients and servers need be the same size. You can make your clients and servers as fat or light as you want. We will discuss how to choose the right size a bit later.

Another characteristics of client/server computing is that you can have a variety of products from different vendors. For example, you can have the LAN operating software from Novell, PC operating software from Microsoft, and database server from IBM, file server from any company, word processors from WordPerfect, computers from Compaq, and printers from HP, all working harmoniously in a client/server relationship. It makes client/server an open system, where you can have a mix of software and hardware from different suppliers, all working together to meet the business needs.

Distributed processing is not limited to a LAN where only a small group of users share resources. The scope can be expanded to connect many enterprise LANs in a WAN (wide area network). In fact, the most popular WAN is the Internet encompassing the whole globe. From your client, typically a Net browser, like Netscape, you can travel the Information Highway, hopping one web server to another. In fact, you don't know where the servers are located or the kind of operating system they are using, or what the hardware is. In fact, you may not even care.

Client/server distributed computing has revolutionized the computing world by first giving users computing power from their desk. And, through it, one can connect to countless networks strung together in a global web.

▮▮▮▮ Advantages

As you can see from our previous discussions, client/server computing is a meeting place of software and hardware. It seems like a complex system. To complicate matters a bit more, there is another layer of software, called *middleware*, which we will look at in the next chapter. This is a convergence of technologies and different products from various suppliers and presents a major challenge in ensuring the computing power is humming all the time. It is equally demanding to develop software for this environment to make sure all the components work together seamlessly. So, the big question is "why does business need this?" Why is client/server computing growing by leaps and bounds? Why the migration from mainframe to client/server? The answers lie in the many advantages it offers to the enterprise, and they are:

● One of the main driving forces of client/server is its promotion of an open and flexible environment where mix-and-match is the rule. This means one is not tied to any proprietary hardware or software. It allows a wide variety of platforms to participate, and consequently, major vendors like IBM, Microsoft, Oracle, and many more are key players in the client/server market. This also means competition keeps the price of computing low.
● The power of the PC has been constantly growing and prices keep coming down. Desktop computing is the other reason for client/server to flourish. It is putting mainframe-like computing power on top of a desk. And users like this trend. The users' likes and dislikes really dictate the success of any technology.
● On powerful workstations, the use of GUI and multimedia applications provides customers user-friendly, intuitive software.
● The client/server environment is a special kind of distributed process called cooperative processing. This allows data to be close to the processing of data. This means less traffic on the network and less expensive hardware for the network.

- It is flexible enough to expand from a small departmental LAN, to enterprise WAN to global network.
- It is also scalable. What does it mean? When needs arise, you can easily add more clients, hardware, servers.

■■■ Disadvantages

Everything is not perfect in the client/server land. To make this model work, you need many layers of software from many different vendors. This can be a challenge for the IS (information system) personnel, especially during down-time and when users are screaming and vendors are finger-pointing.

Distributed processing, especially with cooperative processing, tends to be more complex than non-distributed systems. A common situation is to try to resolve a big problem with oppressive complexity that makes the whole client/server system come to a halt. And this is not acceptable for mission-critical application that demands no down-time. One way to minimize the risk is to reduce a large problem into a set of smaller, interdependent systems, that are easier to manage.

The processing of an application has to be well distributed to achieve optimum throughput. Another common problem with client/server software is assigning a significant amount of logic to the server. When the number of clients hitting their servers with requests increases, it can create a significant bottleneck. The situation gets worse when the server is not given enough resources and the number of clients keeps increasing. A good design of the application with proper distribution of processing among different parts can resolve this problem.

■■■ Looking Ahead

Now that you have had a taste of the client/server world, what next? More changes, of course. This paradigm has a unifying force that is absorbing everything in sight. One time it was predicted that the mainframes were to disappear like the dinosaurs. Instead, the mainframe diehards, which one time existed in their own computing world, are coming back as networked entities, willing to exist with smaller systems like PCS and UNIX computers as equal partners. It is an open system that combines products and technologies from many vendors, such as IBM, Microsoft, and Novell, all working together to meet the needs of the business community.

What are some of technological buzz words? They are database warehouse, datamart, decision support systems, object oriented technologies, networked computers, and so on. Many of today's trends do become hard technologies of tomorrow. DB2, originally developed for the mainframe, has gone through many iterations of change. Now, it conforms more to the client/server model than its original appearance; consequently it is well positioned for the future. Another powerful force of today is the Internet which is based on client/server. All three of them — databases, Internet, and client/server—are converging, thus dividing computing entities into two categories: clients and servers. That's the way it is until the next evolution.

Chapter 2
How Client/Server Works

In the last chapter we briefly looked at the cooperation of processing achieved through the client/server model. The client initiates a request, the server returns the result after processing. This sounds simple but it is not, especially when a network can span several floors of a building or the world. *How does a client access the right server across the network? What are the rules of distribution processing between client and server? Are there standards to ensure quality software in such a heterogeneous ensemble of products? How is data shared among clients and servers running on separate machines?*

These and many more architectural questions will be answered in this chapter. We will learn about the building blocks of the client/server computing model with special attention to DB2 servers and clients.

Client/server is not a product, rather a method according to which distributed application programs are developed. The architecture of this model helps us identify the elements that can be used to build an application. DB2 database server is a product that is built according to the rules of this concept. Similarly, clients for DB2 are built by the same rules.

This chapter will give you the basic ideas of the architecture which are essential in understanding DB2 server and clients.

■■■■ Three Building Blocks

The complexity of client/server model can be reduced to three basic building blocks: a client, a server, and a slash (/ is for middleware) that keeps both talking to each other. Figure 2.1 gives a picture of these elements.

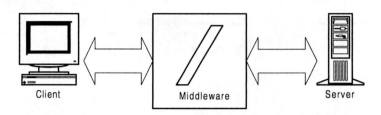

Figure 2.1 Three Basic Building Blocks of Client/Server Model

The client's task is to issue a request for service from a known server. The server processes the request and sends the results back to the client. The slash called the middleware is the glue that keeps the client and server together. Through it, the client finds the appropriate server and the server sends the desired data to the right client.

When is a server is not server? When it turns into a client. For example, the DB2 server becomes a client when it requests file management services from a file server.

Very shortly, we will discuss these three important architectural parts in more detail. Before we do that, let's quickly look at what kinds of applications we can build.

In the next few years, hundreds of millions of machines will be running C/S applications. An application is a self contained software product that performs clearly defined functions. In C/S software, these functions are distributed between client and server, each executing very specific tasks of the application. Since these two kinds of components can be distributed over several computers of a network, each place is called a node.

Next, we will highlight the flexibility of and scalability of client/server in three situations:

Small. A small size client/server application would reside on just one machine. One example would be a GUI interface as client that communicates with a single-user DB2 database. In this case, there is no need for the middleware. This would be appropriate for users of laptop or home desktop computers. The same machine can connect to the outside world servers for mail, data or fax. In this case, the middleware is simple, just the operating software, as shown in Figure 2.2.

```
┌─────────────────────────────┐
│                             │
│       Client/Server         │
│                             │
├─────────────────────────────┤
│                             │
│           O/S               │
│     Windows 95 or NT        │
│    OS/2, Unix, OS/400, etc. │
│                             │
└─────────────────────────────┘
```

Figure 2.2 Small size client/server installation

Medium. The medium architecture is the most suitable for LAN-based departments. It is the most popular and accounts for 80% of client/server installations. A simple example would be many clients managing a multi-user DB2 database. The middleware is kept simple. It can be used to manage inventory and accounts of a small business or department.

Large. A large client/server installation means many clients and servers. The servers could be database servers, Web servers, and ORB. Internet and Intranet are getting a lot of attention these days. As the needs grow, more servers can easily be added. The beauty of the client/server model is that it is upward scalable. It is possible to have many servers that can match the computing power of the mainframe, but at a low cost.

At this large scale, the power of multiserver can be through awesome middleware with low cost and high bandwidth. Such a network must have the following features: networking directory services, network security, remote procedure calls, and network timing services.

▌▌▌▌ Client

Generally, the main role of a client is to interact with the end-users. The client node is designed with functions that enhance the application capacity to meet the needs of the users. It takes advantage of the current software and hardware innovations. The modern workstations come with visual graphics, mouse, microphone, sound, fax/modem, pen-based input, full-motion video, interactive multimedia, and scanners. Usually clients are built to take advantage of these state-of-the-art devices and facilities to make software intuitive and user-friendly.

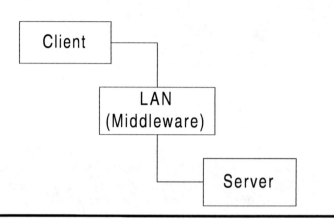

Figure 2.3 Medium size client/server installation

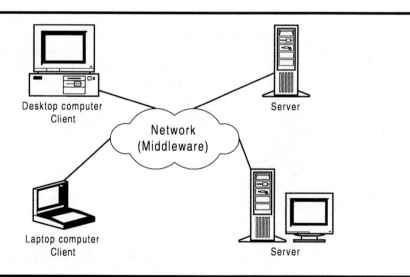

Figure 2.4 Large client/server installation

In the market place, there are many products that build client programs. Some are Visual Basic from Microsoft, PowerBuilder from PowerSoft, and Visual Age from IBM. All of them have the capabilities to implement the presentation logic of an application.

The other role of a client is to request a service from a server. For example, in a customer information application, the client would take a response from a user, request data from the DB2 database, and after receiving the information, present it on the screen. Therefore, some business logic is found in the client so that it knows what kind of requests to make. Typically, a client is a specialized piece of software. For example, a web browser is only used to access a web server. The look, touch, and feel of a customer information client would be different and perform differently than a web browser.

Sometimes a server is called a client when it requests service from another server. For example, a web server may access a DB2 database to get information. The change of role is only in technical terms. Generally, the clients specialize in providing the interface between humans and computers.

What are DB2 clients? Before answering this question, let's look at which operating environment they are most suitable for. Given the client role and functions, naturally the place for DB2 clients would be where the user senses can be most satisfied. They are Windows (3.11, 95, 98), DOS, and OS/2. They have good graphic interfaces and services that produce state-of-the-art clients. DB2 software comes with Client Application Enablers (CAE) for these platforms. We will discuss them in more detail later.

▓▓ Server

In a distributed application, while the client looks pretty, the server is the one slugging all the time to keep everyone happy, if it is designed properly. If not, first you will hear complaints from the users, then the managers, and if the project is canceled, you will see heads roll.

The complexity of the application cannot be underestimated. Servers must be carefully designed and constructed. They should perform, be scalable and available to meet the minimum business requirements.

A robust server must have the capability to manage the clients' requests in the worst cases, yet still meet the design objectives. Some of the characteristics are:

Patiently waiting. A server program is always waiting for a client to make a service request. The request, in the form of messages, comes from the communication infrastructure. At this point some servers initiate a session dedicated for each client. It is also possible to create a dynamic pool of reusable sessions. A server can also have a mix of dedicated and reusable sessions. After the processing is complete, the server passes the result to the appropriate client over the network. A successful server is the one that responds to a client immediately, especially when many requests come from many clients at the same time.

Prompt service. The server must not only respond to many clients, but it must complete the work and return the result promptly. Although possible, it is difficult to achieve acceptable response time with a single-threaded server process. A server that can concurrently execute multiple requests through multitasking can give the best performance during rush hour. Performance throughout the system is very critical to its acceptance among users. Generally, users will accept a few seconds response for every action. Considering high traffic during peak hours and multiple clients, it is recommended transactions be completed in sub-seconds, although it may not be the business requirements.

VIP clients. Not all clients are created equal. Some online transaction processor may require by design a very quick response, while other clients, such as reports or batch jobs, may tolerate slow service. The server must be capable of prioritizing clients' requests, executing with urgency first and, when time permits, it can take care of lower-priority tasks. In a multitasking environment, a server can respond better if it can run some of the less urgent tasks in the background.

Always available. Just like the mainframe data centers, today's servers are expected to be highly available. Some mission-critical applications deployed into a client/server environment are expected to be running all the time. This means that the servers must be robust. It also means that failures and recoveries are transparent and automatic. Even the operation of the server such as backup, recovery, starting and stopping processes, and user administration, all can be done online, with little or no down time.

Keeps growing. One of the main attractions of client/server platform is that applications, especially servers, are scalable. *What does this mean?* It means increase in capacities, performance, throughput, number of users, and so on, as needs arise. The increased demands are realized by adding resources without any change to the application. It is modular in a sense, like adding a room to a house as the family grows, without having to change the foundation.

A server must be designed to provide scalable performance. In other words, it should satisfy the current business requirements, and, in the future, it should be easy to expand. There are two ways of accomplishing this: through vertical scaling or horizontal scaling.

Vertical scaling of a server means you upgrade the hardware. It may mean increasing CPU power, and adding more memory or disk storage. Horizontal scaling is achieved by adding more servers to the application.

OS and The Servers. All the server characteristics that we just looked at are only realized if you choose the right operating system. Choose one that already has some of those fundamental qualities. Otherwise, client/server can be a big disaster; one with lots of bun and little meat. Or, it is like constructing a 10-story building on a 2-story foundation. Eventually, it will collapse. Let's look at some of the server operating system requirements:

- Multiuser.
- Preemptive multi-tasking. The ability to share CPU time and resources among many tasks evenly or based on priority.
- Multi-thread. This allows the server to process many requests, by assigning each work a separate thread. This allows concurrent processing of many client requests.
- Memory protection. This prevents multiple tasks from destroying each other.
- Scalability. It should be easy to add more servers, users, and resources.
- Availability/reliability. The operating system should be robust and should never go down — ideally. At least, it should not crash because of bad behavior of an application. When running mission-critical servers, availability and reliability are of utmost importance.

DB2 server is found on the following operating systems: OS/2, UNIX, Windows 95, Windows 98, and Windows NT.

▐▐▐▐ Middleware

Middleware is a new class of software, the key to distributed processing in a client/server architecture. It is the third building block that enables clients and servers to find and communicate with each other across the network regardless of its size. It is this component that takes a client request and passes it to the right server, and, after completing the work, the server sends the results through the middleware to the client.

Before any request or message circulates the network, a session, also called a connection, must be established to ensure that the server is listening and ready to do some work. From the client or server point of view, all these activities happen without their knowledge. In fact, they need not know how they happen. What does this mean? It is like picking up the phone and dialling a number. When the call is answered at the other end, you just established connect or session in client/server lingo. The parties exchange words like "Hello, hello," to confirm the connection. Then, the two parties have a conversation, sending messages back and forth.

But the participants do not need to know the workings of the telephone system: how the wires are connected or swishing happens. In this analogy, the persons at each end are client and server, and the telephone system is the middleware.

At the minimum, the client and server must have the communication software. In our telephone analogy, they are the handset and the dialler. The person you want to talk to can be next door or on the other side of the world; the process of communication is the same. The same principle applies to the client/server architecture; the network could be a LAN for a small group of people or WAN with nodes scattered around the world.

The middleware is also very flexible to accommodate many different types of applications with diverse servers, such as file, printer, server, OLTP, fax, mail, web, database, and so on. To keep all nodes talking to each other in a comprehensive manner in a wide selection of hardware and software, some standards have to emerge. This is exactly the trend. We will look at some of the standards very shortly.

The middleware has many layers of software, and the number varies from one installation to another. For example, a simple LAN would work with just two layers, but a distributed database across a WAN may need several layers. Here we will discuss three layers that are most appropriate for a distributed database in a client/server environment. They are transport layer, network operating system (NOS), and database services.

Transport layer

This layer is the foundation of the middleware software. Upon it other middleware layers are placed, and clients and servers are attached to it. It is the minimum requirement for a network. This transport layer is made of communication protocol, a kind of language that enables different parties to talk to each other. The protocols that DB2 understands are: IPX/SPX, NetBEUI, APPC, TCP/IP, and named pipes.

IPX/SPX. Novell is the owner of the IPX/SPX, the most popular network protocol. It is also the native protocol for Netware, a LAN protocol from Novell. IPX/SPX consists of two protocols: transport and network. IPX (Internet Packet Exchange) is the network layer. And, SPX (Sequence Packet Exchange) is the transport layer.

NetBEUI. This transport protocol is from IBM. It was mainly developed to work with NetBIOS, a network protocol for PC-based LAN. Sometimes NetBEUI is referred to as NetBIOS, but they are not the same, although they work together.

APPC. The APPC protocol is part of SNA (system network architecture) from IBM. SNA, a truly distributed operating system, was originally built around the mainframe. Now, Advanced peer-to-peer (APPN) creates a SNA network, but without the mainframe-centric hierarchy. The mainframe can be part of it just like another client or server node. APPN uses the APPC protocol for its communication.

TCP/IP. The TCP/IP protocols were developed to allow cooperating computers to share resources across a network. It was developed by a community of researchers centred around the ARPAnet. Certainly the ARPAnet is the best-known TCP/IP network. However, as of June, 1987, at least 130 different vendors had products that support TCP/IP, and thousands of networks of all kinds use it. It is also known as the "Internet protocol suite".

Named Pipes. The named pipes is another way of communicating between clients and servers that reside in the same computer. The exchange of data takes place through API programming in a file-like manner. Processes write and read data to a sequential file. By using named pipes, it is possible for a server to initial one pipe where many receiving clients can read from. The communication is highly reliable and its benefits are highly regarded among OS/2, Windows, and NT client/server programmers as they are part of the interprocess communication.

NOS layer

All the client and server nodes are assigned a node address. Just like a mail address, they are unique within a network. In a network with thousands or even millions of nodes, how does one find the right address? Who manages the directory? What about security? These and other functions will be discussed as part of the network operating system (NOS).

In the early days, the NOS were Netware 3.x and LAN Manager from Novell and Microsoft, respectively. Their main jobs were to share files and printers among DOS client workstations. Some newer servers — like Windows NT, OS/2 server, and UNIXes — are adding network functions that once belonged to separate products. These new functions are directory, security, and distributed files. These additions are suitable for local networks, but for global networks, more facilities are required.

For a truly global network with many architectures, protocols, and operating systems, one standard has emerged. It is Distributed Computing Environment (DCE) from X/Open (formally from Open Software Foundation). In the NOS industry, DCE is an interesting and important development; all the vendors in the open computing market, like Hewlett Packard, IBM, DEC, and Microsoft, are supporting it. In fact, many new versions of OS or NOS are implementing parts of the DCE architecture. In this network-centric computing world, the newer versions of OS will look more like DCE. It includes six key technologies: remote procedure calls, directory service, time services, distributed file system, security services, and thread services (see Figure 2.5).

The importance of the DCE standard is that it gives a framework for many different pieces of hardware and software, from different vendors, to co-exist in a coherent heterogeneous client/server environment. We will briefly describe these technologies. While reading the following sections you will notice that DCE is a collection of the best software from various vendors rather than building it yourself from the ground up.

Remote Procedure Calls. When you make a telephone call, you need a number, and regardless of the distance — whether it is next door or across the world — the calling method is the same. The caller dials a number. After the number is punched, a series of activities takes place under the cover, without the notice of the caller. In the computing network, it is RPC (remote procedure calls) that is responsible for hiding the intricacies of the network calls. To the user, it looks like an ordinary procedure call. When a client requests a service, basically it calls a function or procedure on a remote server and waits for an answer to arrive. The RPCs are synchronous, which means that the client that issued the call must suspend its operation until the result arrives. When a call is issued, the RPC mechanism does the following:

- Collects values for the function parameters
- Forms a message
- Sends the message to the remote server
- Sends the results to the caller after the server has executed the procedure

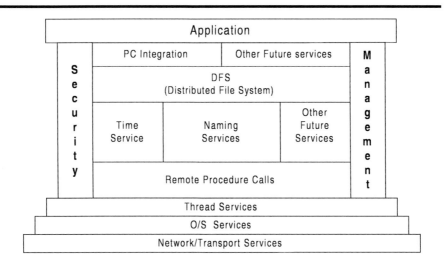

Figure 2.5 DCE Structure

To achieve all these steps, RPC adds pieces of code on the client and server. RPC provides an *Interface Definition Language* (IDL) that is used to describe the functions and parameters of the server exported to its clients.

The IDL compiler takes this information to produce RPC source code. The source code, also called *stub*, comes in two pieces, one for the client and the other for the server. Finally, the stubs and client code and server code are linked together to produce the client software as shown in Figure 2.6.

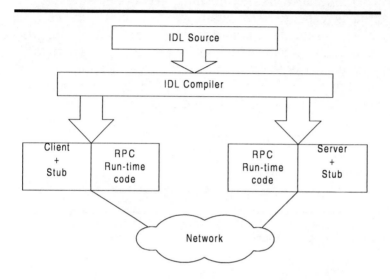

Figure 2.6 IDL compiler generating RPC code and stub

The client stub does the following:

- formats parameters in an RPC packet
- converts data
- sends the requests using the RPC runtime library to the server
- waits for server's reply

The server stub does the following:

- receives the request
- unpacks the parameters
- calls the procedure
- formats the results
- sends the results to the client

The DEC RPC is an adaptation of Hewlett Packard Appolo RPC.

Directory Services. So far we have not answered one fundamental question. How does one find the location of a server? This information is found in the DCE directory servers. This service conforms to the Open System Interconnection (OSI) X.500 world wide directory service standard. It contains information about resources, such as programs, servers, disks, and print queues, and they are called objects. Each object entry in the directory has attributes to describe the object. The directories are organized in a hierarchical order; each directory may contain objects or other directories, just like DOS or UNIX file directories.

DCE divides this distribution environment into smaller units (or domains) called *cell.* A cell consists of client and server workstations, defined by the users. A DCE cell must have at least one Cell Directory Service (CDS).

At a higher level, there is the Global Directory Service (GDS) for a worldwide network. Between the local and global levels, information is passed through the Global Directory Agents (GDA), as shown in Figure 2.7.

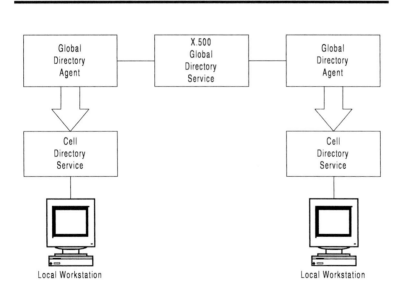

Figure 2.7 Global directory service

All the names in the GDS and CDS are collectively called a *namespace*. The namespace is extensively used by other DCE parts, such as security server, RPC mechanism, and distributed file system. DCE naming services is an adaptation of Digital's DECdns and Siemen's DIR-XX.500.

Time services. The main function of the time services is to synchronize the clocks of all the network nodes to a recognized time standard. The main task of the time servers is to periodically check one another's clock and make adjustments, if needed. The time services come from Digital's Distributed Time Service.

Distributed File System (DFS). The DFS allows a user from one system to connect to one network, to use or change files of another system. In the client/server architecture, the user accessing the storage device is the client and the system where the data is stored is the file server.

When a client requests a file, a copy of the data is stored, or *cached*, in the client system where it can be read or changed. Any modified data at the client site is propagated to the server or any other client using the same file.

DFS allows files to be distributed across a network. Files are considered a resource, therefore, file entries are placed in the namespace of the directory server; DFS uses the DCF security and RPC. The distributed file system came from Transarc's Andrew File System.

Security Services. The DCE security services is called Kerboros to protect the network from intruders. Kerboros is a three headed dog that guards the gates of Hades according to Greek mythology. Like the three heads of the Kerboros monster, the security system consists of three parts: authentication server, security server, and privilege server.

The authentication server is mainly responsible for validating the identity of a client, for example, a user or program. It ensures that the identity is authentic and not one who is pretending to be someone.

The security server maintains a database of clients and associated passwords. In a network, each DCE cell must have a security server in a physically secured place.

The privilege server manages the access level of resources. It maintains users and programs and their privileges to use the facilities. The security server is an adaptation of MIT's Kerberos authentication system.

Thread Services. The ability to run many tasks simultaneously is one of the fundamental characteristics of a network computing environment. Obviously, DCE provides this main function through the thread services. DCE adopted the Concert Multithread Architecture (CMA) from Digital.

This portable thread software runs in the user's space, but calls native thread routines of the OS, such as OS/2, NT, and UNIX.

The DCE thread APIs conform to the POSIX 1003.4a thread standard. This package takes advantage of a multiprocesser environment using shared memory. Semaphores are used to synchronize threads and share memory among them.

Database layer

The database layer is used to make distributed database requests across a network. Several standards have emerged over the years, but there are three that are of particular interest to us. They are DRDA, ODBC, and JDBC:

Distributed Relational Database Architecture (DRDA) is IBM's standard for distributed databases. It is promoting DRDA among many vendors to accomplish federated database interoperability. So many database and gateway vendors, the likes of Oracle, Sybase, Micro Decisionware, IBI, XDB, and Borland, now support DRDA. But DRDA is most popular among DB2 family members; it is the glue that ties them together.

Open Database Connectivity (ODBC) is from Microsoft as a Windows API standard to access SQL databases. In 1992 when it was released, its original objective was to access databases through Windows application. Since then it has made wider appeal and now it is avilible in many platforms, including Windows 3.11, Windows 95, Windows 98, Windows NT, OS/2, Mac, and Unix. Many database vendors, like Microsoft, IBM, Oracle, Sybase, Tandem, and Informix, all support ODBC in their products.

Java Database Connection (JDBC) was first released in March 1996, jointly prepared by Oracle, Sybase, Informix, Sun, and many others. It is a set of Java classes that interfaces to an SQL database, very much like ODBC.

The application of these three standards is discussed in Chapter 8.

▐▐▐ Standards

An open client/server environment, as we just saw, encourages many different technologies, operating systems, layers of middle software that bring all together. Of course, to build an infrastructure with all these different pieces coming from many different vendors is a major challenge. Today, customers want their enterprise system to look wholesome, tying together all their systems regardless of platforms and vendors.

Naturally, when deciding to build a client/server system, one has to look at the interconnectivity or interoperability. Interoperability simply means that products from multiple vendors should be able to talk with one another. It also means applications can be built regardless of operating system or hardware. It avoids locking into a vendor-specific system. The open system should allow scalability as the business needs grow.

To do all these successfully, one has to ensure vendors are conforming to industry standards. Otherwise, it will be time consuming and costly to maintain. We have already looked at some industry standards, for example, DRDA, ODBC, COBRA, Open/X DCE, and so on. There are several organizations that play key roles in defining standards in the open system world. They are:

POSIX (portable operating system interface) for computer environment, from IEEE TCOS, defines consistency across operating systems.

X/Open plays a role in defining compatibility among systems; therefore, it has created Common Application Environment (CAE).

ISO (International Organization for Standards) develops and promotes various standards. One of them is OSI (Open Systems Interconnection).

OMG (Object Management Group) defines framework for object-oriented technology.

OSF (Open Software Foundation) provides technologies for open system environment.

▐▐▐ The Big Picture

This Chapter describes the three main components — client, server, and middleware — of the client/server architecture. Here the level of detail only gives a very basic description of the system, by no means an exhaustive one. There are more aspects of client/server that we have not discussed here. It is a vast subject and numerous good books have been written about it. Here the intention is to discuss the environment essential for DB2 clients, servers, and middleware to function together. Figure 2.8 shows a big picture, combining the parts touched upon so far.

Clients (DCE)	**DB Services** ———————— ODBC, DRDA	Server (DCE)
	NOS ———— DCE	
	Transport Layer ———————— TCP/IP, Named Pipe, APPC	

Figure 2.8 Big picture

These are the parts required to build distributed applications and databases in a local and global network. One aspect of client/server is that it is an evolving model. It is a maturing environment and, as it endures, more software and technologies will be added. The discussion so far is only to prepare you for the following chapters.

Chapter 3
DB2 Clients

In the previous chapters we looked at three important building blocks (client, server, and middleware) which are the essential parts of any client/server application. From now on, we will look at how this software model applies to the DB2 database and applications designed around it.

What is a DB2 client? It is software that accesses a DB2 database server. The DB2 server is a product from IBM and we use it as it is. However, the clients are built by software vendors and developers to access the DB2 database. The clients provide user friendly interfaces to the data. Therefore, DB2 comes with all the utility programs to build these client programs. This chapter discusses the building tools and setup to run a DB2 client.

A client can be developed in many operating systems, such as DOS, Windows 3.11, Windows 95, Windows NT, and many UNIX (AIX, HP-UX, and Solaris) flavors. Here we will discuss clients for Windows and OS/2, the two most popular DB2 client platforms.

▋▋▋ Two Clients

There are two DB2 clients that are available for OS/2, Windows (3.11, 95, and 98). They are *DB2 Client Application Enabler* (CAE) and *DB2 Software Developer's Kit* (SDK).

The application enabler is available to you when you install the DB2 products for Windows and OS/2 and they are:

- DB2 SDK for Windows
- DB2 Single-User for OS/2
- DB2 Server (OS/2 and AIX)
- DDCS Single-User for OS/2

• DDCS Multi-User Gateway (OS/2 and AIX)

The SDK is a development kit to build DB2 clients. In the following sections we will discuss the relationship between the Client Application Enabler and Software Developer's Kit.

■■■ What is DB2 Software Developer's Kit (SDK)?

The SDK is a set of tools and environment needed to develop client applications that access DB2 database servers. These servers must be accessible through the Distributed Relational Database Architecture (DRDA), a standard that we will look at later. Once developed, the programs can either run SDK or DB2 Client Application Enabler as a DB2 client.

The SDK comes with the following:

• Precompilers for C, C++, and COBOL languages. This also includes sample programs with embedded SQL and header files.
• Programming libraries and header files to develop applications with Call Level Interface (DB2 CLI).
• Support to write software in REXX language (only for OS/2 platform).
• Interactive interface with the database through the Command Line Processor to perform SQL statements.
• DB2 Client Application Enabler to build client applications.
• ODBC driver to DB2. This is useful for applications developed with the Microsoft ODBC Software Developer's Kit.
• Documentation on how to use database manager Application Program Interface (API).
• MVS Flagger: A tool that identifies embedded SQL statements in software that are not supported by DB2 for MVS.
• DBA utility tools and Visual Explain.

■■■ What is a DB2 Client Application Enabler?

After a client application is built with the SDK, the Client Application Enabler supplies the run-time software that enables the application to access a DB2 database for OS/2, AIX, HP-UX and Solaris. Through DDCS, to be discussed in Chapter 8, an application can also access DB2 databases in MVS/ESA, VSE,

VM, and OS/400. In addition, a client application can also access non-DB2 databases that conform to the DRDA standard.

It contains the following functions and utilities:

- Runs client application consisting of C, C++, or COBOL programs with embedded SQL, API, or DB2 CLI. It also has ODBC drivers for applications developed with Microsoft ODBC Development Kit.
- Binds a package to a target database.
- Imports data into the database.
- Exports data from the database.
- Catalogs and uncatalogs database and communication protocol, such as, IPX/SPX, NetBIOS, and TCP/IP.
- Lists directories.
- Connects to a remote server.
- Manages database configuration.
- Accesses online information for commands and messages.
- Sends database usage information to DRDA servers.
- Uses **User Profile Management** (UPM) to manage users.

Some of these functions are performed through the **Command Line Processor**.

▌▌▌ Invoking the Command Line Processor

The **Command Line Processor** (CLP) is a program that interfaces the user to the DB2 database. Many of the commands discussed in the following pages are issued through CLP. It can be started in two ways. One is through the DB2 icon. First open the DB2 folder and then click on the **Command Line Processor** icon. Alternately, you can run the program by issuing the command **db2w -tv** from Windows Program Manager or **db2** from the OS/2 command prompt.

Either way, the Command Line Processor is started in interactive mode and you will see the prompt:

```
db2 =>
```

This means the interface is ready to receive any database commands. You can issue any of the commands discussed in Chapter 11. To exit from this program, just enter **quit** or **terminate**. Also you can get further information on any of these commands by issuing a question mark (?) followed by a command, for example,

```
? BIND
```

In the interactive mode, you can issue an operating system command by prefixing it with an exclamation mark (!), for example, **!DIR** for OS/2 or **!ls** for UNIX. To exit from the interactive mode, enter QUIT or TERMINATE at the input prompt. After execution, the DB2 command returns one of the following return codes:

Code	Description
0	Successful
1	Select or fetch statement returned not rows
2	DB2 command or SQL statement warning
4	Encountered error while processing DB2 command or SQL statement
8	DB2 system error

● **Syntax**

```
DB2 [- option)]...
      <db2_command or sql_statement> [\]
      [-- comment ]
        or
DB2 [?phrase or ?message_number
      ?sqlstate or ?class-code]
```

● **Parameters**

option determines the feature the function that DB2 is to perform. The following shows a list of options, followed by the default state of each option and a brief description. The letter to indicate the option can be in lower or upper case, for example, -A is the same as -a. If you invoke DB2 without any option, it goes into the interactive mode. Also, any number of these options can be assigned to the DB2OPTIONS environment variable.

Option	Default	Description
-a	OFF	Display SQLCA data

-c	ON	Automatically commit SQL statement
-e{C or S}	OFF	Display SQLCODE or SQLSTATE. These two options are mutually exclusive.
-f*filename*	OFF	Read the commands from a given file.
-l*filename*	OFF	Log the command to the specified history file.
-o	ON	Display output data and messages to the standard output.
-p	ON	Display a command line process or prompt when in interactive input mode.
-r*filename*	OFF	Write output to a file.
-s	OFF	Stop process if errors occur while executing commands in input file or interactive mode.
-t	OFF	Use the semicolon (;) as the end of a command or statement.
-tdx	OFF	Use 'x' as the end of a command or statement.
-v	OFF	Echo the command to the standard output.
-w	OFF	Display SQL statement warning messages.
-z*filename*	OFF	Write the output, including any messages or error codes, to a file.

db2_command is used to specify the DB2 command you want to execute.

sql_statement is used to specify the SQL statements.

comment is the comment string which is followed by -- (two dashes). The comment is ignored by db2 when processing an SQL statement.

? is used to obtain general help (assistance) information.

?phrase is used to obtain help information on a specific command, such as an SQL statement or topic.

?message_number is used to get a description of a specific message number. A message number is prefixed with one of the following three-character codes.

- DBA — messages for the database administrator
- DB2 — DB2 messages
- SQL — SQL messages

?sqlstate is used to get information about a valid SQLSTATE.
?class_code is used to get information about a valid class code.

● **Example**

In the next example, the SQL statement is used to insert a row in the CLIENTS table. Since there is a -C (suppress commit option), this addition to the database will not become permanent. The -t option indicates that this statement is ended with a semicolon.

```
db2 -C -t INSERT INTO RBA.CLIENTS
        (NAME, CITY, POSTAL_C, PROV)
  VALUES ('RBC','NEWMARKET','L3X1F0','ONTARIO');
```

In the following command, the report data which results from executing the **SELECT** statement is written to the C:\BOOK\OS2REF\CLIENTS OS/2 file. Note that the -t option is missing; therefore, the first line is terminated with a backslash (\), indicating the continuation of the statement into the next line.

```
db2 -R C:\BOOK\OS2REF\CLIENTS SELECT *   \
        FROM RBA.CLIENTS;
```

Let's say we place the next statement in the **select.sql** file.

```
SELECT * FROM RBA.CLIENTS;
```

You can process this statement by giving the following command:

```
db2 -fselect.sql
```

In this case, the -f option tells DB2 to read **select.sql** as the input.

DB2 Client Setup

DB2 Client Setup is a GUI for setting up communication, binding utility files, and changing the database configuration. It is available to you after installing CAE or SDK. To get to it, click on the DB2 icon and then you will see all the items in the DB2 folder, including **Client Setup**, as shown in Figure 3.1.

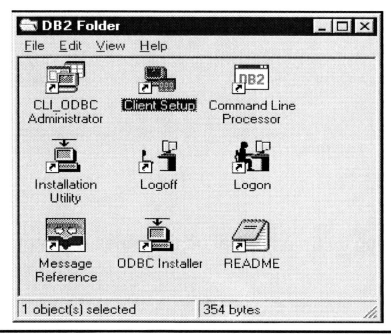

Figure 3.1 The DB2 Folder

Setting up Communication to Access a Local Database

Local database access means that a Windows or OS/2 client application and the DB2 database are on the same workstation. For example, you may want to use a relational database for OS/2 from a WIN-OS2 environment and both are found on the same computer. Also for this arrangement to work, you must have the same version of Application Enabler for Windows and DB2 for OS/2.

With the client and server being physically together, the communication channel is the OS/2 name pipe. To activate this name pipe, you have to add a token to the environment variable DB2COMM on the server side. For example, if the database is only accessed locally, then set the variable in the following way:

```
DB2COMM=NPIPE
```

However, if the server database is used locally and remotely, then you can add more protocol to the variable, for example,

```
DB2COMM=NPIPE,TCPIP
```

DB2 allows you to merge directories of Windows client and DB2 for OS/2. If directories for both are combined, there is no need to catalog the nodes or database.

On the other hand, if you are not using merged catalog, you need to register both the node and database using the command line processor. The commands, discussed in more detail later, are:

```
catalog local node
catalog local database
```

∎∎∎ Setting up Communication to Access a Remote Database

A remote database is on a separate computer than the client application. This necessitates establishing a communication channel between them. As seen in the previous chapter, this channel is made of hardware and software called middleware. The software is the communication protocols that allow a client to talk to a server. These protocols have already been previously discussed in detail and here we will show how to set up the communication on both Windows client and remote DB2 database server.

DB2 server supports the following communication protocols:

- APPC
- IPX/SPX
- NetBIOS
- TCP/IP

The setup can be done in two ways. One is through **DB2 Client Setup** program and the other is through DB2 **Command Line Processor**. It is the administrator's responsibility to set up the communication channel and, once done properly, the middleware is transparent to the user of the client software. One way of checking to see if it is working is for the application to issue a **connect** command to the database.

For each protocol, the following lists the information required for setup and the steps to be executed at both the server and client nodes.

APPC

Information	Description
db2node	A name that you decide identifies the server node, for example, **DB2APPC1**.
sym_dest_name	The symbolic destination name of the remote server node, for example, **NYSERVER**.
database_name	The name of the remote database.
security	The type of APPC security to be used for the connection. The possible choices are NONE, SAME, or PROGRAM. The default is PROGRAM.

Step	Server	Client
1	Set up the environment variable DB2COMM. For example, **DB2COMM=TCPIP,APPC** will enable two protocols.	

Step	Server	Client
2	Create or update the following profiles, only applicable for token ring LAN setup: • Local node characteristics profile • LAN DLC profile • Transaction program definition profile(s) • Mode definition profile	
3		Update the following profiles needed by the client to communicate with a DB2 server or a DDCS for OS/2 multi-user gateway server over a token-ring network: • Local node characteristics profile • Token Ring or Other LAN Types DLC adapter parameter profile • Adapter list profile • Connection to a peer node profile • Partner LUs profile • CPI communications side information profile • Mode definition profile All these changes are done using **Communication Manager**. When a local node starts an APPC connection, the local LU is used as the default LU. Normally, this LU is the same as the node name (control point name) that is configured for the client computer. Optionally, you may want to explicitly specify a local LU.

Step	Server	Client
4	Update the database manager configuration, for example, by issuing the command: **update database manager configuration using tpname NYSERVER**	
5		Catalog the APPC node through **DB2 Client Setup** or by issuing the command: **catalog appc node** In either case, you will need the *db2node*, and *sym_dest_name*.
6		Catalog the database through **DB2 Client Setup** or by issuing the command: **catalog database**

IPX/SPX

Information	Description
db2node	A name that you decide identifies the server node, for example, **DB2IPX1**.
fileserver	The name of the NetWare file server where the database server is registered, for example, **NETWSRV**.
objectname	The object name that represents the database server, for example, **DB2INST1**.
database_name	The name of the remote database.
socket	A hex number that represents the connection end point, for example, **87A2**. It must be unique for

each DB2 server instance and among IPX/SPX applications running on one DB2 server workstation.

Step	Server	Client
1	Set up the environment variable DB2COMM. For example, **DB2COMM=TCPIP,IPXSPX** will enable two protocols.	
2	Update the database manager configuration, for example, by issuing the command: **update database manager configuration using fileserver NETWSRV objectname DB2INST1 socket 87A2**	
3	Register the DB2 server on the Netware file server	
4		Catalog the IPX/SPX node through **DB2 Client Setup** or by issuing the command: **catalog ipxspx node** In either case, you will need the *db2node*, *fileserver*, and *objectname*.
5		Catalog the database through **DB2 Client Setup** or by issuing the command: **catalog database**

NetBIOS

Information	Description
nname	The workstation of the client node, for example, **CLIENT1**.
db2node	A name that you decide identifies the server node, for example, **DB2NET1**.
server_name	The workstation name of the remote database server node, for example, **DB2INST1**.
adapter	The logical LAN adapter number of the adapter at the client workstation, for example, 0.
database_name	The name of the remote database.

Step	Server	Client
1	Set up the environment variable DB2COMM. For example, **DB2COMM=TCPIP,NETBIOS** will enable two protocols.	

2	Update the database manager configuration, for example, by issuing the command:
	  update database
	  manager
	  configuration using
	  nname DB2INST1	

Step	Server	Client
3		Update the database manager configuration, for example, by issuing the command: **update database manager connfiguration using nname CLIENTS** This step could also be done through the **DB2 Client Setup** program.
4		Catalog the NetBIOS node through **DB2 Client Setup** or by issuing the command: **catalog netbios node**
5		Catalog the database through **DB2 Client Setup** or by issuing the command: **catalog database**

TCP/IP

Information	Description
db2node	A name that you decide identifies the server node, for example, **DB2TCP1**.
hostname	The TCP/IP name of the remote database server node, for example, **TCPHOST**.
service_name	The TCP/IP service name for the server instance, for example, **DB2INST1C**.
database_name	The name of the remote database.

Step	Server	Client
1		Determine the IP address of the host, for example, for **TCPHOST** it might be 198.96.129.198.
2	Set up the environment variable DB2COMM. For example, **DB2COMM=APPC,TCPIP** will enable two protocols.	
3	Update the service file. Each database manager instance must have one entry, for example, by adding the following: **DB2INST1C 3700/tcp**	
4		Update the service file, for example, by adding the following: **DB2INST1C 3700/tcp**
5	Update the database manager configuration, for example, by issuing the command: **update database manager configuration using svcename DB2INST1C**	
6		Catalog the NetBIOS node through **DB2 Client Setup** or by issuing the command: **catalog tcpip node**
7		Catalog the database through **DB2 Client Setup** or by issuing the command: **catalog database**

■■■ Running a DB2 Client Program

Before you can run a DB2 client application, there are several steps that need to be taken before it will work. As we saw earlier, one of the main tasks is to set up the communication channel between the client program and the DB2 server. The database could be local or remote to the client application and the setup must be done accordingly.

On both client and server sides, you also have to catalog the databases and nodes, which could mean specifying the communication protocol and updating the configuration files.

You must also verify that the configuration parameters in the database manager configuration file (db2system) and the environment keyword in db2.ini (for Windows) are set correctly.

Before your client program will run, you must ensure that proper database user ID and password is set up. The database engine must be running, which can be accomplished by issuing the db2start command.

You also have to bind the utilities to the database. Finally, you need to run the application programs.

■■■ Binding the Database Utilities

Before a utility or application program can access a database, its bind files must be associated with a particular database. Even the database components, such as **IMPORT**, **EXPORT**, **REORG**, the **Command Line Processor**, **DB2 CLI**, and the binder program, all have associated bind files that must be bound to each database before they can be used with that database. The bind files are grouped together in different **LST** files, each one being specific to a server.

There are two ways of binding the database components to a database, either by using the **DB2 Client Setup** or **Command Line Processor**. The bind files are found in a subdirectory BND of SQLLIB, for example, **\SQLLIB\BND.**

The following commands are issued using CLP to bind two files. First, change the directory to where the bind files are located, for example, SQLLIB\BND directory and issue the following commands:

```
CONNECT TO oneworld
BIND @db2ubind.lst MESSAGES bind.msg GRANT PUBLIC
BIND @db2cli.lst MESSAGES clibind.msg GRANT PUBLIC
CONNECT RESET
```

where

oneworld is the name of the database to which you wish to connect.

db2ubind.lst and **db2cli.lst** are the bind files

bind.msg and **clibind.msg** are the output message files

GRANT PUBLIC grants **EXECUTE** and **BIND** privileges to **PUBLIC**.

When binding files there are a few points to note:

- The BIND command must be run separately for each database that you wish to access.
- If you have different levels or types of clients coexisting on your network, you must bind the utilities from each type of client.
- The utilities only have to be bound to each database once from each type of client.
- The **db2ubind.lst** file contains the list of bind (.bnd) files required to create the packages for the database utilities. The **db2cli.lst** file contains the list of bind (.bnd) files required to create packages for the DB2 CLI and the DB2 ODBC driver.
- Binding may take a few minutes to complete.

▐▐▐▐ Utilities

The following is a list of some useful utility programs that are issued at the command line or in the batch file of a client operating environment. Each provides a brief explanation and the format for how to use it.

Log on DOS or Windows database client

The **SQLLOGN2** command is used to log on to DB2 DOS or Windows database client.

- Syntax

```
SQLLOGN2 [userid [/P=password or *]]
```

- Parameters

  userid is used to specify a valid user ID on the DOS or Windows database client.

  There are a few restrictions on this user ID:

  - It must be unique and no longer than eight characters.
  - It must not start with IBM, SQL, or SYS keywords.
  - It cannot end with the $ character.

  /P=*password*
  This parameter is used to enter the password belonging to the user ID.

  password is made up of 4 to 8 characters.

Start DOS or Windows database client

The **STARTDRQ** command is used to start a DOS or Windows database client.

- Syntax

```
STARTDRQ
```

Stop DOS or Windows database client

The **STOPDRQ** command is used to stop a DOS or Windows database client.

- Syntax

```
STOPDRQ
```

Log off DOS or Windows database client

The **SQLLOGF2** command is used to log off a DB2 DOS or Windows database client.

- Syntax

```
SQLLOGF2
```

■■■ Catalog Commands

The following are commands to catalog a local database and protocols.

Write an entry for a local node to the directory

The **CATALOG LOCAL NODE** command creates an alias name for an instance that resides on the same machine. A local node must be cataloged when there is more than one instance on the same workstation to be accessed from the user's client.

- Syntax

```
CATALOG LOCAL NODE nodename
        INSTANCE instancename
        [WITH "comment-string"]
```

- Parameters

nodename is an alias for the node to be cataloged. This arbitrary name on the user's workstation is used to identify the remote node. It should be meaningful so that it is easy to remember. The name must also conform to the database manager naming conventions.

instancename is the user ID of the owner of another instance on the same workstation.

comment-string is used to describe the node entry in the node directory.

Add an entry for IPX/SPX node to the directory

The **CATALOG IPX/SPX NODE** command adds an Internetwork Packet Exchange/Sequenced Packet Exchange (IPX/SPX) node entry to the node directory. The Novell NetWare IPX/SPX communications protocol is used to access the remote node.

- Syntax

```
CATALOG IPXSPX NODE nodename
        REMOTE  file-server
        SERVER object-name
        [WITH "comment-string"]
```

- Parameters

  nodename is an alias for the node to be cataloged.

  file-server is the name of the NetWare file server where the internetwork address of the database manager instance is registered.

  object-name is the name of the database manager instance stored in the bindery of the NetWare file server. Each database manager instance registered at one NetWare file server must be represented by a unique *object-name*.

  comment-string is used to describe the node entry in the node directory.

Add an entry for TCP/IP node to the directory

The **CATALOG TCP/IP NODE** command is used to write a Transmission Control Protocol/Internet Protocol (TCP/IP) node entry to the node directory. With The TCP/IP communications protocol, you can access the remote node.

- Syntax

```
CATALOG TCPIP NODE nodename
        REMOTE hostname
        SERVER service-name
```

```
[WITH "comment-string"]
```

● Parameters

> *nodename* is an alias of the node to be cataloged. You choose this name on the user's workstation to identify the remote node and it is an arbitrary name. The name should be meaningful such that it is easier to remember. The name must conform to database manager naming conventions.
>
> *hostname* is the hostname of the node where the target database resides. This hostname of the node must be known to the TCP/IP network. The maximum length of the hostname is 255 characters.
>
> *service-name* is the service name of the database manager on the remote node. This name must be the same service name specified in the database manager configuration file on the remote node, and must be specified in the local and remote TCP/IP services file. The maximum length of service-name is 14 characters. This parameter is case sensitive.
>
> "comment-string" is a description of the node entry in the node directory. Choose a comment that says something meaningful about the node being entered. The maximum length of a comment string is 30 characters.

Write an entry for NetBios node to the directory

The **CATALOG NetBios NODE** command is used to write information to the node directory about a remote workstation that uses NetBios (a communication protocol). DB2 reads this information from the node directory to connect an application to a remote database cataloged on this node.

● Syntax

```
CATALOG NetBios NODE nodename
        REMOTE partner-lu
        ADAPTER number
        [IN codepage]
        [WITH "comment-string"]
```

- Parameters

  nodename is used to specify the node name of the workstation. This name should be the same as the one used when the workstation was cataloged.

  partner-lu is used to specify the name of a workstation to which you are trying to connect. This name cannot be longer than eight characters.

  number is used to specify the LAN adapter number, which is 0 or 1.

  codepage is used to specify the code page of the characters found in the comment-string.

  comment-string is used to describe the entry found in the DCS directory. It must be enclosed in quotes (").

- Example

  The following command is used to catalog a remote workstation as a NetBios node.

```
CATALOG NetBios NODE XYZWKST    \
        REMOTE XYZWKST          \
        ADAPTER 0 WITH "XYZ is a NetBios NODE"
```

Write an entry for APPC node to the directory

The **CATALOG APPC** command is used to add an entry to the node directory. An entry contains information about a remote workstation that uses APPC communication protocols. This information is used by DB2 to connect an application program to a remote database cataloged in this node.

- Syntax

```
CATALOG APPC NODE node-name
   [NETWORKID netid] REMOTE partner-lu
   [LOCAL local-lu]   [MODE mode]
   [IN codepage]      [WITH "comment-string"]
```

● Parameters

node-name is used to specify the name of the remote workstation to be cataloged. This name is the same as the one used to catalog a database with the CATALOG DATABASE command. The node name must conform to the DB2 naming conventions.

NETWORKID *netid*
This parameter is used to specify the SNA network ID where the remote LU is to be found.
netid is a string no longer than eight characters and must conform to SNA naming conventions.

REMOTE *partner-lu*
This required parameter is used to specify the SNA partner LU that is needed for connection.
partner-lu is an LU name of the remote node. The length of this name cannot exceed eight characters.

LOCAL *local-lu*
This option parameter is used to specify the alias of the SNA local LU that is used for connection.
local-lu is an LU name in the local node. The length of this name cannot exceed eight characters.

MODE *mode*
This parameter is used to specify the SNA transmission mode used in the connection.
node is the name of the node, and it must be longer than 8 characters. If you omit this parameter, DB2 places the default value of eight blank characters.

codepage is used to specify the code page of the characters found in the comment-string.

comment-string is used to describe the APPC node entry found in the node directory. It must be enclosed in quotes (").

● Example

The following command is used to catalog an APPC node called XYZNODE.

```
CATALOG APPC NODE XYZNODE   \
   REMOTE XYZLU             \
   WITH "Catalog APPC NODE XYZNODE"
```

Write an entry for APPN node information to the directory

The **CATALOG APPN** command is used to add an entry to the node directory. An entry contains information about a remote workstation that uses APPN (Advanced Peer-to-Peer Network) communication protocols. This information is used by DB2 to connect an application program to a remote database cataloged in this node.

● Syntax

```
CATALOG APPN NODE node-name
   [NETWORKID netid] REMOTE partner-lu
   [LOCAL local-lu]   [MODE mode]
   [IN codepage]      [WITH "comment-string"]
```

● Parameters

node-name is used to specify the name of the remote workstation to the catalog. This name is the same as the one used to catalog a database with the **CATALOG DATABASE** command. The node name must conform to DB2 naming conventions.

NETWORKID *netid*
    This parameter is used to specify the SNA (Systems Network Architecture) network ID where the remote LU (logical unit) is to be found.
    netid is a string no longer than eight characters and it must conform to SNA naming conventions.

REMOTE *partner-lu*

This required parameter is used to specify the SNA partner LU (logical unit) that is needed for connection.
partner-lu is an LU name of the remote node. The length of this name cannot exceed eight characters.

LOCAL *local-lu*
This option parameter is used to specify the alias of the SNA local LU that is used for connection.
local-lu is an LU name in the local node. The length of this name cannot exceed eight characters.

MODE *mode*
This parameter is used to specify the SNA transmission mode used in the connection.
node is the name of the node, and it must be longer than eight characters. If you omit this parameter, DB2 places the default value of eight blank characters.

codepage is used to specify the code page of the characters found in the comment-string.

comment-string is used to describe the APPN node entry found in the node directory. It must be enclosed in quotes (").

● Example

The following command is used to catalog an APPN node called XYZNODE.

```
CATALOG APPN NODE XYZNODE   \
   REMOTE XYZLU             \
   WITH "Catalog APPN NODE XYZNODE"
```

Remove node entry from node directory

The **UNCATALOG NODE** command is used to delete an entry from the node directory. This entry was previously added to the directory by the following commands:
● CATALOG NODE or CATALOG APPC NODE

- CATALOG APPN NODE
- CATALOG NetBios NODE

- Syntax

```
UNCATALOG NODE
```

Chapter 4
DB2 Universal Database Server

DB2 is a *relational database management* software. If this sentence does not make sense to you, read on. By the end of this chapter, you will have learned the basic concepts and terms of the relational database management system (RDBMS). But if you are familiar with the world of RDBMS, you may wish to skip this chapter.

In October 1993, IBM introduced DB2, a database manager for the 32-bit OS/2 operating system (it originally appeared in 1988 as DBM). But its legacy goes back many years; in 1981, IBM produced a similar RDBMS, called SQL/DS, for the small size mainframe system; later in 1984, it delivered DB2 for OS/390, another RDBMS for very large mainframe computers. Currently, the DB2 family extends to other operating systems varying in size and complexity; namely DB2 for AIX (IBM's UNIX flavor) and DB2 for OS/400. In recent years, DB2 has been available in many non-IBM platforms, namely, Windows (95, 98, and NT), SCO Unix, HP-UX, Solaris, and Sinix.

As we will see throughout this book, DB2 Universal Database, the name of the current version, is an easy software to use, an advantage we will come to appreciate as we deal with the complexities of a database. This industrial strength program has many of the advance features — and of course includes the basic ones — that a relational database manager has to offer to a wide range of users, from personal to corporate. DB2 comes with a language called SQL (pronounced "sequel"), a very important part of a RDBMS. This is an easy-to-use language to manage a database, whether you are an end-user, programmer, analyst, or administrator. As we will see later, this language is one way to communicate with DB2.

If you have a copy of DB2 in your hands, and are anxious to try some of these features, you may be tempted to skip this chapter. Though DB2 is easy to use, it is still advisable to finish this chapter. It will give you the basics of a relational database server, an understanding essential to derive the most benefit.

■■■ Why DB2 Universal Database?

Since its first appearance in the client/server environment, DB2 has gone through many improvements and versions; the latest, released in June 1997, is called DB2 Universal Database. The original purpose of database was to store business-related data that could be easily manipulated. In the new paradigm, bits and bytes are considered information that can be mined by modern technocrats to gain understanding of realities. This knowledge can vary from discovering customer spending habits to complexities of spatial bodies. New demands are imposed on database vendors; some of them are:

- high performance
- massive parallel processing
- data mining
- data warehousing
- decision support system (DSS)
- object-relational database (ORDBMS)
- WEB server, Internet and Intranet
- online analytical processing (OLAP)

Therefore, DB2 Universal Database is a merging of many DB2 separate products; its ingredients are:

DB2 Common Server Version 2.1. The DB2 Common Server is the main database engine, designed to handle non-traditional, complex, or multimedia data. It supports datatypes, such as text, video, audio, fingerprints, and images. Much of this book is devoted to the capabilities of the DB2 Common Server.

DB2 Parallel Edition Version 1 Release 2. The DB2 Parallel Edition (PE) is shared-nothing implementation of DB2 for AIX. Its main purpose is for high-performance, high-volume queries.

DataHub. DataHub is a tool to administer databases, running on Unix, OS/390, OS/400, and OS/2. Some of its functions are to allow administrators to configure and manage replications, security, backup, recovery, and reorganization.

DataPropagator. DataPropagator is to replicate partial and entire databases.

Net.Data. Net.Data is to develop Web pages which contain data from databases, flat files, and applications.

The overall performance of DB2 has improved by utilizing bitmapped indexed with ANDing. In SMP environment, it can do intra-queries in parallel, and where available, it can use 64-bit memory. To do multidimensional analysis, it supports Rollup and Cube operations, and star join database schemas.

In previous versions, DB2 was lacking administrative tools. Universal Database comes with an enhanced Window-like interface for administrators. The Command Line Processor is improved to provide all kinds of administrative use.

Finally, there are three new functions that make servers highly available. They are point-in-time tablespace recovery, online-reorganization, and database restart. The main advantage is that a database need not come down for recovery or reorganization.

▮▮▮ What Is a Database?

A database is nothing more than a collection of information, organized in a certain way. Most of us have used a database at one time or another without being aware of it. For example, a telephone book is a database, a collection of names, addresses, and telephone numbers. Similarly, a product catalogue and Roledex are all considered databases as they consist of different types of data arranged in a predetermined way.

But a pile of business cards is *not* a database, as it does not conform to any systematic method. For the same reason, your personal library may not be considered a database. However, a public library has a definite method of arranging books; therefore, it is a database.

▮▮▮ What is a Database Software?

If a database on paper like the telephone book works well, why do we need a computer to store information? Depending on the use and nature of data, not all databases need to be computerized. For example, the telephone book is accurate and serves millions, although it is only updated once a year. But, if a business needed up-to-the-minute directory information, the paper system would certainly fail. Or, if a bank wanted to give all its customers an up-to-date picture of every account, again it would be impossible to manually update millions of transactions daily. With a paper and pen system, it would be impossible to enjoy the kind of service we take for granted as a bank customer. In both cases, computers have a unique power to handle massive amounts of data at lighting speed.

There is another weakness of a paper and pen database; say you remember a first name but not the last name, what do you do in such a case? Or, you filed a customer into a database, but you remember only his or her company name and not the last name, how can you reach this file? With software, you can reference data in many different ways, by last name, first name, company name, and so on. You can also sort the data you are retrieving; for example, by customers, company name, zip code, and so on, with little effort. You can easily create good-looking reports.

In summary, database software offers these main advantages:

- It can handle large or small amounts of information.
- It can keep the information as current as you want.
- It can easily and quickly find information.
- It provides many views of data.

These are just a few major advantages; as we will see later, database software gives us far more, including calculation of stored information.

▪▪▪▪ What are the Parts of a Database?

There are many parts to a database, and as it grows in complexity, more components are needed to derive the most benefits. At this time, we will look at the simplest form, consisting of the basic elements that make up a database. As we go through this chapter, we'll examine other facets that make a database efficient, consistent, and secure.

As mentioned earlier, a computerized database has to be organized according to strict rules. Computers are not smart — but they are precise and fast. Therefore, such a database must be designed to conform to a strict structure. Generally, information is divided into small pieces called columns or fields. Each column represents only one type of data. For example, if we computerize a telephone directory, the names, addresses, and phone numbers will each belong to a column. We can give each column a name, for example,

"NAME", "ADDRESS", and "PHONE NUMBER". As well, data of columns are not interchangeable; in other words, an address cannot be in the NAME column, or viceversa.

In database lingo, datatype is simply a piece of data in a category. As we will see later in more detail, there are many kinds of data, such as numbers, a string of characters, voice, or graphics. When we say each column must have a datatype, it means that up-front we decide whether a column will take only numbers, characters, voice, or graphics information. This is important to DB2, so that it can store data in the most efficient way. Once you decide on one type, you cannot store a different kind of data, unless you change the type of the column.

We can choose the phone number column to be numeric, and name and address columns to be strings of characters (characters can be numbers, alphabets, or a combination of both). You have to be careful with the phone numbers; they have to be strictly numbers, without any dash (-), for example, 5552555. If you want dashes, then the datatype has to be characters.

We just defined the name of each table and the type of data each must hold. Now, one set of data for these columns is called a row or record. Conceivably there can be many such rows; each is a collection of related pieces of information, for example, an entry of a person in the directory. Collectively, all these rows sharing the same columns make up a table or file. Figure 4.1 shows the arrangement of columns and rows in a table DIRECTORY.

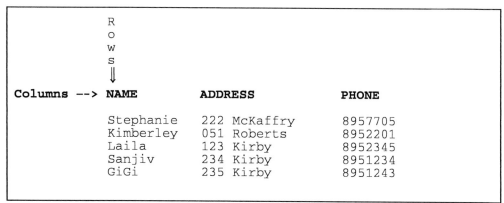

Figure 4.1 Rows and columns of the DIRECTORY table

A database is made of many such table, each designed to hold a category of information. For example, a small employee database could have four tables:

departments, employees, addresses, and employee histories, each having columns to hold small pieces of information only related to that table.

We just looked at some of the elementary steps of designing a database, namely defining a database. The other equally important task is to manage the database, which we will look at next.

■■■ What Is a Database Manager?

Defining a database on paper is only the first step — although an important one — in the process of computerizing information. The next step is to create the database and manage it through additions, changes, and extractions of the information. These and many more steps are done by a database manager like DB2.

The database manager, through the user's instructions, maintains the database. It uses the operating system files to store the information in bits and bytes, but you don't need to know how it does this. As shown in Figure 4.2, it is the link between the users — end-users, programmers, database administrators, and programs — and the database. The user adds and changes rows in tables as required or extract the data in many different ways. For example, you can choose one or more columns or sort the output in certain ways. You can also instruct it to perform calculations on column data. This is a very simplistic view of what a database manager can do. At this point you don't need to care how DB2 accesses the files to meet your request.

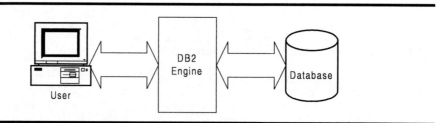

Figure 4.2 Relationship between users, DB2, and the database

In the following chapters, we'll discover the functions of DB2 in these categories:

- Create a database
- Add information to the database

- Change information in a specific record or field
- Delete information from the database
- Perform calculations on fields that have numeric values

■■■ What is a Relational Database?

Previously, we described a table as a collection of related pieces of information in a database. A database is called relational when the tables within it can be interconnected. In database lingo, tables are referred to as *entities*. So we'll use these two words interchangeably throughout this book. Because of this relationship, DB2 lets us do the following:

- Distribute data of a single item, called keys, into several tables and link them together in a meaningful manner. We'll look at this idea in an illustration very shortly.
- Because of this connection, you can ask for information, or *query*, from more than one table at a time. As we will see later, this is a very powerful part of a relational database.
- Establish *one-to-many* relationships, such as all the employees of one department, or all the history entries of one employee. In a more complex database, you can have *many-to-many* relationships, which are not covered in this book.
- In this relationship referred to as a parent-child linkage, there is a risk of losing data when joins are not properly established or data is not removed that has no link to a parent table. To safeguard against this, DB2 allows creation and maintenance of *integrity* of data. Integrity checking also means warning the user when inconsistencies in the data occur.

In the database world, the relationship of the tables can be shown by an entity relationship diagram (ERD). To illustrate what we just discussed, let's look at a simple database called ONEWORLD which maintains information of all the employees of all departments of this company. This database will have the following tables: DEPARTMENTS, EMPLOYEES, EMPL_ADDRESSES, and EMPL_HISTORIES. The relationships of these entities are shown in Figure 4.3.

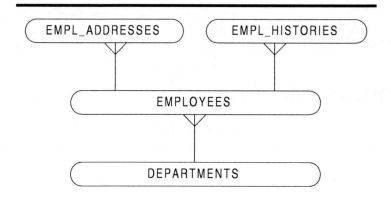

Figure 4.3 Entity Relationship diagram (ERD)

Let's look at a few points about this diagram. Each block represents an entity and a line shows that a link exists between two entities. For example, DEPARTMENTS is joined to EMPLOYEES but not to EMPL_HISTORIES. The Crow's foot at the end of the relationship line indicates an association with one or more occurrences; for example, one department may have one or many employees.

Typically this diagram is called a *data model*, which gives a business view of data. This helps one understand the relationship of data, especially when there are hundreds of entities in a database. We'll use this model as a design to walk through many aspects of DB2.

▐▐▌ Parts of DB2

There are many parts to DB2. we have already discussed some of them, such as tables, columns, and rows. A database is made of more parts (called objects in database lingo), with such names as tablespace, package, stored procedure, function, schema, and trigger. To make DB2 work for us in the fullest, while taking advantage of the relational database features, it is imperative to have a clear understanding of these parts. In this section we'll describe the basic concepts; however, the commands to implement these ideas are postponed until the following chapters.

Table

From the user's point of view, a table is a collection of related pieces of data. Although DB2 may physically store the information differently, as far as we are concerned, looking at updating or adding data to the database, we perceive the database in terms of tables, columns, and rows. In a database, each table has a name. In our sample **ONEWORLD** database, there are four tables: **DEPARTMENTS**, **EMPLOYEES**, **EMPL_ADDRESSES**, and **EMPL_HISTORIES**.

As we go through many different aspects of DB2, you will notice that we must follow many rules. One of them is naming conventions of tables. We do that next. Whatever we say about table names also applies to views, columns and indexes. A table name must be unique within a database. It cannot be more than 18 characters long. It must start with a letter (A to Z) or with one of the special characters (@, #, or $). That takes care of the first character, the rest of the name can be made of the following:

- Any A to Z letters
- Any numbers from 0 to 9
- Special characters @, #, and $

When DB2 stores a name in each catalog, it converts the letters to upper characters.

Each table can be imagined to be a grid of rows and columns, as shown earlier in Figure 4.1. A row is made of pieces of information corresponding to consecutive columns, each representing a datatype. A column has data along many rows, but the type is the same in all cases.

Before we use a table, we have to define the columns in a very precise way — what kind of values they are allowed to hold — which we will do next.

Column

To define a column, you have to decide upon three different points: name, datatype and key. Choosing a name is very important, especially because DB2 allows up to 255 columns in a table. Although you are not allowed to repeat a name within a table, you can use the same name in different tables or databases. A column name can be up to 18 characters, made of alphabets, numbers, and special characters, as discussed earlier. In a large database, with hundred of tables, designers devote considerable amounts of time come up with appropriate names; at a glance the name should tell what kind of data it is holding.

As mentioned earlier, a column is associated with only one datatype. DB2 supports many datatypes, and for the sake of remembering them, they can be grouped into these categories: number, string, graphics, date, and user-defined (version 2.1 and above).

A column must always hold data — it cannot have nothing. But there are many cases when there is no data available for a column in a particular row; for example, in our EMPLOYEES table there is a column for middle name, but not everyone has a middle name. In such a case, the column can be filled with a null value which is simply a filler; for example zero for number datatype, a blank for strings and so on. On the other hand, you may want some columns to always hold a real value and not nulls, for example the employee number or department number. When defining a column, you can specify whether it is allowed to hold NULL or NOT NULL values.

Sometimes a column is used to do an additional job in addition to holding the data. A column can be primary or foreign keys. We'll look at keys shortly.

With what we know about tables and columns, we can define all the columns of the EMPLOYEES table of our sample database. Figures 4.4 shows the column name, datatype, and a brief description of each column in this table. The number in brackets at the end of a datatype indicates the maximum length for a field, for example six digits for DEPARTMENT_NUM and up to 20 characters for FIRST_NAME.

Note that under datatype, NOT NULL means that this column can only have real values. In cases where these key words are not present, it means null values are allowed in case real values are not available.

```
Columns             Datatype              Description

DEPARTMENT_NUM      Numeric (6) NOT NULL  Department number
EMPLOYEE_ID         String (10) NOT NULL  Employee number
FIRST_NAME          String (20)           First name
MIDDLE_NAME         String (20)           Middle name
SURNAME             String (20)           Surname
BIRTH_DATE          Date                  Birth date
AGE                 Numeric (3)           Employee age
```

Figure 4.4 Columns of EMPLOYEES table

Similarly, we can define the columns of DEPARTMENTS, EMPL_HISTORIES, and EMPL_ADDRESSES. Figure 4.5 is the definition of DEPARTMENTS.

```
Columns              Datatype              Description

DEPARTMENT_NUM    Numeric (6) NOT NULL   Department number
DEPT_NAME         String (20)            Department name
MANAGER           String (10)            Manager
LOCATION          String (20)            Place of business
```

Figure 4.5 Columns of DEPARTMENTS table

View

There are certain situations when you want to limit access to one or more tables to certain users. For instance, everyone in our sample company may be able to read an employee name from the EMPLOYEES table, but you may want to hide the confidential material except for for access by a select few. Rearranging the way data from one or more tables is seen is done by a concept called a *view*. A *view* is a different way of presenting data derived from one or more base tables or other views. Views do not have a physical existence like tables; rather they are considered virtual tables. Like a table, a view has a name. For example, Figure 4.6 shows a view called EMPLOYEE_NAME, derived from EMPLOYEE table (see Figure 4.4). This view has only three columns: FIRST_NAME, MIDDLE_NAME, and SURNAME.

```
Columns           Datatype         Description

FIRST_NAME      String (20)      First name
MIDDLE_NAME     String (20)      Middle name
SURNAME         String (20)      Surname
```

Figure 4.6 Data for EMPLOYEE_NAME view

Index

Let's say we want to get a row from the DEPARTMENTS table, where DEPARTMENT_NUM='1000'. DB2 finds the row by scanning the table from top to bottom and, when found, the data is delivered without any delay because this table has only six rows. Even if you had a few thousand rows, again the computer is fast enough to find it in a short time. How long will it take to scan a table with one million rows? This size is not inconceivable. The speed of access will be significant and it will depend on the power of the computer. There is a faster way to access data in a table using *index*. An *index* is a set of pointers to the rows. Each index is based on data from one or more columns of a table. They are called pointers.

Once it is created, DB2 automatically maintains and uses it whenever appropriate. In general, it is faster to access data with an index than without. An index is a separate part (or object) from a table. It can be created during or after a table is defined in the database.

An index cannot be made for a view; however, if a view is derived from a base table that has an index, the operation on that view may be improved.

There are two kinds of indexes: unique or duplicate. A unique index ensures that two or more rows do not have the same pointers or keys. This also means the combination of column values that make up the pointers is unique. With a duplicate index, it is possible to have one or more pointers be the same.

Key

When discussing columns earlier, we briefly mentioned the primary key. Before we move on to the next topic of referential integrity, we have to understand this and other keys that are essential to a relational database. There are two kinds of keys: *primary keys* and *foreign keys*. These keys can be viewed as roads that link two or many tables together.

A primary key is made of one or many columns of a table to ensure that a row can be uniquely identified. This is a method to access or modify databases with great precision. If there are two persons called Smith, and you are updating the record of one of them, you want to make sure that you are handling the right row. For example, in Figure 4.7, every row can be uniquely identified with the values found in the DEPARTMENT_NUM column. This is easy because we choose unique department numbers. But, column values are not always unique. Let's look at another scenario. Figure 4.8 shows a table with phone number, first name, last name, and city for each row.

```
DEPARTMENT_NUM DEPT_NAME                        MANAGER LOCATION

          1000 Tex-Mex Restaurant              1000-JK Rodeo Circle
          1001 Jimmy The Greek Restaurant      1001-JO Greek Village
          1002 Authentic Chinese Food          1002-MT China Town
          1003 Reduce, Recycle and Reuse       1003-RG Ecology Fair
          1004 Virtual Reality                 1004-BG Futuristic World
          1005 Spiritual Transformation        1005-PZ Heaven On Earth
```

Figure 4.7 Data for the DEPARTMENTS table

As you can see, none of these columns contain unique values. Now, to identify a row without any doubt of accessing the right one, we have to do something different. We make a primary key using phone number, first name, and last name. With this combination of these columns making the primary key, we can uniquely identify any row.

```
Phone number   First name   Last name   City

922-7777       Ray          Wingett     Peterborough
922-7777       Maddie       Wingett     Peterborough
922-7777       Lee          Wingett     Peterborough
922-7778       Bob          Hutchcraft  Peterborough
922-7778       Emma         Hutchcraft  Peterborough
922-7778       Lee          Hutchcraft  Peterborough
```

Figure 4.8 Example of duplicate column values

A *foreign key* consists of columns in one table that are the same as the primary key in another table. This establishes a link between two tables to join data from both. Figure 4.9 shows that DEPARTMENT_NUM — found in two tables — is the link between DEPARTMENTS and EMPLOYEES tables. In DEPARTMENTS it is a primary key and a foreign key in EMPLOYEES.

```
Tables           Columns          Keys

DEPARTMENTS      DEPARTMENT_NUM   Primary key

EMPLOYEES        EMPLOYEE_ID      Primary key
                 DEPARTMENT_NUM   Foreign key to
                                  DEPARTMENT_NUM
                                  in DEPARTMENTS table
```

Figure 4.9 Primary and foreign key relationships

Because of this association of keys, we can classify tables into three categories: parent, child, and independent. The parent table is the one that has the primary key, such as DEPARTMENTS. EMPLOYEES is a child or dependent table. A child can also be a parent with relation to another table. An independent table is neither a parent nor a child, for example, Figure 4.10 shows FRUIT is such a table.

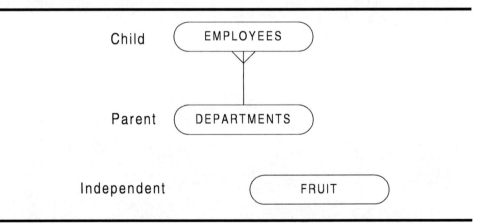

Figure 4.10 Parent, child and independent tables

This parent-child relationship does not preclude getting any piece of data from other parent or child tables. The greatest advantage of this join is to combine data from two or more tables.

Tablespace

The DB2 engine stores all the data and definitions of the database objects in files. *Tablespaces* are created to link the physical locations of data and abstract concepts of tables, columns, indexes and so on. Eventually, every piece of information ends up in files. Therefore one of the first tasks in creating a database is to set up a logical layer between the data and the storage devices. In other words, when creating tablespaces you use files and devices; tables are associated with one or many tablespaces and not directly with files.

A database can have many tablespaces called, for example, ONEWORLD_DATA1, ONEWORLD_INDEX, USER_DATA, TEMP, TOOLS_DATA, and so on. You can store different types of data and give appropriates names that will help identify their purposes. To optimize the performance, you may want to spread a tablespace over many devices. For instance, less accessed data can go to slower devices and those with heavily used tables can go to faster disks. You can also backup an entire tablespace that may contain many tables.

A tablespace is allocated in terms of *extents*. An extent is made of a collection of pages. Each page size is 4,096 (4K). The default extent size of a tablespace is 32 pages (128 KB). Once an extent size is established, it *cannot be* changed.

Package

A *package* is another database object that contains executable forms of SQL statements found in a program. Each program corresponds to one package that has DB2 references of how to access tables. A package is created by the BIND statement, stored in the database system catalog tables. When building an application that accesses DB2 objects, it be part of a package or group of packages.

Stored Procedure

A *stored procedure* is an application program residing in the database server that can be executed by a client program. Data to the stored procedure is passed when it is called by a client program and then, after execution on the server, the result is passed to the client. While the execution is taking place, no interaction is permitted by the client. A stored procedure can be written in any of the following languages: C, C++, COBOL, FORTRAN, REXX, and Java. After the program is built and installed on the server, it is then ready to be invoked by the client.

Function

DB2 comes with many built-in *functions* which, when invoked, returns a result given a set of values. They do many common tasks such as calculating averages and sums, counting rows, conversions and more. It may happen that these functions may satisfy a special business or scientific need. In this case, the DB2 users can create their own function with the CREATE FUNCTION statement.

Trigger

A *trigger*, as the name suggests, is a set of actions that are executed when a change in the database occurs. This change is specific to a table. Triggers are executed by DB2 in the background as a result of changes to the database. Triggers are very useful; some of the ways of using them are:

- Validate input data
- Generate values for a new row automatically
- Read from another table for cross-referencing
- Write to a log table

Schema

A huge database can have thousands of objects, including tables, views, packages, functions, and triggers. A *schema* is a way of dividing the objects in logical groups. For example, an accounting database may have the following schemas: PAYROLL, INVOICE, GL, AR, and AP. All the objects for payroll are created under PAYROLL, for invoicing under INVOICE, and so on. When referencing any object in an application, a two-part naming convention must be used. For example, EMPLOYEES table for PAYROLL schema is referenced by PAYROLL.EMPLOYEES. This convention is only used with tables, views, user-defined data types, user-defined functions, packages, and functions.

■■■ Table and Referential Integrity

One of the greatest challenges to maintain is the soundness of a database — so that the data remains wholesome as it undergoes constant changes. DB2 provides two kinds of integrity checks: table integrity and referential integrity.

Table integrity means that if a column is a primary key, it must have a value in every row; such a column cannot have a null value. If you try to add a field (designated as NOT NULL) with a null value, DB2 will reject it. For example, you cannot add a row in the DEPARTMENTS table without a department number or an employee to the EMPLOYEES table without an employee ID. This ensures the integrity of the tables or entities.

Referential integrity means that the relationship between tables is consistent. A foreign key value in a table must have a corresponding primary key value in a parent table. DB2 gives a hand in accomplishing this referential integrity by allowing us to define constraints. When creating a table (we'll see in Chapter 5) you name the columns that make up a foreign key and associated it to a primary key. At this point, you give this constraint a name or DB2 will do it for you. DB2 also registers it in its catalog in addition to enforcing the referential integrity automatically; however, it is optional. DB2 will not enforce the referential rules unless allowed to. If enforced, any violation is reported.

What are the referential rules? They apply only to the column(s) that participate in it, namely those that make the primary and foreign keys. They only apply when a row is inserted, updated or deleted. Now, let's examine the importance of these operations on both parent and dependent tables. There are two kinds of operation that do not abide by the referential integrity constraints: one is deleting a row from a dependent table and the other is inserting a new row to a parent table. The reason is that every time you add a parent record, it does not need a child row to exit; for example, the moment we add a new department, it does not immediately have to have an employee or an address in the database. This information can be added later, but the existence of a row in the dependent table is not relevant at all at that moment.

However, if you add a row in a child table, the foreign key of that record must have a value that matches a primary key of a parent table. In other words, an employee record must belong to a department; therefore, an employee row must be added with a department number. Similarly, every row in EMPL_ADDRESSES must belong to an employee. This check is done automatically by DB2, resulting in a failure if records with inconsistent keys are added. This also applies when you change a foreign key — it must correspond to a primary key. Earlier, we said the existence of a primary key does not depend on a foreign key. What happens if a primary key, which has records in the dependent tables, is deleted or changed? For example, a department number is removed or renumbered. When the referential constraints are on, any such update or deletion will fail. Because if these operations are to proceed, the rows in the child table will become orphans; lacking data integrity.

There are two ways to delete or change a primary key. One is to turn off the referential constraints, then perform the operations on the primary key of the parent table. When this is over turn the constraints on.

The other way is to use the DB2 cascade option. It states that if a record in a parent table is either removed or changed, the operation will be expanded to all the rows in the dependent table(s), having a foreign key corresponding to the primary key of the row in the parent table. For example, with the cascade option, if we delete or change the DEPARTMENT_NUM of DEPARTMENTS, a similar operation will happen in the EMPLOYEES table.

■■■ Structure Query Language (SQL)

So far we have dipped into many concepts of DB2, such as tables, columns, keys, and referential integrity. These are called data structures and data integrity. So far we have avoided data manipulation. How do we create a table, index or key? How can we add or change a row? These and other objects come into existence in a database with a special language called Structured Query Language (SQL, pronounced 'sequel'). SQL is the standard language for relational DBMS, with its commands (or statements) divided into three categories: data manipulation language (DML), data definition language (DDL), and data control language (DCL).

The user issues these SQL commands to DB2 to manage the database. In the coming chapters, we'll use them extensively to manipulate our sample database.

DML

The SQL statements in the DML are for managing the data of the database. The statements are SELECT, INSERT, and UPDATE. SELECT is for getting the data from columns of one or more tables. The DML's INSERT statement adds into a table; UPDATE changes any one of them.

DDL

The DDL statements are for DB2 objects. These objects are the structures upon which the data rests. They are like the walls, floors, roof of a house where contents, such as furniture, beds, and lamps can be placed. These objects are be the tables, indexes, views, stored procedures, packages, tablespaces, and triggers. The DDL gives you the commands to create, change or remove any of these objects. The SQL statements are CREATE, ALTER, and DROP.

DCL

The DCL statements are different from the last two categories. They are to manage the security of the data — what a user is able to do to the data in a table or view. The category offers two statements: GRANT and REVOKE. They allow you to grant or revoke privileges of a user regarding tables and views.

Chapter 5
Design and Create a Database

Like many things in life, we start with an idea and eventually make it into real objects that can touched, seen, and felt. A database is no different. Designing and creating a database is very much like building a house: the project must undergo different stages. In this chapter, we'll examine all the steps needed in designing a database, constructing the necessary parts, and preparing for any changes that we may contemplate.

■■■ Database Design

In a database design one must consider two components: logical database and physical database. Put in a simple form, the former is the idea (the blue print) and the latter is the physical parts (like the walls, doors, wiring etc.). After you decide on these two aspects, you have determined the database requirements of the business. These requirements take a certain shape after detailed analysis of the needs of a business. The method is the same regardless of the size of the database, whether it is a personal or enterprise warehouse of information.

The logical design process can be broken down into four phases:

- Identify the business information needs
- Define database requirements
- Reduce duplication through normalization
- Establish referential integrity rules

In discussing these phases in the following sections, we'll revisit some of the database concepts talked about in Chapter 4, and look at them again in terms of database design processes.

▮▮▮ Identify the Business Information Needs

In this first phase of logical design, the goal is to understand the database needs of a business. Here, business means the end-user of the information, for example, an enterprise, department or personal use. At this stage we are not concerned about the physical aspects of the database, like the tables, columns, index, or even the model of the computer. In this phase, the focus is on drawing an accurate picture of the business data through interviews and analysis of all manuals and reports. At the end of this process, we define the business information in terms of structures and rules. For the sake of simplicity, we divide this phase into two small tasks: business entities and relationships.

Business entities. In this task, we place business data into different categories. In fact, we have already looked at this in the previous chapter when defining entities or tables of the ONEWORLD company. We grouped the information in terms of departments, employees, employee history, and addresses.

   Generally, an entity is information related to a business that has to be maintained and it could be anything, such as person, place, or concepts. The entities for an order entry department would be customers, orders, products, suppliers, and so on. The different pieces of information that go into an entity are called attributes. For instance, a customer entity will have customer name, address, credit limit, etc.

Relationships. The next step is to decide upon the relationship between the entities. Again, we delved into this particular aspect in the previous chapter when describing the relationship of RDBMS. The point to remember in this process is that the connection between entities only makes sense in the context of the business and its rules.

▮▮▮ Define Database Requirements

In this step of the logical design, we translate business entities into data entities. In terms of a database entities translate to entities and attributes of the entities become columns. We also define the relationship between the tables using primary key and foreign key. Again, we worked out all these issues of relationship of RDBMS in Chapter 4.

   This is important. To refresh our memory, we'll go over some of these points, but this time in terms of logical design of a database. Taking the

ONEWORLD database as an example, the department entity becomes the DEPARTMENTS table. It has four attributes (or columns). It is a parent table for the EMPLOYEES table. DEPARTMENTS has a primary key called DEPARTMENT_NUM. The child table EMPLOYEES has seven attributes. It has an attribute called DEPARTMENT_NUM, which is a foreign key, linked to DEPARTMENT_NUM of the DEPARTMENTS table. Figure 5.1 shows the attributes and the relationship between these two tables. The EMPLOYEES entity has EMPLOYEE_ID as a primary key, and one of the reasons we need this key is because it is a parent table to EMPL_HISTORIES and EMPL_ADDRESSES.

```
DEPARTMENTS (parent table)        EMPLOYEES (child table)

DEPARTMENT_NUM (primary key)      DEPARTMENT_NUM (foreign key)
DEPT_NAME                         EMPLOYEE_ID (primary key)
MANAGER                           FIRST_NAME
LOCATION                          MIDDLE_NAME
                                  SURNAME
                                  BIRTH_DATE
                                  AGE
```

Figure 5.1 Attributes of DEPARTMENTS and EMPLOYEES entities

Similarly, other entities — as part of the logical design — are defined showing any relationship among them.

▮▮▮ Reduce Duplication Through Normalization

The purpose of this stage of the logical design is to reduce duplication of data that is not part of a key. *What does this mean?* The reasoning behind this is to reduce the problem inherent in updating the same data in many places. One cannot be too strict about this rule; in practice it is important to keep in mind performance, as it can deteriorate with an overly normalized database.

First we'll look at what normalization means, followed by pros and cons of normalization. To start, let's create a table called OLD_DEPARTMENTS, which has the columns as shown in Figure 5.2.

```
OLD_DEPARTMENTS

DEPARTMENT_NUM
DEPT_NAME
MANAGER
LOCATION
EMPLOYEE_ID
FIRST_NAME
MIDDLE_NAME
SURNAME
BIRTH_DATE
AGE
```

Figure 5.2 Columns of the OLD_DEPARTMENTS table to illustrate duplicate data

As you can see, it has information for both departments and employees. In one department, there will be one or many employees' records; therefore, each time you add a row, you have to duplicate the department information. Each time you change one or more column values about a department, you have to make the same change for each row of the particular department.

To normalize the data, we create two tables: DEPARTMENTS and EMPLOYEES where the key data is not duplicated. These tables are normalized, the columns of each table are shown in Figure 5.3.

```
Entity          Attributes

DEPARTMENTS
                DEPARTMENT_NUM
                DEPT_NAME
                MANAGER
                LOCATION

EMPLOYEES
                DEPARTMENT_NUM
                EMPLOYEE_ID
                FIRST_NAME
                MIDDLE_NAME
                SURNAME
                BIRTH_DATE
                AGE
```

Figure 5.3 Attributes of DEPARTMENTS and EMPLOYEES entities (normalized)

In this case, the data is split into two tables; most of the department data is not duplicated with each employee record. The department number is found in both tables — the link between them. With these two tables, if you want to update the department data, you change only one row in the DEPARTMENTS table, not multiple instances, as in the previous case.

This works fine when you have to link only a few tables (about 4), to extract data. It becomes a problem when many tables (about 10) are linked together to retrieve data. Joining many tables reduces the performance of the database considerably. To improve the performance, you have to denormalize the database to an extent that will reduce the number of joins. Denormalization is beyond the scope of this book. However, it is accomplished by duplicating only some data; this helps keep maintenance of the data less costly in terms of access time. If you need more information on this issue, refer to a book on database design.

▐▐▐ Establish Referential Integrity Rules

The last stage of a logical design is to establish referential integrity. We dealt with this issue sufficiently in the last chapter. We also gave the referential integrity consideration for our ONEWORLD sample database. Refer to it for more information.

▐▐▐ Physical Design

In the preceding sections, we described the method guiding you through different stages of a database logical design. After defining the entities, relationships, normalization and referential integrity, you are ready to deal with the physical design. At this stage, one looks at performance; perhaps some refinement may be required, which means revisiting the logical design one or more times. Once the database design has reached its final stage, you can create the objects that make up the actual database. In the rest of this chapter, we'll look at how to create various objects with the Data Definition Language (DDL) of SQL.

▇▇▇ Creating a Database

Once the logical design is finalized, it is time to create a database. A database contains all the objects — such as tables, views, keys, and so on — that we defined earlier. In DB2, we do so with the CREATE DATABASE statement. But, before we do that, we must start the DB2 manager. Next, enter the command:

```
CREATE DATABASE ONEWORLD
    ON D
  WITH "The database for one world"
```

Since there can be many databases with DB2, we have to give ours a name, for example,"ONEWORLD". There are a few rules to remember about the database name. It should not exceed 8 characters, the first of which should be A through Z, @, #, or $. Any other characters can be A through Z, 0 to 9, @, #, and $.

After the ON keyword, we specify the drive which DB2 can use as storage. In this case it is D, where all the information of ONEWORLD database will be kept in files. We need not be concerned with how DB2 maintains its files — the name or types of file. But make sure that there is enough space to store all the data, keeping in mind the future growth rate of the database.

The WITH keyword gives us a way of adding a comment about a database being created. This information is kept in the data dictionary for reference.

Whether a command is successful or not, DB2 acknowledges with a message as shown in Figure 5.3.

When issuing the CREATE DATABASE command, you will be asked for a **userid** and a **password**.

This command not only creates the database, but does a number of other things. It creates the system catalog tables and recovery log. It catalogs the database name in the volume database directory on the drive where the database was created and in the system database directory. The userid you provided becomes the creator of the database and it grants this user privileges to create tables and to connect to the database.

▇▇▇ Connecting to the Database

After creating a database, we want to do something with it, like creating a table or an index, entering data or changing data. For the SQL statement to do any of these operations, you must be connected to the database. Throughout this book, to execute a SQL statement it is assumed that the connection to the database is already established, in one of the following ways:

- Using the CONNECT TO statement
- Using environment variable

Now, let's see how each of them work.

```
A successful command:

   CREATE DATABASE ONEWORLD ON D  \
     WITH "The database for one world"

   CREATE DATABASE Completed successfully


An unsuccessful command:

   CREATE DATABASE ONEWORLD ON D  \
     WITH "The database for one world"

   SQL1001N "ONEWORLD" is not a valid database name.
   SQLSTATE=22503
```

Figure 5.3 Create ONEWORLD database

▪▪▪▪ Using the CONNECT TO Statement

The CONNECT TO statement can connect you to any database. Subsequently, you can issue any SQL statement against that database. To connect to the ONEWORLD database, we type:

```
CONNECT TO ONEWORLD
```

In this command, we supply the database name with which you are about to work. Remember, once connected to one database, you can switch to another database by giving another CONNECT TO command, for example,

```
CONNECT TO NEWWORLD
```

▉▉▉ Using Environment Variable

This is an implicit way of connecting to a database, and it is also the way you would normally connect. If you are not explicitly connected, DB2 will try to connect for you, whenever an SQL command is issued. This will only happen if SQLDBDFT variable is enabled. You enable it by associating a database name to it in your CONGIF.SYS file, for example,

```
SET SQLDBDFT = ONEWORLD
```

Another way to accomplish the same thing is to give the command:

```
SET SQLDBDFT = ONEWORLD
```

at the command line before starting DB2.

▉▉▉ Creating Tables

Now we are ready to create tables for our ONEWORLD database. To do so, we use the CREATE TABLE statement. It is probably one of the most used statements by database users, programmers, and administrators. Let's use this statement to create the DEPARTMENTS table of the ONEWORLD database by issuing the command:

```
CREATE TABLE DEPARTMENTS (
    DEPARTMENT_NUM    INT        NOT NULL PRIMARY KEY
    ,DEPT_NAME        CHAR(20)   NOT NULL WITH DEFAULT
    ,MANAGER          CHAR(10)   NOT NULL WITH DEFAULT
    ,LOCATION         CHAR(20)   NOT NULL WITH DEFAULT
                          )
```

We give DEPARTMENTS as the table name after the CREATE TABLE. Next, we list all the column names, enclosed in parentheses. This table has 4 columns: DEPARTMENT_NUM, DEPT_NAME, MANAGER, LOCATION. For each column, we specify a name, followed by its datatype (e.g. INT, CHAR(20), CHAR(10), etc.) If the datatype is characters, we give a length. For your reference, Figures 5.4 is a list of datatypes that DB2 accepts.

Numeric data

SMALLINT	For small whole numbers between -32768 and +32767
INTEGER or INT	For very large whole numbers between -2147483648 and +2147483647.
DECIMAL(p,q) or DEC(p,q)	Decimal numbers where p is the number of digits (1 to 15) before the decimal point. And q is the number of digits after the decimal point, and it can be 0 to whatever p is.
FLOAT	For floating-point number

String data

CHARACTER(n) or CHAR(n)	For fixed-length character string, where n is the length. n can be between 1 and 254.
VARCHAR(n)	For variable-length character string, where n can be between 1 and 4000.
LONG VARCHAR	For variable-length character string and this type is used for very long string, up to 32700 characters.

Graphics data

GRAPHIC(n)	For fixed-length graphic character string, where n is between 1 and 127.
VARGRAPHIC(n)	For variable-length graphic character string, where n is between 1 and 2000.
LONG VARGRAPHIC	For variable length graphic character string, and this type is used for very long string, up to 16350 characters.

Date/Time Data

DATE	For date including day, month, and year. The format depends on the country, for example, for USA it is *mm/dd/yyyy*. *mm* is the month, *dd* is the day, and *yyyy* is the year.
TIME	Time in hours, minutes, and seconds.
TIMESTAMP	For date and time. The format is: *yyyy-mm-dd-hh.mm.ss.nnnnnn*, where *yyyy* is the year, *mm* the month, *dd* the day, *hh* the hour, *mm* the month, *ss* the seconds, and *nnnnnn* the microseconds.

Large Objects

BLOB	This type is used to hold data up to two gigabytes long.
CLOB	This type is used to hold data up to two gigabytes long.
DBLOB	This type is used to hold double-byte character string up to one gigabytes long.

Figure 5.4 Datatypes of DB2

The NOT NULL for the DEPARTMENT_NUM column tells DB2 to store valid numbers in this field for any row. DB2 will not accept a null for it. The NOT NULL WITH DEFAULT for the rest of the columns means that null values are allowed; however, if a value is not available when inserting a row, DB2 will put a default value as listed in Figure 5.5. In this command, we designate DEPARTMENT_NUM as the primary key.

```
Datatype                              Default value

Numeric                               0
Fixed length character string         Blanks
Variable length character string      Blanks
   [The length of such a string is set to 0]
Date                                  Current date
Time                                  Current time
Timestamp                             Current date and time
Large Object string                   Blanks
```

Figure 5.5 Default values for DB2 datatypes.

After DB2 executes this command, we have the DEPARTMENTS table in the ONEWORLD database. Next, we create the other tables: EMPLOYEES, EMPL_HISTORIES, and EMPL_ADDRESSES. Again, we use the definitions from our logical design, discussed earlier, to create these tables. Figure 5.6 shows the creation of the EMPLOYEES table. Here, there are a few things worth noting. NOT NULL WITH DEFAULT is optional and is not included. It means that if you have not put any values, these columns will have anything (probably garbage). We have also used two new datatypes, SMALLINT and DATE.

```
CREATE TABLE EMPLOYEES(
   DEPARTMENT_NUM    INT         NOT NULL,
   EMPLOYEE_ID       CHAR(10)    NOT NULL PRIMARY KEY,
   FIRST_NAME        CHAR(20),
   MIDDLE_NAME       CHAR(20),
   SURNAME           CHAR(20),
   BIRTH_DATE        DATE,
   AGE               SMALLINT)

CREATE TABLE EMPL_HISTORIES(
   DEPARTMENT_NUM    INT         NOT NULL,
   EMPLOYEE_ID       CHAR(10)    NOT NULL PRIMARY KEY,
   POSITION          CHAR(15)    NOT NULL,
   START_DATE        DATE,
   END_DATE          DATE,
   SALARY            INT )

CREATE TABLE EMPL_ADDRESSES(
   DEPARTMENT_NUM    INT         NOT NULL,
   EMPLOYEE_ID       CHAR(10)    NOT NULL PRIMARY KEY,
   STREET_LINE1      CHAR(20),
   CITY              CHAR(20),
   STATE_PROV        CHAR(15),
   ZIP_CODE          CHAR(9) )
```

Figure 3.6 Commands to create the EMPLOYEES, EMPL_HISTORIES, and EMPL_ADDRESSES table

■■■ Creating Views

As mentioned before, a view does not have a real existence; rather it is derived from one or more real tables. A view is a virtual table, which exists in definition only in the DB2 catalog. You can access a view just like a real table, and when it is referred to, DB2 accesses it in terms of the view definition.

A view is created with the CREATE VIEW statement. We'll create one view called DEPARTMENT_001 with the command:

```
CREATE VIEW DEPARTMENT_001
  ( DEPT_NUM, NAME, AGE )
 AS SELECT A.DEPARTMENT_NUM,
           B.SURNAME,
           B.AGE
      FROM DEPARTMENTS A,
```

```
                    EMPLOYEES    B
        WHERE  A.DEPARTMENT_NUM  =  001
              AND  A.DEPARTMENT_NUM  =  B.DEPARTMENT_NUM
```

The DEPARTMENT_001 view has three columns: DEPT_NUM, NAME, and AGE, enclosed in parentheses. The next part of this command is to get the data from DEPARTMENTS and EMPLOYEES, using the SELECT statement. So far we have not discussed the SELECT statement, which we'll do in the next chapter. For now, all we can say is that the SELECT statement is used to match the view columns with the columns of the real tables whenever the view is used. Figure 5.7 shows the columns of the view that correspond to the ones of DEPARTMENTS and EMPLOYEES.

```
View columns          Real columns          Real table

DEPT_NUM              DEPARTMENT_NUM        DEPARTMENTS
NAME                  SURNAME               EMPLOYEES
AGE                   AGE                   EMPLOYEES
```

Figure 5.7 Columns of DEPARTMENT_001 view corresponding to the real tables

Note that the column names of the view can be the same or different from the real table. Also, if you don't specify a column name for a view, DB2 will assume the real table column names are to be used.

The WITH CHECK OPTION is not required; if used, DB2 verifies all updates against the view definition before updating a row. This option will prevent any illogical operation against the view, although the request may be legal.

▮▮▮ Creating Indexes

Indexes improve the efficiency of data access. When an index for a table is created, DB2 maintains a path to each row. As the rows are added or removed, a related pointer is built or deleted. When retrieving part or all the information of one or many rows, DB2 uses the index, if one is available, to reach the information. Otherwise, it will scan the whole table to find the data. This is not very efficient, especially if a table is populated with thousands or millions of rows.

We create an index with the **CREATE INDEX** statement. For instance, for the DEPARTMENTS table, we issue the command:

```
CREATE UNIQUE INDEX IDX_DEPARTMENT_NUM
    ON DEPARTMENTS(DEPARTMENT_NUM ASC)
```

Let's examine the different parts of this statement. The UNIQUE keyword is optional, and if present, DB2 will not allow duplicate entries in the index. This is one way of ensuring that two or more departments do not have the same number. If we omit UNIQUE, DB2 will allow duplicate entries in the index. Entries in an index do not necessarily have to be unique; there are situations when duplicates are allowed by design.

We give this index the name IDX_DEPARTMENT_NUM. The ON clause is used to give the name of the table, followed by one or more columns names enclosed in parentheses. In this case, only the DEPARTMENT_NUM is used as an index and DESC indicates that the entries are kept in descending order. This order is used when retrieving the data.

When an index is present, DB2 automatically uses it; there is no explicit way of saying whether to use an index or not. Indexes are created with judgement. Someone designing these indexes must understand the techniques DB2 uses to access data; therefore, indexes are built with efficient access of data in mind.

Similarly, we create an index for each of the other tables: EMPLOYEES, EMPL_HISTORIES, and EMPL_ADDRESSES. An index can be built with one or many columns, depending on how the columns are used to extract the data. As shown in Figure 5.8, the IDX_EMPLOYEES, IDX_EMPL_HISTORIES, and IDX_EMPL_ADDRESSES indexes are made of two columns. We specify the order to be in ascending order with ASC. Note that the indexes for EMPL_HISTORIES and EMPL_ADDRESSES are not unique, as one employee can have more than one address or history record.

```
CREATE UNIQUE INDEX IDX_EMPLOYEES
    ON EMPLOYEES
    (DEPARTMENT_NUM, EMPLOYEE_ID ASC)

CREATE INDEX IDX_EMPL_HISTORIES
    ON EMPL_HISTORIES
    (DEPARTMENT_NUM, EMPLOYEE_ID ASC)

CREATE INDEX IDX_EMPL_ADDRESSES
    ON EMPL_ADDRESSES
    (DEPARTMENT_NUM, EMPLOYEE_ID ASC)
```

Figure 5.8 Command to create indexes for EMPLOYEES, EMPL_HISTORIES, and EMPL_ADDRESSES tables

▮▮▮▮ Primary and Foreign Keys

If we want to specify the referential integrity rules for a table, we use the CREATE TABLE or ALTER TABLE statement. In our ONEWORLD database, we have DEPARTMENTS table as a parent table and EMPLOYEES as a child table. Creating a foreign key assumes the primary key of a parent table already exists, which happens to be in DEPARTMENTS.

Now, let's create the EMPLOYEES table with the referential integrity constraints, with the command:

```
CREATE TABLE EMPLOYEES(
    DEPARTMENT_NUM      INT        NOT NULL,
    EMPLOYEE_ID         CHAR(10)   NOT NULL PRIMARY KEY,
    FIRST_NAME          CHAR(20),
    MIDDLE_NAME         CHAR(20),
    SURNAME             CHAR(20),
    BIRTH_DATE          DATE,
    AGE                 SMALLINT,
        foreign key dept_num (department_num)
        references departments on delete restrict
                    )
```

We saw this statement before, and here the difference is the addition to enable the integrity constraint (in small letters). Let's look at the two extra lines. Notice that the constraints part is placed after the last definition of the columns. We give the constraint a name; let's call it DEPT_NUM, and the column associated with it is DEPARTMENT_NUM. The next step is to establish the reference to the parent table, which is DEPARTMENTS. The DELETE RESTRICT means that a department cannot be deleted from the DEPARTMENTS table if there are any employees in that department. This is an extra step to maintain integrity.

■■■ Changing the Database Design

Once a database is implemented, it is rare that there is no room for improvement. Once the first implementation reaches its final stage and you see the design at work, you'll see its strong and weak points. A design can go through many changes, until it reaches a high level of satisfaction among users (expecting everyone to be completely happy with a design is perhaps unreasonable).Consequently, the rework may happen in these areas:

- Adding columns to an existing table
- Adding primary and foreign keys
- Dropping primary and foreign keys
- Dropping views, tables, synonyms, and indexes
- Dropping database

In this section we'll discuss how to accomplish these and other tasks.

■■■ Adding Columns to an Existing Table

We add a column to an existing table with the ALTER TABLE statement. To illustrate this point, let's add two new columns called START_DATE and REGION to the DEPARTMENTS table with the command:

```
ALTER TABLE DEPARTMENTS
   ADD ( START_DATE DATE NOT NULL WITH DEFAULT,
         REGION  CHAR(10) )
```

In this command, you specify the column information similar to the CREATE TABLE statement, with column name, datatype, and any constraint, placed in brackets after the ADD clause.

▐▐▐ Adding Primary and Foreign Keys

The primary and foreign keys are added to an existing table using the ALTER TABLE statement. In it, we focus on the PRIMARY KEY and REFERENCES clauses. Let's add the primary and foreign key for the EMPL_HISTORIES table, assuming it has been created without a primary key, with the command:

```
ALTER TABLE EMPL_HISTORIES
     PRIMARY KEY ( POSITION )
     FOREIGN KEY EMPL_ID (EMPLOYEE_ID)
     REFERENCES  EMPLOYEES on delete restrict
```

After executing this command, POSITION becomes the primary key and EMPLOYEE_ID the foreign key. And the EMPL_HISTORIES becomes a child table of EMPLOYEES.

Before you execute this statement, make sure that EMPL_HISTORIES does not have a primary key. Learning how to eliminate a primary key is what we are going to do next.

▐▐▐ Dropping Primary and Foreign Keys

The primary and foreign key can be removed from an existing table with the ALTER TABLE statement. In this, we focus on the DROP PRIMARY KEY and DROP FOREIGN KEY clause of this statement. Executing these statements has many repercussions; one needs the ALTER privilege on the dependent table and parent table (we'll look at privileges later). Dropping a primary or foreign key will also cancel the referential relation between the parent and child tables. It may also drop any related index.

Let's drop the primary and foreign key, which we created previously, for the EMP_HISTORIES table; for example:

```
ALTER TABLE EMPL_HISTORIES
     DROP PRIMARY KEY
     DROP FOREIGN KEY EMPL_ID
```

Note that we supply the name of constraint EMPL_ID when dropping the foreign key.

▪▪▪ Dropping a Non-key Column

DB2 does not have a single direct statement to remove a column that is not a primary or foreign key. There are two ways of dropping a non-key column. One is to drop the table and re-create it, omitting the column you want to remove. The other is to create a view whereby the view columns do not have the column you want to drop.

▪▪▪ Dropping a Table

A table is removed from a database with the DROP TABLE statement; for example:

```
DROP TABLE EMPLOYEES
```

removes the EMPLOYEES table from the ONEWORLD database. Here, we do not name the database, but it is assumed once we connect the database. But if you want to be more specific, you can issue a command with the database, for example,

```
DROP TABLE ONEWORLD.EMPLOYEES
```

When DB2 drops a table, it also does many other operations, which you should to be aware of:

- All the rows of the table are deleted
- All the columns are dropped
- An existing index for the table is also removed
- Any view based on the table is dropped
- All the referential constraints, if the table is a parent or child, is dropped
- A privilege related to the table, or view based on the table, is removed from the DB2 catalog.

▪▪▪ Changing An Index

There is no statement to change an index. To modify one, you first remove it from the DB2 catalog with the DROP INDEX, for example, to drop the IDX_EMPLOYEES we use the command:

```
DROP INDEX IDX_EMPLOYEES
```

To redo the same index, you use the CREATE INDEX statement:

```
CREATE UNIQUE INDEX IDX_EMPLOYEES
    ON EMPLOYEES (DEPARTMENT_NUM, SURNAME ASC)
```

In the new IDX_EMPLOYEES index, DEPARTMENT_NUM and SURNAME are columns combined together to form the index.

▮▮▮ Changing a View

There is no statement to change a view. The only way to accomplish this is to drop the view with the DROP VIEW statement, for example,

```
DROP VIEW DEPARTMENT_001
```

Then you re-create it with the CREATE VIEW command.

▮▮▮ Dropping a Database

Finally, we may want to change some characteristics of a database, for instance, the directory where DB2 keeps the file. The only way to alter a database is drop it and re-create it. Once deleted, all the objects, data files, and catalog entries are gone. Therefore, one must be very careful when dropping a database. It is done with the DROP DATABASE statement. For example,

```
DROP DATABASE ONEWORLD
```

will delete the ONEWORLD database.

Chapter 6
Maintaining a Database

In the last chapter, we went through various steps of designing a database. We illustrated how to build different parts of ONEWORLD, our sample database used throughout this book. But with no data in it, it is like a new house with empty rooms. Now it's the time to populate the tables with information. Unlike a house, the content of a database changes constantly: in some cases within seconds and others within days, months or years. The changes could happen in many ways: it could be simply by adding a new row into a table, changing an existing one, or purging stale data that is no longer required.

A database is a repository of information built with a particular purpose in mind. Regardless of the objective — whether it be for personal or corporate use — the addition, change, and retrieval of the data will happen according to certain design. It could be mean storing a personal directory or millions of transactions worth billions of dollars. Or it may simply be a quick check of the name or position of an employee and you may want the data to be retrieved in a certain format.

As mentioned before, to manage the data we use the DML (data management language) of SQL. In this chapter, our focus will be to explore four important statements: INSERT, UPDATE, DELETE, and SELECT. We'll discuss how to use these statements — with illustrations — to perform the following:

- Add data to a table
- Change data
- Delete data
- Extract data

■■■ Adding Data to a Table

A row of data is added to a table with the INSERT statement. INSERT is issued in two ways. One way is to give the values for all or some of the columns. To insert a row of data into the DEPARTMENTS table, we use the command:

```
INSERT INTO DEPARTMENTS
          (DEPARTMENT_NUM,DEPT_NAME,MANAGER,LOCATION)
    VALUES (1000,'Tex-Mex Restaurant','1000-JK','Rodeo Circle')
```

In this statement there are a few points to note. One is that the data you supply must be enclosed in parentheses, placed after the VALUES clause. Next, each field is separated by a comma. A field that is numeric data, such as DEPARTMENT_NUM, must not be enclosed in quotes, but string data must be in quotes only if there are spaces in it. If there is no data for a field, you can type NULL instead or place nothing for that field, for example

```
INSERT INTO DEPARTMENTS
          (DEPARTMENT_NUM,DEPT_NAME,MANAGER,LOCATION)
     VALUES (1000,NULL,,'Rodeo Circle')
```

In this INSERT statement, no values are given for DEPT_NAME and MANAGER.

Since we are giving the values for all the columns, there is no need to list all the column names. This insert will work the same way with this command:

```
INSERT INTO DEPARTMENTS
VALUES (1000,'Tex-Mex Restaurant','1000-JK','Rodeo Circle')
```

But if you have values for some columns, then you have to list the columns, for example,

```
INSERT INTO DEPARTMENTS
          (DEPARTMENT_NUM,DEPT_NAME,LOCATION)
     VALUES (1000,'Tex-Mex Restaurant','Rodeo Circle')
```

In this case, we omitted the value for MANAGER. This row will have no value for MANAGER. Or you can place NULL instead, for example,

```
INSERT INTO DEPARTMENTS VALUES
          (1000,'Tex-Mex Restaurant',NULL,'Rodeo Circle')
```

When inserting values to a row, make sure the datatype defined for the column is compatible with the datatype you provide; for example, numbers will not be acceptable where a string is required and vice versa.

The second way to use INSERT is without the VALUES clause, but with a SELECT statement. The SELECT statement retrieves data from one or more tables. We'll look at SELECT statement in detail later in this chapter. When INSERT is combined with SELECT, you are copying data from one or more tables to another, for example,

```
INSERT INTO EMPL_HISTORIES
        ( DEPARTMENT_NUM
        ,EMPLOYEE_ID )
          ( SELECT DEPARTMENT_NUM
                 ,EMPLOYEE_ID
            FROM EMPLOYEES )
```

This copies data from EMPLOYEES to EMPL_HISTORIES. Here, we transfer data for only two columns; of course, you have many more.

Now, we can insert data into all the tables, as shown in Figure 6.1.

```
DEPARTMENTS:
   insert into departments(DEPARTMENT_NUM,DEPT_NAME,MANAGER,LOCATION)
    VALUES(1000,'Tex-Mex Restaurant','1000-JK','Rodeo Circle')
   insert into departments(DEPARTMENT_NUM,DEPT_NAME,MANAGER,LOCATION)
    VALUES(1001,'Jimmy The Greek Restaurant','1001-JO','Greek
   Village')
   insert into departments(DEPARTMENT_NUM,DEPT_NAME,MANAGER,LOCATION)
    VALUES(1002,'Authentic Chinese Food','1002-MT','China Town')
   insert into departments(DEPARTMENT_NUM,DEPT_NAME,MANAGER,LOCATION)
    VALUES(1003,'Reduce, Recycle and Reuse','1003-RG','Ecology Fair')
   insert into departments(DEPARTMENT_NUM,DEPT_NAME,MANAGER,LOCATION)
    VALUES(1004,'Virtual reality','1004-BG','Futuristic World')
   insert into departments(DEPARTMENT_NUM,DEPT_NAME,MANAGER,LOCATION)
    VALUES(1005,'Spiritual Transformation','1005-PZ','Heaven On
   Earth')

EMPLOYEES:
   insert into EMPLOYEES
   (EMPLOYEE_ID,DEPARTMENT_NUM,FIRST_NAME,MIDDLE_NAME,SURNAME,BIRTH_D
   ATE,AGE)
   VALUES('1000-JK',1000,'John',NULL,'Kennedy','1945-02-03',50)
   insert into EMPLOYEES
   (EMPLOYEE_ID,DEPARTMENT_NUM,FIRST_NAME,MIDDLE_NAME,SURNAME,BIRTH_D
   ATE,AGE)
   VALUES('1000-IS',1000,'Itsu','Frank','Sony','1960-01-20',35)
   insert into EMPLOYEES
   (EMPLOYEE_ID,DEPARTMENT_NUM,FIRST_NAME,MIDDLE_NAME,SURNAME,BIRTH_D
   ATE,AGE)
   VALUES('1001-JO',1001,'Jimmy',NULL,'Onasis','1950-02-24',45)
```

```
    insert into EMPLOYEES
    (EMPLOYEE_ID,DEPARTMENT_NUM,FIRST_NAME,MIDDLE_NAME,SURNAME,BIRTH_D
    ATE,AGE)
    VALUES('1002-MT',1002,'Mao','Tse','Tung','1962-12-31',33)
    insert into EMPLOYEES
    (EMPLOYEE_ID,DEPARTMENT_NUM,FIRST_NAME,MIDDLE_NAME,SURNAME,BIRTH_D
    ATE,AGE)
    VALUES('1003-RG',1003,'Raj',NULL,'Gandhi','1955-01-02',40)
    insert into EMPLOYEES
    (EMPLOYEE_ID,DEPARTMENT_NUM,FIRST_NAME,MIDDLE_NAME,SURNAME,BIRTH_D
    ATE,AGE)
    VALUES('1004-BG',1004,'Billy',NULL,'Gates','1956-12-01',39)
    insert into EMPLOYEES
    (EMPLOYEE_ID,DEPARTMENT_NUM,FIRST_NAME,MIDDLE_NAME,SURNAME,BIRTH_D
    ATE,AGE)
    VALUES('1005-PG',1005,'Paul',NULL,'Zen','1954-09-02',41)
```

EMPL_HISTORIES:
```
    insert into EMPL_HISTORIES
    (EMPLOYEE_ID,DEPARTMENT_NUM,POSITION,START_DATE,END_DATE,SALARY)
    VALUES('1000-JK',1000,'Manager','1990-02-01',NULL,30100)
    insert into EMPL_HISTORIES
    (EMPLOYEE_ID,DEPARTMENT_NUM,POSITION,START_DATE,END_DATE,SALARY)
    VALUES('1000-JK',1000,'Cook','1985-05-01','1990-01-31',25000)
    insert into EMPL_HISTORIES
    (EMPLOYEE_ID,DEPARTMENT_NUM,POSITION,START_DATE,END_DATE,SALARY)
    VALUES
    ('1000-JK',1000,'Cashier','1982-02-23','1985-04-30',22000)
    insert into EMPL_HISTORIES
    (EMPLOYEE_ID,DEPARTMENT_NUM,POSITION,START_DATE,END_DATE,SALARY)
    VALUES('1000-IS',1000,'Cashier','1990-02-01',NULL,26000)
    insert into EMPL_HISTORIES
    (EMPLOYEE_ID,DEPARTMENT_NUM,POSITION,START_DATE,END_DATE,SALARY)
    VALUES('1001-JO',1001,'Manager','1992-01-01',NULL,30200)
    insert into EMPL_HISTORIES
    (EMPLOYEE_ID,DEPARTMENT_NUM,POSITION,START_DATE,END_DATE,SALARY)
    VALUES('1002-MT',1002,'Manager','1991-02-10',NULL,30300)
    insert into EMPL_HISTORIES
    (EMPLOYEE_ID,DEPARTMENT_NUM,POSITION,START_DATE,END_DATE,SALARY)
    VALUES('1003-RG',1003,'Manager','1986-03-10',NULL,30400)
    insert into EMPL_HISTORIES
    (EMPLOYEE_ID,DEPARTMENT_NUM,POSITION,START_DATE,END_DATE,SALARY)
    VALUES('1004-BG',1004,'Manager','1992-02-05',NULL,30200)
    insert into EMPL_HISTORIES
    (EMPLOYEE_ID,DEPARTMENT_NUM,POSITION,START_DATE,END_DATE,SALARY)
    VALUES('1004-BG',1004,'Analyst','1991-01-01','1992-02-24',25000)
    insert into EMPL_HISTORIES
    (EMPLOYEE_ID,DEPARTMENT_NUM,POSITION,START_DATE,END_DATE,SALARY)
    VALUES('1004-BG',1004,'Programmer','1990-01-01','1990-12-31',20000
    )
    insert into EMPL_HISTORIES
    (EMPLOYEE_ID,DEPARTMENT_NUM,POSITION,START_DATE,END_DATE,SALARY)
    VALUES('1005-PZ',1005,'Manager','1975-06-07',NULL,30700)
```

EMPL_ADDRESSES:
```
    insert into EMPL_ADDRESSES
    (EMPLOYEE_ID,DEPARTMENT_NUM,STREET_LINE1,CITY,STATE_PROV,ZIP_CODE
```

```
) values ('1000-JK',1000,'123 Peace Blvd.','New World Expo'
,'ON','L3X-1Y1');
insert into EMPL_ADDRESSES
(EMPLOYEE_ID,DEPARTMENT_NUM,STREET_LINE1,CITY,STATE_PROV,ZIP_CODE
) values ('1000-IS',1000,'609 Unity Ave.','New World Expo'
,'ON','L3X-1T2');
insert into EMPL_ADDRESSES
(EMPLOYEE_ID,DEPARTMENT_NUM,STREET_LINE1,CITY,STATE_PROV,ZIP_CODE
) values ('1001-JO',1001,'851 Harmony Rd.','New World Expo'
,'ON','L3X-5S1');
insert into EMPL_ADDRESSES
(EMPLOYEE_ID,DEPARTMENT_NUM,STREET_LINE1,CITY,STATE_PROV,ZIP_CODE
) values ('1002-MT',1002,'923 Charity Rd.','New World Expo'
 'ON','L3X-9P1');
```

Figure 6.1 Inserting data into the ONEWORLD database

■■■ Changing Data

After you have added data to a table, there is a chance you may want to update it. The data in a table is altered with the UPDATE statement. When you issue this statement, it may change none or many rows, depending on the structure of the statement. For example,

```
UPDATE EMPL_HISTORIES
    SET SALARY = SALARY + 10
```

This will add 10 to the current value in every row. Figure 6.2 shows the values before and after the addition.

Sometimes you may not want to change all the rows, but only some of them. You limit the change with a search condition. We use the WHERE clause to search rows that meet a certain criteria and then apply the changes to them. Let's say we want to give a raise of $10 only to the managers; we issue the command:

```
UPDATE EMPL_HISTORIES
    SET SALARY    = SALARY + 10
  WHERE POSITION = 'Manager'
    AND END_DATE = NULL
```

There are two parts to this WHERE clause. The POSITION = 'Manager' means the record must belong to a manager and the END_DATE must have a NULL value. Remember this table may have one or more records for each employee, especially those that received promotions. Each position will have a start and end date, except in the row of the latest position where the end date will not be determined yet. In database terms it will be NULL.

```
Before          After
-------         -------
30100           30110
25000           25010
22000           22010
26000           26010
30200           30210
30300           30310
30400           30410
30200           30210
25000           25010
20000           20010
30700           30710
```

Figure 6.2 Values before and after the UPDATE statement

Now, let's verify the result.

Statement:

```
SELECT * FROM EMPL_HISTORIES
```

Result:

DEPARTMENT_NUM	EMPLOYEE_ID	POSITION	START_DATE	END_DATE	SALARY
1000	1000-JK	Manager	01-FEB-90		30110
1000	1000-JK	Cook	01-MAY-85	31-JAN-90	25000
1000	1000-JK	Cashier	23-FEB-82	30-APR-85	22000
1000	1000-IS	Cashier	01-FEB-90		26000
1001	1001-JO	Manager	01-JAN-92		30210
1002	1002-MT	Manager	10-FEB-91		30310
1003	1003-RG	Manager	10-MAR-86		30410
1004	1004-BG	Manager	05-FEB-92		30210
1004	1004-BG	Analyst	01-JAN-91	24-FEB-92	25000
1004	1004-BG	Programmer	01-JAN-90	31-DEC-90	20000
1005	1005-JK	Manager	07-JUN-75		30710

The salary of only 6 rows changed. As seen in the previous query, only six rows have 'Manager' as position and the END_DATE as NULL.

▐▐▐▐ Deleting Data

There will come a time when you may want to prune your database, removing all the dead wood. We remove data from a table with the DELETE statement. Let's say you want to get rid of the rows from the DEPARTMENTS table; the command is:

```
DELETE DEPARTMENTS
```

With the DELETE statement, you can also remove data selectively with a WHERE clause. To delete all the the rows in DEPARTMENTS for a department that does not exist, say 1000, we give the command:

```
DELETE DEPARTMENTS
 WHERE DEPARTMENT_NUM = 1000
```

We know that this statement will remove only one row because the DEPARTMENTS table should have one row for each department. Let's view the data in this table after the previous delete operation.

Statement:

```
SELECT * FROM DEPARTMENTS
```

Result:

```
DEPARTMENT_NUM DEPT_NAME                    MANAGER LOCATION
-------------- ---------                    ------- --------
          1001 Jimmy The Greek Restaurant  1001-JO Greek Village
          1002 Authentic Chinese Food      1002-MT China Town
          1003 Reduce, Recycle and Reuse   1003-RG Ecology Fair
          1004 Virtual reality             1004-BG Futuristic World
          1005 Spiritual Transformation    1005-PZ Heaven On Earth
```

From this query, we see that the records for department 1000 are gone.

If we want to delete all the rows in EMPLOYEES table for the department 1000, we execute:

```
DELETE EMPLOYEES
 WHERE DEPARTMENT_NUM = 1000
```

This will remove 2 rows, because we know that there are only two employees for department 1000. After this operation, we check the data in EMPLOYEES.

Statement:

```
SELECT * FROM EMPLOYEES
```

Result:

```
DEPARTMENT_NUM EMPLOYEE_I FIRST_NAME MIDDLE_NAME  SURNAME BIRTH_DATE AGE
-------------- ---------- ---------- -----------  ------- ---------- ---
          1001 1001-JO    Jimmy                   Onasis  24-FEB-50   45
          1002 1002-MT    Mao        Tse          Tung    31-DEC-62   33
          1003 1003-RG    Raj                     Gandhi  02-JAN-55   40
```

When data is removed from the DELETE statement, the entire row(s) is removed and not part of it. If you want to get rid of values of some columns, then set those columns to NULL with the UPDATE statement. When you remove a table from a database with the DROP TABLE statement, it also deletes all the rows from that table.

▮▮▮ Retrieving Data

When we want to get data out of a database, we use the SELECT statement. In fact, we have used it a few times earlier; this time we'll go over the nitty-gritty points of this very important statement. SELECT is considered to the heart of SQL. It has many facets and can be used with INSERT, UPDATE, and DELETE statements. It will take many chapters to discuss all the aspects of this versatile command; in the rest of this chapter and the next one, we will only be able to cover some of the basic points.

If we want to get all the information from a table, we do the following steps.

Statement:

```
SELECT * from DEPARTMENTS
```

Result:

```
DEPARTMENT_NUM DEPT_NAME                   MANAGER  LOCATION
-------------- ---------                   -------  --------
          1000 Tex-Mex Restaurant          1000-JK  Rodeo Circle
          1001 Jimmy The Greek Restaurant  1001-JO  Greek Village
          1002 Authentic Chinese Food      1002-MT  China Town
          1003 Reduce, Recycle and Reuse   1003-RG  Ecology Fair
          1004 Virtual reality             1004-BG  Futuristic World
          1005 Spiritual Transformation    1005-PZ  Heaven On Earth
```

The asterix (*) after SELECT means to retrieve data from all the columns. This shows all the data we inserted earlier into the DEPARTMENTS table. Next, we issue similar commands to look at data from other tables of the ONEWORLD database.

Statement:

```
SELECT * from EMPLOYEES
```

Result:

```
DEPARTMENT_NUM EMPLOYEE_ID FIRST_NAME MIDDLE_NAME SURNAME BIRTH_DATE AGE
-------------- ----------- ---------- ----------- ------- ---------- ---
          1000 1000-JK     John                   Kennedy 03-FEB-45   50
          1000 1000-IS     Itsu       Frank       Sony    20-JAN-60   35
          1001 1001-JO     Jimmy                  Onasis  24-FEB-50   45
          1002 1002-MT     Mao        Tse         Tung    31-DEC-62   33
          1003 1003-RG     Raj                    Gandhi  02-JAN-55   40
          1004 1004-BG     Billy                  Gates   01-DEC-56   39
          1005 1005-PZ     Paul                   Zen     02-SEP-54   41
```

Statement:

```
SELECT * from EMPL_HISTORIES
```

Result:

```
DEPARTMENT_NUM EMPLOYEE_ID POSITION     START_DATE END_DATE     SALARY
-------------- ----------- --------     ---------- --------     ------
          1000 1000-JK     Manager      01-FEB-90               30100
          1000 1000-JK     Cook         01-MAY-85  31-JAN-90    25000
          1000 1000-JK     Cashier      23-FEB-82  30-APR-85    22000
          1000 1000-IS     Cashier      01-FEB-90               26000
          1001 1001-JO     Manager      01-JAN-92               30200
          1002 1002-MT     Manager      10-FEB-91               30300
          1003 1003-RG     Manager      10-MAR-86               30400
          1004 1004-BG     Manager      05-FEB-92               30200
          1004 1004-BG     Analyst      01-JAN-91  24-FEB-92    25000
          1004 1004-BG     Programmer   01-JAN-90  31-DEC-90    20000
          1005 1005-JK     Manager      07-JUN-75               30700
```

Statement:

```
SELECT * from EMPL_ADDRESSES
```

Result:

```
DEPARTMENT_NUM EMPLOYEE_ID STREET_LINE1     CITY      STATE_PROV ZIP_CODE
-------------- ----------- ------------     ----      ---------- --------
          1000 1000-JK     123 Peace Blvd.  New World Expo ON    L3X-1Y1
          1000 1000-IS     609 Unity Ave.   New World Expo ON    L3X-1T2
          1001 1001-JO     851 Harmony Rd.  New World Expo ON    L3X-5S1
          1002 1002-MT     923 Charity Rd.  New World Expo ON    L3X-9P1
```

There are times when you do not want to get the data from *all* the columns. To access only some columns, you simply name the column rather than asterix (*) after SELECT. The name can be in any order, for example,

Statement:

```
SELECT LOCATION
          ,DEPT_NAME
   FROM DEPARTMENTS
```

Result:

```
LOCATION              DEPT_NAME
--------              ---------
Rodeo Circle          Tex-Mex Restaurant
Greek Village         Jimmy The Greek Restaurant
China Town            Authentic Chinese Food
Ecology Fair          Reduce, Recycle and Reuse
Futuristic World      Virtual reality
Heaven On Earth       Spiritual Transformation
```

The examples we just looked at are some of the simplest forms of the SELECT statement. The SELECT statement has the capacity to do much more: retrieve data according to certain criteria, order the output in a certain order or group the result in certain ways. When combining these and other functionalities, the SELECT command can become quite long and complicated. The basic concepts we'll discuss here will be enough to get you using SELECT, but by no means would we have covered all the nuances and variations of this powerful SQL statement. Also, we'll look at how it can be used with other statements, such as INSERT, UPDATE, and DELETE.

We'll start with its general form, which gives all the main parts. They are called clauses. They look like this:

```
SELECT ...
   FROM ...
   WHERE ...
   GROUP BY ...
   HAVING ...
   ORDER BY ...
```

As you may have noticed, only SELECT and FROM clauses are required and the rest are optional. In the following pages we'll discuss each of them.

The SELECT clause

The SELECT clause is mandatory and is always preceded by an asterix (*) or a list of columns. You can also add a comment or function (we'll discuss function later) after the SELECT clause, for example,

Statement:

```
SELECT  MANAGER
        , 'is the manager for'
        , DEPT_NAME
   FROM  DEPARTMENTS
```

Result:

```
MANAGER    'IS THE MANAGER FOR' DEPT_NAME
-------    -------------------- ---------
1000-JK    is the manager for   Tex-Mex Restaurant
1001-JO    is the manager for   Jimmy The Greek Restaurant
1002-MT    is the manager for   Authentic Chinese Food
1003-RG    is the manager for   Reduce, Recycle and Reuse
1004-BG    is the manager for   Virtual Reality
1005-PZ    is the manager for   Spiritual Transformation
```

What we did in this statement is to add a literal 'is the manager for' instead of a column name. As you can see in the result, the literal appears on each line, but the data for each column is from the table.

There are times when the result of a SELECT would give you duplicate rows, as is possible when retrieving from EMPL_HISTORIES, for example,

Statement:

```
SELECT EMPLOYEE_ID
   FROM EMPL_HISTORIES
```

Result:

```
EMPLOYEE_ID
----------
1000-JK
1000-JK
1000-JK
1000-IS
1001-JO
1002-MT
1003-RG
1004-BG
1004-BG
1004-BG
1005-PZ
```

To eliminate the duplicates we use the DISTINCT keyword, for example,

Statement:

```
SELECT DISTINCT EMPLOYEE_ID
   FROM EMPL_HISTORIES
```

```
Result:

EMPLOYEE_ID
-----------
1000-IS
1000-JK
1001-JO
1002-MT
1003-RG
1004-BG
1005-PZ
```

The WHERE clause

As we saw earlier, the SELECT clause is to choose the column(s) of a table from which data is extracted. Now let's examine closely this very important WHERE clause. Its main function is to limit the number of rows. The result can be from no row selected to many rows retrieved. To do this, the WHERE clause contains a search condition that satisfies every row. We specify the search condition with different operators: comparison operators, AND, OR, BETWEEN, IN and LIKE operators. They are familiar English common words and the concepts behind them are easy to understand.

Comparison operators

There are operators as shown in Figure 6.3.

Operator	Meaning
=	Equal to
<>	Not equal to
>	Greater than
>=	Greater than or equal to
<=	Less than or equal to

Figure 6.3 Comparison Operators in the WHERE clause

Basically, these operators compare two values, which could be both from columns, one from a column and the other a fixed value, or both fixed values. An example of comparing a content to a column value would be:

Statement:

```
SELECT  SURNAME
   FROM  EMPLOYEES
  WHERE  DEPARTMENT_NUM = 1000
```

Result:

```
SURNAME
-------
Kennedy
Sony
```

DB2 takes a look at all the rows of the EMPLOYEES table and, when it finds the DEPARTMENT_NUM equals to 1000, it gives us the value of SURNAME for that row. In this case, it gives us 2 names that satisfy this condition. We just used the equal to operator. Similarly, we can use the not equal to (<>) operator, as in the following:

Statement:

```
SELECT  SURNAME
   FROM  EMPLOYEES
  WHERE  DEPARTMENT_NUM <> 1000
```

Result:

```
SURNAME
-------
Onasis
Tung
Gandhi
Gates
Zen
```

The result is different; fives rows were selected and none of them belong to department 1000. One thing to remember about the comparison operators is that the datatypes of both sides of the operator must be the same: comparing numbers with numbers, strings with strings, date with date, and so on. If they are not compatible, DB2 will give an error message.

AND and OR operators

If a WHERE clause has more than one condition, they must be stringed together with AND or OR. AND simply means that the conditions on both sides of AND must be true. When you use OR instead, one of the two conditions must be true. Let's see how this works with the example:

Statement:

```
SELECT SURNAME
   FROM EMPLOYEES
  WHERE DEPARTMENT_NUM = 1000
    AND EMPLOYEE_ID = '1000-JK'
```

Result:

```
SURNAME
-------
Kennedy
```

In this WHERE clause, we have two conditions: DEPARTMENT_NUM = 1000 and EMPOYEE_ID = '1000-JK'. The result is that only one row satisfies these two conditions. From this row, the value of SURNAME is returned.

Now, let's separate these two condition with an OR as in:

Statement:

```
SELECT SURNAME
   FROM EMPLOYEES
  WHERE DEPARTMENT_NUM = 1000
     OR EMPLOYEE_ID    = '1000-JK'
```

Result:

```
SURNAME
-------
Kennedy
Sony
```

In this case, the value of SURNAME is shown from the row that satisfies either the condition DEPARTMENT_NUM = 1000 or POSITION = '1000-JK'. We have two rows that satisfy this condition.

BETWEEN operator

The BETWEEN in operator is used when you are looking for a value in a certain range. To understand this better let's look at an example.

Statement:

```
SELECT EMPLOYEE_ID,
       POSITION
  FROM EMPL_HISTORIES
 WHERE START_DATE  BETWEEN '1971-01-01'
                   AND     '1995-01-01'
```

Result:

```
EMPLOYEE_ID POSITION
----------  ---------
1000-JK     Manager
1000-JK     Cook
1000-JK     Cashier
1000-IS     Cashier
1001-JO     Manager
1002-MT     Manager
1003-RG     Manager
1004-BG     Manager
1004-BG     Analyst
1004-BG     Programmer
1005-PZ     Manager
```

In this SELECT statement, we see the values of EMPLOYEE_ID and POSITION from the rows that have the START_DATE between two dates: '1971-01-01' AND '1995-01-01'.

IN operator

The IN operator is similar to BETWEEN, except you give specific values rather than a range, for example,

Statement:

```
SELECT  POSITION
  FROM EMPL_HISTORIES
 WHERE EMPLOYEE_ID IN ('1000-JK','1000-IS','1004-BG')
```

Result:

```
POSITION
--------
Manager
Cook
Cashier
Cashier
Manager
Analyst
Programmer
```

In this case, you get the position for employees where the EMPLOYEE_ID is 1000-JK, 1000-IS, or 1004-BG.

LIKE operator

The LIKE operator is useful when you are not sure of a name or an address. In such a case, you use a wild card when searching for a value. The wild card symbol is the percent sign (%). for any string having none to many characters. An example of the like operator is:

Statement:

```
SELECT EMPLOYEE_ID, SURNAME
  FROM EMPLOYEES
  WHERE SURNAME LIKE 'Ga%'
```

Result:

```
EMPLOYEE_ID SURNAME
----------- --------
1003-JK     Gandhi
1004-BG     Gates
```

In this case, the rows that are chosen have 'Ga' in the first two characters of the SURNAME.

Now, with an underscore (_) we can be more wild. You can have one or more underscores sa part of the wild card string, which means that at the position where underscore is found, it can be any character. Let's look at an example:

Statement:

```
SELECT EMPLOYEE_ID, SURNAME
   FROM EMPLOYEES
   WHERE SURNAME LIKE '_un%'
```

Result:

```
EMPLOYEE_I SURNAME
---------- -------
1002-MT    Tung
```

This means that we don't care what the first character is.

Ordering the data

Ordering the data that we request from DB2 is important in many instances. The SELECT statement has the ORDER BY clause that tells DB2 how we want the data arranged. If you don't specify the ORDER BY, DB2 will simply give the data the way it is stored, without any extra effort in arranging it. It may have a certain order to it, but you may not necessarily like it.

The ORDER BY clause uses the column values to order the result and it can be either in ascending (ASC) or descending (DESC) order. If you omit a specific order, the default is ascending order.

The column values can be specified by the name or a position. The position or name refers to the column name listed after the SELECT clause, and if an asterix (*) is present instead, it refers to the column names as defined in the table. The position starts with 1 referring to the first column, 2 for the second and so on.

In the ORDER BY clause, you can have more than one name or position. The ordering is done within each column. Next, we'll look at four examples of ordering data.

```
Without ORDER BY
```

Statement:

```
SELECT EMPLOYEE_ID
       START_DATE
   FROM EMPL_HISTORIES
```

```
START_DATE
----------
1000-JK
1000-JK
1000-JK
1000-IS
1001-JO
1002-MT
1003-RG
1004-BG
1004-BG
1004-BG
1005-PZ
```

In the first example, we select EMPLOYEE_ID and START_DATE from EMPLOYEES without the ORDER BY clause. We are presented with the data as it is stored in DB2 files. Here, DB2 does not attempt to order the output.

```
With ORDER BY and specify a column name.
```

Statement:

```
SELECT EMPLOYEE_ID
       START_DATE
  FROM EMPL_HISTORIES
 ORDER BY EMPLOYEE_ID
```

Result:

```
START_DATE
----------
1000-IS
1000-JK
1000-JK
1000-JK
1001-JO
1002-MT
1003-RG
1004-BG
1004-BG
1004-BG
1005-PZ
```

In the next example, we add the ORDER BY to the previous example, and the result has changed. The employee numbers are listed from the lowest to the highest order.

```
With ORDER BY and specify a position
```

Statement:

```
SELECT EMPLOYEE_ID
       START_DATE
  FROM EMPL_HISTORIES
 ORDER BY 1
```

Result:

```
START_DATE
----------
1000-IS
1000-JK
1000-JK
1000-JK
1001-JO
1002-MT
1003-RG
1004-BG
1004-BG
1004-BG
1005-PZ
```

In the following example, we change the ORDER BY clause to specify a position rather than a column name. The result is the same as the previous example.

```
With ORDER BY and specify two column names.
```

Statement:

```
SELECT EMPLOYEE_ID
      ,START_DATE
  FROM EMPL_HISTORIES
 ORDER BY EMPLOYEE_ID DESC, START_DATE ASC
```

Result:

```
EMPLOYEE_ID    START_DATE
----------     ----------
1005-PZ        1975-06-07
1004-BG        1990-01-01
1004-BG        1991-01-01
1004-BG        1992-02-05
1003-RG        1986-03-10
1002-MT        1991-02-10
1001-JO        1992-01-01
1000-JK        1982-02-23
1000-JK        1985-05-01
1000-JK        1990-02-01
1000-IS        1990-02-01
```

In the last example, we specify two column names, each with an explicit way to order the result. DESC means descending order and ASC means ascending order. The result shows that the employee IDs are listed in descending order and within each employee, the start date is listed in ascending order.

GROUP BY clause

The GROUP BY is used to group rows together according to one or more categories. The category is determined by the value of a column. This is an optional clause of the SELECT statement, placed following the WHERE clause, if one exists. To illustrate this, let's try a query without and one with this clause.

Statement:

```
SELECT MAX(SALARY)
    FROM EMPL_HISTORIES
```

Result:

```
MAX(SALARY)
-----------
      30700
```

Now, we introduce a new word MAX, don't let it throw you off. MAX is a function — we'll discuss function a bit later — that returns the maximum value for a column, for example, SALARY.

As you can see, the statement returns one value without the GROUP BY. Basically, it goes through all the salaries and picks the highest number. In the next example, it groups the salaries by employee IDs and then finds the maximum values for each employee.

Statement:

```
SELECT MAX(SALARY), EMPLOYEE_ID
    FROM EMPL_HISTORIES
    GROUP BY EMPLOYEE_ID
```

Result:

```
MAX(SALARY) EMPLOYEE_ID
----------- -----------
      26000 1000-IS
```

```
30100 1000-JK
30200 1001-JO
30300 1002-MT
30400 1003-RG
30200 1004-BG
30700 1005-JK
```

Therefore we get a maximum value for each employee. To understand how this works, let's look at EMPL_HISTORIES without the GROUP BY clause and MAX function.

Statement:

```
SELECT SALARY, EMPLOYEE_ID
   FROM EMPL_HISTORIES
```

Result:

```
SALARY EMPLOYEE_I
------ ----------
 30100 1000-JK
 25000 1000-JK
 22000 1000-JK
 26000 1000-IS
 30200 1001-JO
 30300 1002-MT
 30400 1003-RG
 30200 1004-BG
 25000 1004-BG
 20000 1004-BG
 30700 1005-JK
```

In this list, we see three salaries for 1000-JK. With MAX and GROUP BY, we receive only 30100, the maximum salary for 1000-JK. Next, we have only one salary item for 1000-IS, therefore, we get 26000 as the maximum value. Similarly, for 1004-BG, we receive 30200 for this employee.

HAVING clause

The HAVING clause is a way of giving a condition for a group of rows rather than a single row. It is optional and placed after GROUP BY. HAVING works with group, while WHERE is for rows. To illustrate this, we are changing our previous example a bit to add the HAVING clause.

Statement:

```
SELECT MAX(SALARY), EMPLOYEE_ID
  FROM EMPL_HISTORIES
  GROUP BY EMPLOYEE_ID
  HAVING MAX(SALARY) > 30200
```

Result:

```
MAX(SALARY) EMPLOYEE_ID
----------- -----------
      30300 1002-MT
      30400 1003-RG
      30700 1005-JK
```

The HAVING clause makes sure that a group satisfies the condition MAX(SALARY) > 30200. As you can see, all the maximum salaries are greater than 30200.

▥ Arithmetic

We have already seen some examples of calculations with SQL statements, for example, when we previously discussed the UPDATE statement. DB2 allows arithmetic operations on columns, constants, or combinations of both. The arithmetic operations allowed by DB2 are shown in Figure 6.4.

```
Operator    Meaning

   +        Addition
   -        Subtraction
   *        Multiplication
   /        Division
```

Figure 6.4 Arithmetic operators

Now, let's look at the workings of arithmetic operators with the following two examples:

Statement:

```
SELECT SALARY + 100
  FROM EMPL_HISTORIES
```

Result:

```
SALARY+100
----------
     30200
     25100
     22100
     26100
     30300
     30400
     30500
     30300
     25100
     20100
     30800
```

In the first example, 100 is added to the value of SALARY in each row of EMPLOYEE and shown to us. This addition is part of the SELECT clause.

In the next example, 5 months is subtracted from the current date and then the result is compared to the values of START_DATE. In this case, the subtraction is part of the WHERE clause.

Statement:

```
SELECT EMPLOYEE_ID
      ,SALARY
      ,START_DATE
  FROM EMPL_HISTORIES
 WHERE START_DATE > CURRENT - MONTH
```

Result:

```
for current date is 1992-02-10

EMPLOYEE_ID      SALARY START_DATE
-----------      ------ ----------
1000-JK          30100 1990-02-01
1000-JK          25000 1985-05-01
1000-JK          22000 1982-02-23
1000-IS          26000 1990-02-01
1002-MT          30300 1991-02-10
1003-RG          30400 1986-03-10
1004-BG          25000 1991-01-01
1004-BG          20000 1990-01-01
1005-PZ          30700 1975-06-07
```

▐▐▐▐ Functions

DB2 gives us special types of processing called functions. There are several of them and each does a specific task, but all of them act upon the values of a column. In fact, we looked at one earlier called MAX(). You may have noticed that the SUM() and AVG() functions must be used with columns whose datatype is numeric, such as DECIMAL, INT, and SMALLINT.

The other thing to note is that a function can only be used with the SELECT and HAVING clauses. Now, let's see how function works.

Statement:

```
SELECT COUNT(*)
   FROM EMPLOYEES
```

Result:

```
COUNT(*)
----------
         7
```

In this example, we used the COUNT() function (the parentheses indicates a function) to count the number of rows in the EMPLOYEES table. COUNT() is one of the most commonly used functions.

Statement:

```
SELECT EMPLOYEE_ID
       ,COUNT(*)
   FROM EMPL_HISTORIES
   GROUP BY EMPLOYEE_ID
```

Result:

```
EMPLOYEE_ID   COUNT(*)
-----------   --------
1000-IS          1
1000-JK          3
1001-JO          1
1002-MT          1
1003-RG          1
1004-BG          3
1005-JK          1
```

In this case, we counted rows for each EMPLOYEE_ID. Now, let's use a function in the HAVING clause.

Statement:

```
SELECT EMPLOYEE_ID
      ,COUNT(*)
  FROM EMPL_HISTORIES
  GROUP BY EMPLOYEE_ID
HAVING COUNT(*) < 2
```

Result:

```
EMPLOYEE_ID    COUNT(*)
-----------    --------
1000-IS            1
1001-JO            1
1002-MT            1
1003-RG            1
1005-JK            1
```

This result of this example is different than the previous one because, the count is less than 2. And, this is because of the HAVING COUNT(*) < 2. SUM is another useful function. It adds all the values of a column, for example,

Statement:

```
SELECT SUM(SALARY)
  FROM EMPL_HISTORIES
```

Result:

```
SUM(SALARY)
-----------
     299900
```

We have looked briefly at functions; DB2 has many more built-in functions and all of them are described in Chapter 10.

■■■ Making Changes Permanent

So far, we have looked at how we can change data in tables with INSERT, DELETE and UPDATE statements. Obviously, the SELECT statement does not change any information in the database. *When does a change become permanent?* Is it right after a change operation? Actually, DB2 gives us a chance to change our mind after issuing these statements and gives the user the control over whether to make an insert or update operation permanent or not with the COMMIT or ROLLBACK statement.

A COMMIT will make any number of previous changes permanent. In the following two statements,

```
UPDATE   EMPL_HISTORIES
   SET   SALARY = SALARY + 10 ;
COMMIT;
```

COMMIT tells DB2 to make the UPDATE statement permanent. There is no turn back from here.

However, if you want to discard a change, use the ROLLBACK statement. In the next two statements,

```
UPDATE   EMPL_HISTORIES
   SET   SALARY = SALARY + 10 ;
ROLLBACK;
```

ROLLBACK simply ignores the effect of the UPDATE statement.

In a program, COMMIT and ROLLBACK are judiciously used, depending largely on the situation. Normally, you would not commit after every statement; this will affect the performance negatively. Rather, you commit after a unit of *work. What is a unit of work?* It is defined as a transaction, the basic building block. To elaborate a bit, let's look at a banking transaction: transferring $100 from a savings account to a checking account. This transaction is complete only if the debit from the savings account and the credit to the checking account are successful. Only then do you want to make the changes of this transaction permanent with a COMMIT. This also ensures the consistency of the data. On the other hand, if something goes wrong while processing this transaction, you want to rollback any change.

There are situations when commit and rollback operations happen automatically. If a program is terminated successfully , and a commit is not issued, DB2 will make all the changes permanent for this program. On the other hand, when a program aborts, any change that is not committed will be rolled back by DB2.

Chapter 7
Advanced SQL

In the last chapter, we discussed the basic concepts of the SELECT statement. In this chapter, we'll discuss three complicated aspects of the SELECT statement. They sound complicated, but after gaining a clear understanding, you will find they are easy to use. You will appreciate their capabilities. They are subselect, UNION and joins. To illustrate these aspects of the SELECT statement, we'll use the ONEWORLD data. We will also look at more SQL statements, those to create and drop database objects, and those to grant and revoke privileges.

▊▊▊ Subselect

The *subselect* statement is a way of answering one question before answering another one. Once, I asked my daughter what she wanted for her birthday. She replied, "I want everything that Kim got for her birthday." Before deciding what to buy, I had to question her what Kim, her friend, received for her birthday.

A subselect, also known as a subquery, gives you the information that you need about something else. A subselect can be part of many statements, for instance, SELECT, UPDATE, INSERT or DELETE. A subselect is a clause, not a statement, though its syntax is the same as a SELECT statement. But it is part of another statement. Now, let's look at three examples to demonstrate the use of a subselect.

Statement:

```
SELECT AVG(SALARY)
  FROM EMPL_HISTORIES
```

Result:

```
AVG(SALARY)
-----------
 27263.6364
```

Statement:

```
SELECT EMPLOYEE_ID,SALARY
   FROM EMPL_HISTORIES
  WHERE SALARY >  27263.6364
```

Result:

```
EMPLOYEE_ID     SALARY
-----------     ------
1000-JK         30100
1001-JO         30200
1002-MT         30300
1003-RG         30400
1004-BG         30200
1005-PZ         30700
```

Statement:

```
SELECT EMPLOYEE_ID,SALARY
   FROM EMPL_HISTORIES
  WHERE SALARY > (SELECT AVG(SALARY)
                    FROM EMPL_HISTORIES)
```

Result:

```
EMPLOYEE_ID     SALARY
-----------     ------
1000-JK         30100
1001-JO         30200
1002-MT         30300
1003-RG         30400
1004-BG         30200
1005-PZ         30700
```

The first example gives us the average (27263.6364) of all the salaries from the EMPL_HISTORIES table. The next SELECT statement shows the employees whose salary is greater than the average we just found from the first example. Now, the third statement combines the first two, replacing 27263.6364 with a subselect which is the same as the first select statement.

Subselect is always enclosed with parentheses, as part of a WHERE or HAVING clause. For the sake of simplicity, we'll only look at how subselect works with the WHERE clause. You may recall that whatever we say about the WHERE clause also applies to the HAVING clause.

In the third statement, two statements are combined into one. *Why would you need to do this?* DB2 accepts one statement at a time; this alternate way gives us the ability to place one statement within another in a nested way.

In the above example, and as in any SELECT statement, the expression after the WHERE clause is evaluated before determining which row satisfies the search condition before it is retrieved. In this case the search condition containing the subselect "SELECT AVG(SALARY) FROM EMPL_HISTORIES", is calculated before any employee ID is given to us. After calculating the average salary, for every row that has a salary greater than 27263.6364, employee information extracted is given to us. The results from the two previous SELECT statements are the same.

DB2 allows many subselects in one statement in a nested manner:

Statement:

```
SELECT EMPLOYEE_ID,SALARY,DEPARTMENT_NUM
  FROM EMPL_HISTORIES
 WHERE SALARY > ( SELECT AVG(SALARY)
                   FROM EMPL_HISTORIES
                  WHERE EMPLOYEE_ID IN
                        (SELECT EMPLOYEE_ID
                          FROM EMPLOYEES
                         WHERE DEPARTMENT_NUM = 1000))
```

Result:

EMPLOYEE_ID	SALARY	DEPARTMENT_NUM
1000-JK	30100	1000
1000-IS	26000	1000
1001-JO	30200	1001
1002-MT	30300	1002
1003-RG	30400	1003
1004-BG	30200	1004
1005-PZ	30700	1005

Earlier we mentioned that the subselect is an answer to one question before another is resolved. In this example, we are using subselect to get two pieces of information from two different tables: EMPL_HISTORIES and EMPLOYEES. Simply put, it extracts all the employee IDs with a salary greater than the average salary of the EMPL_HISTORIES table and belonging to the department 1000 from the EMPLOYEES table.

This SELECT statement with two subselects does look a bit confusing. Let's analyze it by breaking it down into smaller pieces and executing each subselect separately.

Statement:

```
SELECT  EMPLOYEE_ID
  FROM  EMPLOYEES
 WHERE  DEPARTMENT_NUM = 1000
```

Result:

```
EMPLOYEE_ID
-----------
1000-JK
1000-IS
```

This innermost subselect gives a list of all the employees that belong to department 1000. The next example is to calculate the average salary of the department. We take the employee IDs we found in the previous example, and plug them in after the WHERE IN clause. Don't forget to enclose them in parentheses.

Statement:

```
SELECT  AVG(SALARY)
  FROM  EMPL_HISTORIES
 WHERE  EMPLOYEE_ID IN ('1000-JK','1000-IS')
```

Result:

```
AVG(SALARY)
-----------
      25775
```

This gives us the average of 25775.

Next, we execute the SELECT statement without the WHERE clause, thereby discarding the subselect.

Statement:

```
SELECT  EMPLOYEE_ID,  SALARY,DEPARTMENT_NUM
  FROM  EMPL_HISTORIES
 WHERE  SALARY > 25775
```

Result:

```
EMPLOYEE_ID    SALARY DEPARTMENT_NUM
----------- ---------- --------------
1000-JK        30100           1000
1000-IS        26000           1000
1001-JO        30200           1001
1002-MT        30300           1002
1003-RG        30400           1003
1004-BG        30200           1004
1005-PZ        30700           1005
```

It gives a list of all the employee IDs and their salary for all the departments.

Now, when we put the subselect back in, the only rows selected will be the ones that are highlighted. From it we only get the employee IDs that we asked for, where the salaries are greater than 25775 and they belong to department 1000.

Subselect with INSERT and UPDATE statements

Now, let's look at a subselect with other than a SELECT statement. One of the most useful ways is to combine an INSERT statement with a subselect to copy data from one table to another. For example, the follow INSERT statement:

Statement:

```
INSERT INTO TMP_DEPARTMENTS
    (SELECT * FROM DEPARTMENTS )
```

Result:

```
 5 rows inserted
```

copies data from DEPARTMENTS table to TMP_DEPARTMENTS. Here, we assume that TMP_DEPARTMENTS already exists and the definition of both tables is the same.

Next, we will use a subselect with an UPDATE statement, for example,

Statement:

```
UPDATE EMPL_HISTORIES
   SET SALARY = SALARY + 1000
 WHERE SALARY < (SELECT AVG(SALARY)
                 FROM  EMPL_HISTORIES)
```

Result:

```
5 rows updated
```

Here, you are being generous and giving those employees whose salary is less than the average a raise of $1000. We calculate the average salary with the subselect.

When using a subselect, there are three points to keep in mind:

- Compatible datatypes
- One or multiple returns
- EXIST clause

Let's go through each of these:

Compatible datatypes

As we have seen in the previous chapter, while discussing the WHERE clause, the datatype of the columns and literals on both sides of any operator (=, >=, >, <, <>, or <=) must be the same. In other words, if one is numeric, the other should be numeric. Characters should be matched with characters. Similarly, make sure that the datatypes of the return value from a subselect matche the expression on the other side of the operator.

In the example,

Statement:

```
SELECT EMPLOYEE_ID,SALARY
   FROM EMPL_HISTORIES
  WHERE SALARY > (SELECT AVG(SALARY)
                   FROM EMPL_HISTORIES )
```

Result:

```
EMPLOYEE_ID     SALARY
----------- ----------
1000-JK         30100
1001-JO         30200
1002-MT         30300
1003-RG         30400
1004-BG         30200
1005-PZ         30700
```

The datatypes are compatible in SALARY and the results of AVG(SALARY) are all numeric. Now, let's look at one with an incompatible datatype:

Statement:

```
SELECT EMPLOYEE_ID, SALARY
   FROM EMPL_HISTORIES
  WHERE SALARY > (SELECT POSITION
                    FROM EMPL_HISTORIES
                      WHERE EMPLOYEE_ID = '1005-JK')
```

Result:

```
ERROR: invalid number
```

This statement gives us an error as expected indicating incompatible datatypes. SALARY is numeric and POSITION, returned from the subselect, is a string of characters.

One or multiple returns

A subselect may return none or many values, depending on its search condition in the WHERE clause. However, the WHERE clause of the outer SELECT may only expect one value.

Statement:

```
SELECT   EMPLOYEE_ID,SALARY
   FROM   EMPL_HISTORIES
  WHERE   SALARY > (SELECT SALARY
                      FROM EMPL_HISTORIES
                      WHERE DEPARTMENT_NUM = 5000)
```

Result:

```
no rows selected
```

Statement:

```
SELECT   EMPLOYEE_ID,SALARY
   FROM   EMPL_HISTORIES
  WHERE   SALARY > (SELECT SALARY
                      FROM EMPL_HISTORIES
                      WHERE DEPARTMENT_NUM = 1000)
```

Result:

```
ERROR:  single-row subquery returns more than one row
```

Actually this example does not make sense. Why would someone do this? But, it demonstrates the point we are trying to make about one and multiple values returned from a subselect. This command will not execute successfully because the subselect returned more than one values, but the WHERE clause expected only one to be substituted.

EXIST clause

Before we finish with subselect, we have another aspect, the EXIST subclause of the WHERE clause. So far, we have looked at variations of the subselect that are evaluated once or many times and the result is substituted in the WHERE clause of the outer select. With EXIST, DB2 determines whether a row exists or not. It does not return a particular value from the subselect; rather it determines whether it is in a table or not. Let's explore this a bit further with an example:

Statement:

```
SELECT EMPLOYEE_ID,SURNAME
   FROM EMPLOYEES A
  WHERE EXISTS (SELECT *
                  FROM EMPL_HISTORIES B
                 WHERE POSITION = 'Manager'
                   AND A.EMPLOYEE_ID = B.EMPLOYEE_ID)
```

Result:

```
EMPLOYEE_ID SURNAME
----------- -------
1000-JK     Kennedy
1001-JO     Onasis
1002-MT     Tung
1003-RG     Gandhi
1004-BG     Gates
1005-PZ     Zen
```

It is important to note that the subselect does not take a column name, rather an asterix(*). In this example, we want the employee ID and surname from the EMPLOYEES table, of those whose position is manager. The position information is found in the EMPL_HISTORIES table. The result is 6 employee IDs, each one holding the position of manager.

Now let's examine another example:

Statement:

```
SELECT EMPLOYEE_ID,SURNAME
  FROM EMPLOYEES A
 WHERE EXISTS (SELECT *
                FROM EMPL_HISTORIES B
               WHERE POSITION = 'President'
                 AND A.EMPLOYEE_ID = B.EMPLOYEE_ID)
```

Result:

```
no rows selected
```

This time we did not get any employee IDs because in the EMPL_HISTORIES table, none of the rows has the POSITION column with value 'President'. Let's verify this.

To verify the result of the previous two examples, let's look in the EMPL_HISTORIES table, all the employee IDs and positions. Sure enough, there are six employees who are managers and none of them are president.

Statement:

```
SELECT EMPLOYEE_ID,POSITION
  FROM EMPL_HISTORIES
```

Result:

```
EMPLOYEE_ID POSITION
----------  --------
1000-JK     Manager
1000-JK     Cook
1000-JK     Cashier
1000-IS     Cashier
1001-JO     Manager
1002-MT     Manager
1003-RG     Manager
1004-BG     Manager
1004-BG     Analyst
1004-BG     Programmer
1005-PZ     Manager
```

What is the advantage of EXISTS? The EXISTS and subsequent subselect can be substituted with POSITION = 'Clerk' and the result would be the same.

In practice, the use of EXISTS with a subselect is not common, but it is useful with its opposite: NOT EXISTS.

Statement:

```
SELECT EMPLOYEE_ID,SURNAME
  FROM EMPLOYEES A
 WHERE NOT EXISTS (SELECT *
                     FROM EMPL_HISTORIES B
                    WHERE POSITION     = 'Cook'
                      AND A.EMPLOYEE_ID = B.EMPLOYEE_ID)
```

Result:

```
EMPLOYEE_ID SURNAME
----------  -------
1000-IS     Sony
1001-JO     Onasis
1002-JK     Tung
1003-JK     Gandhi
1004-BG     Gates
1005-PZ     Zen
```

With this statement, we check with the employee IDs in EMPLOYEES that do not have a row with the position 'Cook' in the EMPL_HISTORIES table. The result is that all the employees except 1000-JK are listed. We try the same statement, but with the NOT EXIST subclause and the result is exactly the opposite — only 1000-JK is selected.

Let's explore a bit further how this NOT EXISTS works. Remember that we are extracting the data from EMPLOYEES and checking the existence or non-existence of a row with the subselect in EMPL_HISTORIES. To start, let's list all the relevant columns from each of these two tables. Only 1000-JK of the first column has the same employee ID with the position of 'Cook'.

Statement:

```
SELECT EMPLOYEE_ID          SELECT EMPLOYEE_ID,POSITION
  FROM EMPLOYEES              FROM EMPL_HISTORIES
```

Result:

```
EMPLOYEE_ID                 EMPLOYEE_ID POSITION
----------                  ----------  --------
1000-JK                     1000-JK     Manager
1000-IS                     1000-JK     Cook
1001-JO                     1000-JK     Cashier
1002-JK                     1000-IS     Cashier
1003-JK                     1001-JO     Manager
1004-BG                     1002-MT     Manager
1005-PZ                     1003-RG     Manager
                            1004-BG     Manager
```

```
1004-BG      Analyst
1004-BG      Programmer
1005-PZ      Manager
```

▌▌▌▌ Union

There are situations when you have two or more SELECT statements and you want to merge the results so that the output comes out together. The keyword to merge them is UNION. Let's examine this with an example, followed by some of the rules that you have to abide by when using UNION.

Statement:

```
SELECT EMPLOYEE_ID, START_DATE, 'Start date'
  FROM EMPL_HISTORIES
 WHERE POSITION = 'Manager'
UNION
SELECT EMPLOYEE_ID, END_DATE, 'End date'
  FROM EMPL_HISTORIES
 WHERE POSITION = 'Manager'
```

Result:

```
EMPLOYEE_ID DATE
----------- ----------
1000-JK     1990-02-01  Start date
1000-JK                 End date
1001-JO     1992-01-01  Start date
1001-JO                 End date
1002-MT     1991-02-10  Start date
1002-MT                 End date
1003-RG     1986-03-10  Start date
1003-RG                 End date
1004-BG     1992-02-05  Start date
1004-BG                 End date
1005-PZ     1975-06-07  Start date
1005-PZ                 End date
```

In this example there are two SELECT statements. The first one gets EMPLOYEE_ID, START_DATE, and a literal 'Start Date' from the EMPL_HISTORIES table where the positions are 'Manager'. The second one is the same as the first, except that in the SELECT clause, START_DATE and 'Start Date' are replaced with END_DATE and 'End Date'.

In a union, DB2 executes each statement separately, creating an intermediate result. Then the results of these tables are combined together without any duplicate rows. There are three rules to follow in a union. One is that the number of column names in all the UNIONed statements must be the same. In addition, columns in the same relative position must be of the same datatypes. Finally, if you include an ORDER BY clause, you must place it in the last SELECT statement. In the clause, you can only name the position and not the column name by which the ordering takes place.

Let's look at an example of a union with ORDER BY clause.

Statement:

```
SELECT EMPLOYEE_ID, START_DATE, 'Start date'
  FROM EMPL_HISTORIES
 WHERE POSITION = 'Manager'
UNION
SELECT EMPLOYEE_ID, END_DATE, 'End date'
  FROM EMPL_HISTORIES
 WHERE POSITION = 'Manager'
 ORDER BY 1 DESC
```

Result:

```
EMPLOYEE_ID DATE
----------  -----
1005-PZ     1975-06-07  Start date
1005-PZ                 End date
1004-BG     1992-02-05  Start date
1004-BG                 End date
1003-RG     1986-03-10  Start date
1003-RG                 End date
1002-MT     1991-02-10  Start date
1002-MT                 End date
1001-JO     1992-01-01  Start date
1001-JO                 End date
1000-JK     1990-02-01  Start date
1000-JK                 End date
```

This example is the same as the previous, except we included the ORDER BY clause, resulting in a descending order by EMPLOYEE_ID.

▬▬▬ Joins

In the previous section, in a nutshell, we showed how UNION works to combine rows from two SELECT statements. Now, let's look at how we can merge columns from two or more tables. Whatever we do with tables also applies to views; combining information for columns of tables is called a join operation.

Joining tables to extract data is very central to a relational database. In Chapter 4, we said that in RDBMS, relationships are established between two tables — also called entities — with common columns in both tables. We use these common columns to join tables for retrieving data from both tables.

Similarly, we can join more than two tables, and we can choose any number of columns from each one. The linkage between tables is established by conditions of the WHERE clause. As you may recall, in a SELECT statement, the WHERE is not mandatory. This applies to a join operation. But if you omit the condition, you will get data without proper relationship. Now, let's do a join operation using DEPARTMENTS and EMPLOYEES. With this example, we'll further explore the data from more than one table.

Statement:

```
SELECT   A.DEPT_NAME,
         B.EMPLOYEE_ID,
         A.MANAGER,
         B.SURNAME
  FROM   DEPARTMENTS A,
         EMPLOYEES B
 WHERE   A.DEPARTMENT_NUM = B.DEPARTMENT_NUM
```

Result:

```
DEPT_NAME                       EMPLOYEE_ID MANAGER    SURNAME
------------------------------- ----------- ---------- -------
Tex-Mex Restaurant              1000-JK     1000-JK    Kennedy
Tex-Mex Restaurant              1000-IS     1000-JK    Sony
Jimmy The Greek Restaurant      1001-JO     1001-JO    Onasis
Authentic Chinese Food          1002-JK     1002-MT    Tung
Reduce, Recycle and Reuse       1003-JK     1003-RG    Gandhi
Virtual reality                 1004-BG     1004-BG    Gates
Spiritual Transformation        1005-PZ     1005-PZ    Zen
```

You will notice that the tables to be linked are found in the FROM clause. Also, there is letter A after DEPARTMENTS and B after EMPLOYEES. These letters are called correlation names (also called aliases), which are not always required, but are necessary in this case. A correlation name lasts only as long as a statement is being executed. You could have the full table name but it is preferred to use a temporary short name like A, B, A1, EM and so on. It should be unique within a statement; you can't use one alias for two or more tables.

Why do we need a correlation name? We have the same column name (DEPARTMENT_NUM) in both tables. The correlation name is a way of indicating to DB2 which names associate with a table. The identification is done by placing the correlation name after the table name in the FROM clause.

In the SELECT statement, the association is made between the table and the column name by placing the correlation name before the column name with a period in between. You will notice that the correlation names are placed before all the column names in the SELECT clause; it is not necessary where ambiguity does not exists, but it is placed there for the sake of clarity. Similarly, the correlation name is always required in the WHERE clause where ambiguity exists, and is not needed where column names are unique.

In the above example, DEPARTMENT_NUM is the primary key in the DEPARTMENTS table, but in EMPLOYEES, it is a foreign key; both columns have the same name.

The join operation is a very important aspect of relational database and gaining a sound understanding of this central issue will make retrieval of data from multiple tables easier. Let's investigate how DB2 arrived at the result after executing the previous SELECT statement. What happens when the statement is issued without the WHERE clause?

Statement:

```
    SELECT   A.DEPT_NAME,
             B.EMPLOYEE_ID,
             A.MANAGER,
             B.SURNAME
      FROM   DEPARTMENTS A,
             EMPLOYEES B
```

Result:

DEPT_NAME	EMPLOYEE_ID	MANAGER	SURNAME
Tex-Mex Restaurant	1000-JK	1000-JK	Kennedy
Jimmy The Greek Restaurant	1000-JK	1001-JO	Kennedy
Authentic Chinese Food	1000-JK	1002-MT	Kennedy
Reduce, Recycle and Reuse	1000-JK	1003-RG	Kennedy
Virtual reality	1000-JK	1004-BG	Kennedy
Spiritual Transformation	1000-JK	1005-PZ	Kennedy
Tex-Mex Restaurant	1000-IS	1000-JK	Sony
Jimmy The Greek Restaurant	1000-IS	1001-JO	Sony
Authentic Chinese Food	1000-IS	1002-MT	Sony
Reduce, Recycle and Reuse	1000-IS	1003-RG	Sony
Virtual reality	1000-IS	1004-BG	Sony
Spiritual Transformation	1000-IS	1005-PZ	Sony
Tex-Mex Restaurant	1001-JO	1000-JK	Onasis
Jimmy The Greek Restaurant	1001-JO	1001-JO	Onasis
Authentic Chinese Food	1001-JO	1002-MT	Onasis
Reduce, Recycle and Reuse	1001-JO	1003-RG	Onasis
Virtual reality	1001-JO	1004-BG	Onasis
Spiritual Transformation	1001-JO	1005-PZ	Onasis
Tex-Mex Restaurant	1002-JK	1000-JK	Tung

Jimmy The Greek Restaurant	1002-JK	1001-JO	Tung
Authentic Chinese Food	1002-JK	1002-MT	Tung
Reduce, Recycle and Reuse	1002-JK	1003-RG	Tung
Virtual reality	1002-JK	1004-BG	Tung
Spiritual Transformation	1002-JK	1005-PZ	Tung
Tex-Mex Restaurant	1003-JK	1000-JK	Gandhi
Jimmy The Greek Restaurant	1003-JK	1001-JO	Gandhi
Authentic Chinese Food	1003-JK	1002-MT	Gandhi
Reduce, Recycle and Reuse	1003-JK	1003-RG	Gandhi
Virtual reality	1003-JK	1004-BG	Gandhi
Spiritual Transformation	1003-JK	1005-PZ	Gandhi
Tex-Mex Restaurant	1004-BG	1000-JK	Gates
Jimmy The Greek Restaurant	1004-BG	1001-JO	Gates
Authentic Chinese Food	1004-BG	1002-MT	Gates
Reduce, Recycle and Reuse	1004-BG	1003-RG	Gates
Virtual reality	1004-BG	1004-BG	Gates
Spiritual Transformation	1004-BG	1005-PZ	Gates
Tex-Mex Restaurant	1005-PG	1000-JK	Zen
Jimmy The Greek Restaurant	1005-PG	1001-JO	Zen
Authentic Chinese Food	1005-PG	1002-MT	Zen
Reduce, Recycle and Reuse	1005-PG	1003-RG	Zen
Virtual reality	1005-PG	1004-BG	Zen
Spiritual Transformation	1005-PZ	1005-PZ	Zen

The list of results is much longer than with a WHERE clause. The reason is that DB2 is not asked to retrieve the data according to rules. With the WHERE clause, DB2 chooses only the rows that meet the search condition.

▌▌▌ Outer Joins

The joins that we looked at in the previous section have one thing in common. If a row exists in one table, but not in the other, the information from such a row is not included in the result table. There are many situations when this is exactly what you want. Such a join is called an inner join.

There is another kind of join called *outer join*. In this case, if there is no match among join tables, the information is still included in the result table. There are three kinds of outer joins:

Left outer join. It includes rows from the left table that were not matched to the rows in the right table.
Right outer join. It includes rows from the right table that were not matched to the rows in the left table.
Full outer join. It includes rows from the left and right tables that did not have matches in the other table.

■■■ Table Check Constraints

In earlier chapters, we discussed constraints in the database required by the business rules. They mainly applied to primary and foreign key constraints which are commonly known as referential integrity constraints. With DB2, there is a new mechanism called table check *constraint*. It is a way of checking each row of a table or an individual column. This constraint is added to the database with the CREATE TABLE or ALTER TABLE statements. The following is an example of adding the SALARY_CAP constraint to the EMPL_HISTORIES table. The condition is that the salary of a manager cannot be more than $50,000:

```
ALTER TABLE EMPL_HISTORIES
      ADD   CONSTRAINT SALARY_CAP
      CHECK (SALARY > 50000 AND POSITION = 'Manager')
```

With this rule enabled, DB2 will give a constraint violation error whenever the salary of a manager exceeds $50,000 in the EMPL_HISTORIES table. This can happen when updating or inserting rows.

As soon as the previous statement is executed, the rules take effect, and existing rows are checked to make sure they do not violate this new constraint. However, you may choose to defer the checking with the SET CONSTRAINTS statement. This statement is used to turn constraint checking on or off.

In the next example, we set the constraints at the time the table is created. At the column level, we check that the value for DEPARTMENT_NUM is always between 1 and 200. At table level, we also add the previous SALARY_CAP constraint.

```
CREATE ....
   DEPARTMENT_NUM   SMALLINT
   CHECK (DEPARTMENT_NUM BETWEEN 1 and 200)
              .
              .
              .
   CHECK (SALARY > 50000 AND POSITION = 'Manager')
```

■■■ Large Objects

In the information age, storing large amounts of data as a single entity is becoming common. These objects can be audio, graphics, photos, and documents of size in the order of megabytes. DB2 supports large objects (LOB) which consists of three datatypes: Binary Large Objects (BLOB), Character Large Objects (CLOB), and Double Byte Character Large Objects (DBCLOB). These types can accommodate up to 2 gigabytes of information and are maintained by DB2 like any other type.

In the next example, the statement creates a table named PROFILE, which is defined to contain information about people:

```
CREATE TABLE PROFILE
      (NAME   CHAR(30),
       PICTURE  BLOB (4000000000) NOT LOGGED COMPACT,
       DESCRIPTION CLOB(50000) )
```

In this table we use two large object columns: PICTURE and DESCRIPTION. The former is binary information up to 4 megabytes and the other is text up to 50,000 bytes.

■■■ Create Database Objects

This section shows the SQL statements to create database objects. Some of them we have already seen before, but only at the introductory level. Here, we will explore these types of statement in full.

Define an alias

The CREATE ALIAS statement is used to define an alias for a table, view, or another alias.

● Syntax

```
CREATE <ALIAS or SYNONYM> alias-name
       FOR <table-name
             or
            view-name
             or
            alias-name2
          >
```

● Parameters

alias-name is the name of the alias that is being defined.

table-name is the table for which a new alias is being defined.

view-name is the view for which a new alias is being defined.

alias-name2 is an existing alias for which a new alias is being defined.

● Usage

Embedded in an application, or dynamically prepared and executed.

● Example

In the following example, SNOOPY creates an alias to a table S1:

```
CREATE ALIAS A1 FOR S1
```

The alias SNOOPY.A1 is created for SNOOPY.S1

Define a user type

The CREATE DISTINCT TYPE statement is used to define a distinct type. This new type is always based upon a built-in type. If the definition of the new type is successful, the statement also creates functions to cast between the distinct types and the source type. It also generates support for the comparison operators for use with the distinct type.

● Syntax

```
CREATE DISTINCT TYPE distinct-type-name
                AS source-data-type
                [WITH COMPARISONS]
```

● Parameters

distinct-type-name is the name of a new type and it should not be the same as the source or built-in type, such as INTEGER, CHAR, DOUBLE and so on.

source-data-type is of the following built-in datatypes:

```
INTEGER or INT
SMALLINT
FLOAT or DOUBLE or DOUBLE PRECISION
DECIMAL(n,n) or DEC(n,n) or NUMERIC(n,n) or NUM(n,n)
CHAR(n) or VARCHAR(n) or LONG VARCHAR [FOR BIT DATA]
GRAPHIC(n)
VARGRAPHIC(n)
DATE
TIME
TIMESTAMP
BLOB(n<K or M or G>) or CLOB(n<K or M or G>) or
     DBCLOB(n<K or M or G>)
```

where *n* is an integer.

WITH COMPARISONS means that the statement will generate operators (=,<>,<,<=,>, and >=) for comparing values related to distinct types. If the source datatypes is BLOB, CLOB, DBCLOB, LONG VARCHAR, or LONG VARGRAPHIC, then you must not use this parameter.

● Usage

Embedded in an application, or dynamically prepared and executed.

● Example

The following statements create DOLLAR, NAME and MILES as distinct types. Note that in each case the source type is different.

```
CREATE DISTINCT TYPE DOLLAR AS INTEGER  WITH COMPARISONS;
CREATE DISTINCT TYPE NAME   AS CHAR(40) WITH COMPARISONS;
CREATE DISTINCT TYPE MILES  AS DOUBLE   WITH COMPARISONS;
```

Record database activities

The CREATE EVENT MONITOR statement is used to define a monitor to trace the activities of a database. Within the definition, you can name a place where the records of the monitor should be recorded.

● Syntax

```
CREATE EVENT MONITOR event-monitor-name
     FOR < < DATABASE
```

```
                    or
                    TABLES
                    or
                    DEADLOCKS
                    or
                    TABLESPACES
                >,...
            or
        < CONNECTIONS
          or
          STATEMENTS
          or
          TRANSACTIONS
        > WHERE event-condition
      >,...
WRITE TO <PIPE pipe-name or FILE path-name file-option>
        <MANUALSTART or AUTOSTART>


where event-condition is:

        <AND or OR> [NOT] <APPL_ID or AUTH_ID or APPL_NAME>
                    < =   or
                      <>  or
                      >=  or
                      <   or
                      <=  or
                      LIKE or
                      NOT LIKE
                    > comparison-string

file-option is:

    [MAXFILES< NONE or number-of-files >]
    [MAXFILES< NONE or pages >]
    [BUFFERSIZE pages] [BLOCKED or NONBLOCKED]
    [APPEND or REPLACE]
```

● Parameters

event-monitor-name is the name of a new event that you want to create. It cannot be a monitor name that already exists in the catalog.

DATABASE means to record a database event when the last application disconnects from the database.

TABLES means to record changes to a table.

DEADLOCKS means to record a deadlock.

TABLESPACES means to record an event for each tablespace when the last application disconnects from the database.

CONNECTIONS means to record a connection event when an application disconnects from the database.

STATEMENTS means to record an event after the SQL statement is executed.

TRANSACTIONS means to record an event when ever a COMMIT or ROLLBACK statement is executed.

WHERE is used to define an event condition for CONNECTION, STATEMENT, or TRANSACTION events. The condition returns TRUE or FALSE.

APPL_ID means to compare the application ID with the comparison string, which determines whether or not to log a CONNECTION, STATEMENT or TRANSACTION event.

AUTH_ID means to compare the authorization ID with the comparison string, which determines whether or not to log a CONNECTION, STATEMENT or TRANSACTION event.

APPL_NAME means to compare the application program name with the comparison string, which determines whether or not to log a CONNECTION, STATEMENT or TRANSACTION event.

WRITE TO is used to specify the destination of event records.

PIPE means a pipe as the destination of event records.

pipe-name is the name of a pipe to which records are written. The pipe name should conform to syntax.

FILE means a file is to receive event records. All files have the extension.EVT. The first file is 00000000.EVT.

path-name is the name of the directory where files for event data are created.

file-option specifies the file format.

MAXFILES is used to specify the number of files to be created.

NONE means to create event files as many as needed — without any limit. This is the default.

number-of-files is the maximum number of files for event data.

MAXFILESIZE is to specify the page limit.

NONE means that there is no limit to the file size of the event data.

pages is the number of 4k-byte pages for file size. The default is 200 pages.

BUFFERSIZE is used to specify the buffer size.

pages is number of 4k-byte pages for monitor buffer.

BLOCKED means that each agent that generates an event should wait for an event buffer to be written out to disk if the agent determines that both event buffers are full. BLOCKED is the default.

NONBLOCKED means that each agent that generates an event should not wait for an event buffer to be written out to disk if the agent determines that both event buffers are full.

APPEND means to add data to an existing file.

REPLACE means to erase all existing event data files and start with 00000000.EVT.

MANUALSTART means that the event monitor not to is started automatically each time the database is started.

AUTOSTART means that the event monitor is started automatically each time the database is started.

- Usage

  Embedded in an application, issued interactively, or dynamically prepared and executed.

- Example

  In the following example, the EMP_INFO monitor event is created. This event collects data for the database and SQL statements for the EMPL application, owned by BGATES. The data is appended to existing event files found in directory \event\emp_info. A maximum of 25 files is to be created and each file will not be longer than 1024 4K pages. The file I/O must not be blocked.

  ```
  CREATE EVENT MONITOR EMP_INFO
          FOR DATABASE, STATEMENTS
          WHERE APPL_NAME = 'EMPL' AND AUTH_ID ='BGATES'
          TO FILE 'd:\event\emp_info
              MAXFILES 25
              MAXFILESIZE 1024
              NONBLOCKED
              APPEND
  ```

Register a user-defined function

DB2 comes with many built-in functions and they return a result if given a set of values. One example of such a function is to find the maximum salary of employees. This function is called MAX, which we have seen earlier in this chapter. Other functions that we have seen are MIN and COUNT. Chapter 10 is a reference of all the built-in functions.

It may happen that these functions may satisfy a special business or scientific need. In this case, the DB2 users can create their own function with the CREATE FUNCTION statement.

- Syntax

  ```
  CREATE FUNCTION function-name (data-type1,...)
          RETURNS data-type2
          [CAST FROM data-type3]
          [SPECIFIC specific-name]
          < external-function-direct-ref
                      or
  ```

```
                function-indirect-ref
         >

    external-function-direct-ref:

   EXTERNAL
      NAME 'string'
      LANGUAGE C
      PARAMETER STYLE DB2SQL
      <NOT VARIANT or VARIANT>
      <FENCED or NOT FENCED>
      <NOT NULL CALL or NULL CALL>
      NO SQL
      <NO EXTERNAL ACTION or EXTERNAL ACTION>
      <NO SCRATCHPAD or SCRATCHPAD>
      <NO FINAL CALL or FINAL CALL>

  function-indirect-ref:

     SOURCE <function-name
                  or
              SPECIFIC specific-name
                  or
              function-name(data-type3,...)
            >
```

- Parameters

  function-name is the unqualified or qualified name of a function that is being defined. An unqualified type is just a function name of a maximum length of 18 characters. A qualified type is a schema-name followed by a period and the function name.

  data-type1 is the datatype of each parameter of the function. Each parameter is an input and you can have none to many of them. The parameters are enclosed by parentheses. If no parameter is specified, the parentheses are still coded.

  RETURNS is used to name the datatype of the function output. It is important in terms of type when the optional CAST FROM clause is specified in the function definition.

  data-type2 is the datatype of the return. There are four cases to consider in conjunction with the CAST FROM clause for both external and source function.

They are:

- No CAST FROM with external function
- No CAST FROM with source function
- CAST FROM with external function
- CAST FROM with source function

CAST FROM is used to return a different datatype than one specified in the RETURN clause.

data-type3 is a datatype different than that specified in the RETURN clause. To better understand this, let's look at this example,

```
CREATE FUNCTION GET_START_DATE(CHAR(6))
        RETURNS DATE CAST FROM CHAR(10)
```

The functions returns a value of CHAR(10) datatype to the database. Subsequently, the database converts this value to a DATE datatype before returning it to the calling statement.

SPECIFIC is used to give a function that is being defined as unique. This name is not used to invoke the function; rather it is used when sourcing this function, dropping the function, or commenting on the function.

specific-name is a qualified or unqualified name and it can be the same as *function-name*.

EXTERNAL means that for the function being registered, its code is written in an external programming language, such as C.

NAME is used to specify the name of the library and the function within it.

'string' is the library specification, followed by an exclamation mark, and the function name (e.g. `funclib!clear`). You can also specify a full path for the library, for example, `d:\mylib\funclib`. During execution, DB2 will load `funclib.dll` into memory and expects clear function to be in it.

LANGUAGE C means that DB2 will use the C language of calling a function. Actually this is the only language interface used.

PARAMETER STYLE DB2SQL is the convention used in passing parameters to and returning values from an external function. This is documented in DBl:YOW-006.

NOT VARIANT means that the function always returns the same results for given argument values.

VARIANT means that the returns depend on the state values that affect the results.

FENCED means the function is not safe to run in the DB2 operating environment process and address space. This is the default.

NOT FENCED means the function is safe to run in the DB2 operating environment process and address space.

NOT NULL CALL means that if any one of the arguments is null, then the user-defined function is not invoked. It returns a null value.

NULL CALL means the user-defined function is called, regardless of the arguments. It will return a null value or a normal value.

NO SQL means the function cannot issue any SQL statements.

NO EXTERNAL ACTION indicates that the function does not change the state of an object not managed by DB2. The objects are files, send a message, or ring a bell.

EXTERNAL ACTION indicates that the function changes the state of an object not managed by DB2. The objects are files, send a message, or ring a bell.

NO SCRATCHPAD means a scratch pad is not provided for an external function.

SCRATCHPAD means scratch pad is provided for an external function.

NO FINAL CALL means a final call to the function is not required.

FINAL CALL means a final call to the function is required to free any resources used by the function.

SOURCE means that this function is implemented by another function (called the source function).

function-name is the name of the source function, which must be known to DB2.

SPECIFIC is used to name the particular user-defined function that is to be used as the source.

specific-name is a qualified or unqualified name.

function-name is a unique name of the source function.

data-type3 is a datatype associated with the source function. For a source function, there may be none to many datatypes, each corresponding to a parameter.

- Usage

  Embedded in an application, or dynamically prepared and executed.

- Example

  In the following example, the **calculate()** function is registered with the CREATE FUNCTION statement. This function accepts two parameters: int and float datatypes and returns a float value. It is an external function implemented in C language. The external name is cal, found in myfunc library. The rest of the keywords are default options.

  ```
  CREATE FUNCTION calculate(int, float)
              RETURNS float
              EXTERNAL
                 NAME 'myfunc!cal'
                 LANGUAGE C
                 PARAMETER STYLE DB2SQL
                 NOT VARIANT
                 NO SQL
                 NO EXTERNAL ACTION
  ```

Let's say you create another function called CHARCOUNT to count the number of characters in a column. After registering it, we will use it in a query, for example,

Statement:

```
SELECT SURNAME
        ,CHARCOUNT(SURNAME)
    FROM EMPLOYEES
```

Result:

```
SURNAME              CHARCOUNT(SURNAME)
------               -----------------

Kennedy              7
Sony                 4
Onasis               6
Tung                 4
Gandhi               6
Gates                5
Zen                  3
```

In this example, the user-defined CHARCOUNT function calculates the number of characters for each SURNAME value in the EMPLOYEES table.

Create an index on a table

The **CREATE INDEX** statement creates an index on an existing table of the DB2 database.

● Syntax

```
CREATE [UNIQUE] INDEX index-name
ON table-name
[(column-name <ASC or DESC>,...)]
```

● Parameters

UNIQUE
This creates only unique index keys.

INDEX *index-name*
> This specifies the name of an index for which an index space is created. *index-name* is the name of the index, which does not exist in the DB2 catalog.

ON *table-name*
> This specifies the name of the table on which the index is to be created. *table-name* is the name of a table already described in the DB2 catalog.

column-name is the name of a column that is to be part of the index key. You can enter one or more column names that are part of a table definition. The maximum number of columns you can enter in this statement is 16. Following each name, you can specify the order of index entries.

ASC means to store the index entries in ascending order. ASC is the default.

DESC means to store the index entries in descending order.

- Usage

  Embedded in an application program, and dynamically prepared and executed.

- Example

  The following example creates an index IXCLIENTS on the table CLIENTS. Also, it specifies having only unique index keys. In this case, the column name is CLIENTID and the index entries are to be stored in descending order.

  ```
  CREATE UNIQUE INDEX IXCLIENTS
     ON CLIENTS
     (CLIENTID DESC)
  ```

Create a table for a database

The **CREATE TABLE** statement creates a table within a DB2 database. This statement also lets you create one or more columns with specific datatypes for each column. With this, you can also add table level constraints, such as check and primary key.

● Syntax

```
CREATE TABLE table-name
             ( < col-name data_type
                 <NOT NULL WITH DEFAULT or FOR BIT DATA>
                 [lob-options]
                 [CONSTRAINT constraint-name]
                 [PRIMARY KEY
                       or
                  REFERENCES table-name (col_name2,...)
                                   rule-clause
                       or
                  CHECK(check-condition)
                 ]
              >,...)
             [[CONSTRAINT constraint-name]
                   PRIMARY KEY (col-name3,...)]
             [[CONSTRAINT constraint-name]
                   FOREIGN KEY (col-name4,...)
                   REFERENCES table-name (col_name5,...)
                                   rule-clause]
             [[CONSTRAINT constraint-name]
                   CHECK (check-condition)]
             [DATA CAPTURE NONE or DATA CAPTURE CHANGES]
             [IN tablespace-name1 INDEX IN tablespace-name2]
             [LONG IN tablespace-name3]


  lob-options-clause:

     [LOGGED or NOT LOGGED]
     [NOT COMPACT or COMPACT]

  rule-clause:

     ON DELETE <NO ACTION or RESTRICT or CASCADE or SET NULL>
     ON UPDATE <NO ACTION or RESTRICT>
```

● Parameters

table-name is the name of the table you want to create. It must not exist in the DB2 catalog. The creator of the table has all the privileges.

col-name is a unique name for a column with the table.

data-type is one of the datatypes found in the following list:

```
INTEGER      SMALLINT          FLOAT
DECIMAL      CHAR              VARCHAR
GRAPHIC      VARGRAPHIC        LONG
VARGRAPHIC   LONG VARCHAR      CLOB
DATE         TIME
TIMESTAMP    BLOB
DBCLOB       user-defined type
```

NOT NULL prevents columns from having null, values but does not specify a default.

FOR BIT DATA defines data as binary values. It may be used for data exchange between systems.

PRIMARY KEY(*col-name*,...) specifies that primary keys are made of the column names to be used as indexes.

col-name is the name of an existing column of the table. You can list one or more columns, and these specified columns must not be defined with NOT NULL.

NOT NULL WITH DEFAULT allows columns to have default values instead of null values. The DB2 default values for datatypes are as follows:

Data type	Default value
Numeric	0
Fixed-length character string	Blanks
Variable-length character string	A string of length 0
Date	January 1, 0001
Time	0 hour, 0 minute, and 0 second
Timestamp	January 1, 0001, 0 hour, 0 minute, 0 second, and 0 microsecond

lob-options specifies the large object (LOB) datatypes, namely BLOB, CLOB, and DBCLOB.

LOGGED means that the changes made to a column with LOB datatype are logged.

The logged data can be used for recovery with the RESTORE DATABASE command. This is the default.

NOT LOGGED means that the changes made to a column with LOB datatype must not be logged.

COMPACT means that the data for LOB column must take the least amount of disk space, freeing any free disk pages in the last group used by the data.

NOT COMPACT means to add extra empty space in the LOB column data, which helps in future changes of this data.

CONSTRAINT is used to specify a new constraint named in this CREATE TABLE statement or an existing constraint, defined previously. As you may have noticed, this parameter is used with other options, such as columns, primary key, foreign key, and check.

PRIMARY KEY, when associated with a column, specifies that the column is a primary key; consequently, it is automatically indexed.

REFERENCES *table-name* (*col-name*,...)
   This parameter defines a column as a foreign key.

   table-name is the name of the parent table to which this column is a foreign key.

   col-name is the column (primary key) in the parent table linked to this column.

rule-clause specifies the action to be performed on dependent tables.

ON DELETE is used to name an action to be done on a dependent table when a row is deleted from the parent table.

   NO ACTION means to do nothing on the dependent table. This is the default.

   RESTRICT means not to delete row from the dependent table.

   CASCADE means to propagate deletion to dependent tables.

SET NULL means to set the column in the dependent table to a null value.

ON UPDATE is used to name an action to be done on a dependent table when a row is updated on the parent table.

NO ACTION means to enforce the rule after all other constraints.

RESTRICT means to enforce the rule before all other constraints.

CHECK (*check-condition*) specifies a validation that is performed for this column.

check-condition is the condition for the validation.

PRIMARY KEY (*col-name3*,...)
This parameter is used to define multiple columns as a primary key. As shown in the syntax, optionally, you can create primary key constraint.

col-name3 is the column name which is part of the table being created.

FOREIGN KEY (*col-name4*,...)
This parameter is used to associate a constraint with foreign key. As shown in the syntax, the definition also includes reference to parent table and rules.

DATA CAPTURE NONE means not to write extra information for data propagation to the log.

DATA CAPTURE CHANGES means to write extra information for data propagation to the log.

IN is used to specify tablespace information when creating a table.

tablespace-name1 is the name of an existing tablespace with REGULAR attribute.

INDEX IN is used to identify a tablespace where the index is to be created.

tablespace-name2 is the name of an existing tablespace, with REGULAR attribute, where index is created.

LONG IN is used to identify a tablespace where long objects are stored. These objects are columns with LONG VARCHAR, LONG VARGRAPHIC, LOB datatypes, or distinct types derived from any of these long datatypes.

tablespace-name3 is the name of an existing table where the long objects are to be stored.

● Usage

Embedded in an application program, dynamically prepared and executed, and issued interactively.

● Example

The following creates a table called CLIENTS. This table has four columns: CLIENTS_ID, CLIENTS_ADDR, CLIENTS_CITY, and CLIENTS_C. Each column allows default values. The primary key consists of the content of column CLIENTS_ID.

```
CREATE TABLE CLIENTS
   (CLIENTS_ID    SMALLINT      NOT NULL WITH DEFAULT,
    CLIENTS_ADDR  CHAR (20)     NOT NULL WITH DEFAULT,
    CLIENTS_CITY  CHAR (25)     NOT NULL WITH DEFAULT,
    CLIENTS_C     VARCHAR (25)  NOT NULL WITH DEFAULT)
    PRIMARY KEY (CLIENTS_ID)
```

Define a new tablespace

The **CREATE TABLESPACE** statement is used to define a new tablespace in an existing database. It does the following:

- ● Assign containers to this tablespace.
- ● Catalog the definition and attributes of the tablespace.

- Syntax

```
CREATE < REGULAR or LONG or TEMPORARY >
        TABLESPACE tablespace-name
        MANAGED BY
            < SYSTEM USING (container-string1,...)
                            or
              DATABASE USING (FILE 'container-string2'
                                   number-of-pages,...)
            >
        [EXTENTSIZE number-of-pages]
        [PREFETCHSIZE number-of-pages]
        [OVERHEAD <24.1 or number-of-milliseconds>]
        [TRANSFERRATE <0.9 or number-of-milliseconds>]
```

- Parameters

REGULAR means to store all data except for temporary tables.

LONG means to store data for tables with LOB columns. The tablespace must have the DMS tablespace attributes.

TEMPORARY means to store data of temporary tables. A database must have at least one temporary tablespace.

tablespace-name is the name of the tablespace that is to be created. The name must be the same as an existing one.

MANAGED BY is to specify the management of the tablespace space: system managed space (SMS) or database managed space (DMS).

SYSTEM means the tablespace is managed by the system managed space (SMS).

USING is the name of the files that are assigned to the system managed tablespace.

container-string1 is a filename with full pathname or relative to the database directory. If a directory does not exist, DB2 will create it. If it exists, it will be overwritten. A smaller file will be extended.

DATABASE means the tablespace is managed by the database (DMS).

USING (FILE *'container-string2' number-of-pages,...*)
This parameter specifies storage space.

FILE means that the container is a filename.

container-string2 is a filename with full pathname or relative to the database directory. If a directory does not exist, DB2 will create it. If it exists, it will be overwritten. A smaller file will be extended.

number-of-pages is the number of 4K pages that will be added to the file.

EXTENTSIZE specifies the number of 4K pages that a tablespace is extended before writing to the next file. The default value is taken from the DFT_EXTENT_SZ configuration parameter.

PREFETCHSIZE is used to specify the number of 4K pages that will be read from the tablespace when data prefetching is being done. Prefetching means that DB2 anticipates the data for a query and it reads it before the query actually requests it. The default value is taken from the DFT_PREFETCH_SZ configuration parameter.

OVERHEAD is used to specify the I/O controller overhead and disk seek and latency time in milliseconds. The time value can be an integer, decimal, or floating-point number.

TRANSFERRATE is used to specify the time to read one 4K page into memory, in milliseconds. The time value can be an integer, decimal, or floating-point number.

● Usage

Embedded in an application or issued interactively. It can also be dynamically prepared and executed.

● Example

In the following example, a tablespace called ONEWORLD is created. Its space is managed by the system (SMS) and uses 3 directories on three separate drives. The extent size is 128 and prefetch size is 64.

```
CREATE   TABLESPACE ONEWORLD
         MANAGED BY SYSTEM
         USING ('c:\ow_tbsp','d:\ow_tbsp','e:\ow_tbsp')
         EXTENTSIZE  128
         PREFETCHSIZE 64
```

Create a database trigger

The CREATE TRIGGER statement is used to create a trigger in a database. A *trigger*, as the name suggests, is a set of actions that are executed when a change in the database occurs. This change is specific to a table. Triggers are executed by DB2 in the background as result of an INSERT, DELETE, or UPDATE operation. Triggers are very useful. Some of the ways of using them are:

- Validate input data
- Generate values for a new row automatically
- Read from other table for cross-referencing
- Write to a log table

Triggers are not arbitrarily implemented; rather they are part of the database design required by the business rules. If properly done, using them can result in faster software development as they can be used to do repetitive chores at a global level. They can also make application and data easier to maintain.

There are several types of triggers. They can be defined to execute *before* or *after* a DELETE, INSERT, or UPDATE operation. A trigger is defined with the CREATE TRIGGER statement, which includes a set of SQL statements called a *triggered action.* The after triggers are defined to execute the action for each row or once for each row. These triggers are used to propagate as needed to perform other tasks. The before triggers are defined to perform the triggered action for each row. This kind of trigger before an INSERT, UPDATE, or DELETE allows you to verify some value before performing a triggered operation or to change a value before it is stored in the database.

- General format

```
CREATE TRIGGER trigger-name
   <NO CASCADE BEFORE or AFTER>
   <INSERT  or
```

```
   DELETE   or
   UPDATE   [OF column-name,...]
>

ON table-name

[REFERENCING < OLD [AS] correlation-name
                       or
              NEW [AS] correlation-name
                       or
              OLD_TABLE [AS] identifier
                       or
              NEW_TABLE [AS] identifier
            >...
<FOR EACH ROW  or FOR EACH STATEMENT>
MODE DB2SQL trigger-action
```

trigger-action:

```
[WHEN (search-condition)]
<trigger-sql-statement
        or
 BEGIN ATOMIC
 trigger-sql-statement;
   .
   .
   .
END
```

- Parameters

  trigger-name is the name of the trigger that you want to create.

  NO CASCADE BEFORE means to execute the action of the trigger before any change to the database occurs. It also means that the action of this trigger must not activate other triggers.

  AFTER means to execute the action of the trigger after any change to the database occurs.

  INSERT means that action of the trigger is activated whenever changes to the specified base table are due to an INSERT operation.

  DELETE means that action of the trigger is activated whenever changes to the specified base table are due to a DELETE operation.

UPDATE means that action of the trigger is activated whenever changes to the specified base table are due to an UPDATE operation. Optionally, you can add a list of columns with this parameter. If included, the trigger will be activated only when these columns change; otherwise, the trigger is activated when any column changes.

column-name is the column name of the base table and any update to it will activate the trigger action. You can list more than one column name.

table-name is the name of a table for which this trigger is defined. This name must be a base table or an alias; it must not be a catalog table.

REFERENCING is to define the scope of the trigger. Therefore, it is used to specify the correlation names and table names.

OLD AS is used to specify a correlation name which identifies the row state prior to the trigger SQL operations.

NEW AS is used to specify a correlation name which identifies the row state as modified by the trigger SQL operations.

correlation-name is a name that identifies an old or new state of a row. It is used with the OLD AS and NEW AS parameter; and, they are different in both cases.

OLD_TABLE AS is used to specify a temporary table name which identifies a set of rows before the trigger SQL operation takes place.

NEW_TABLE AS is used to specify a temporary table name which identifies a set of affected rows as modified by the trigger SQL operation.

identifier is a temporary table name that identifies a set of rows before and after trigger SQL operations take place.

FOR EACH ROW means that the trigger SQL operation is applied once to each row of the table.

FOR EACH STATEMENT means that the trigger SQL operation is applied only once for the whole statement.

MODE DB2SQL is the mode of the triggers.

trigger-sql-statement consists of one or more SQL statements that are executed as part of the trigger action. If there are more than one statement, they must be enclosed with BEGIN ATOMIC and END keywords.

WHEN specifies a condition. After it is evaluated, it is a way of determining whether a trigger action is activated.

search-condition is an expression that can be evaluated to true, false, or unknown.

BEGIN ATOMIC marks the start of SQL statements that form the body of the trigger action.

END marks the end of SQL statement.

- Usage

Embedded in an application, issued interactively, or dynamically prepared and executed.

- Example

Let's look at an example. We define a trigger called RECORD_HISTORY, activated after the POSITION column of the EMPL_HISTORIES table is updated. The third line specifies the name that should be used as a qualifier of the column name for the new value (NEWPOS) and the old value (OLDPOS). The fourth line tells us that this after trigger is activated for each row. The triggered action consists of two statements: UPDATE and INSERT. When the position of an employee changes, the END_DATE of the current position is updated with the current date. The INSERT is to initiate a new record for the new position.

```
CREATE TRIGGER RECORD_HISTORY
        AFTER UPDATE OF POSITION ON EMPL_HISTORIES
        REFERENCING NEW AS NEWPOS OLD AS OLDPOS
        FOR EACH ROW MODE DB2SQL
        BEGIN ATOMIC
            UPDATE EMPL_HISTORIES
                SET OLDPOS.END_DATE = CURRENT TIMESTAMP;
            INSERT INTO EMPL_HISTORIES
```

```
          VALUES(NEWPOS.EMPLOYEE_ID,
                 NEWPOS.DEPARTMENT_NUM,
                 'NEWPOS',
                 CURRENT TIMESTAMP,
                 NULL,
                 0);
    END
```

Create a view from a table or view

The **CREATE VIEW** statement derives a virtual table from one or more tables or views.

- Syntax

```
CREATE VIEW view-name [(column-name,...)]
        AS subselect-statement
           [WITH-CHECK-OPTION]
           WITH common-table-expression,... subselect
```

- Parameters

view-name is the view you want to create.

column-name is a unique name of a column within a table. You can have one or more columns in this statement.

AS *subselect-statement*
This defines the view in association with the **SELECT** statement.

subselect-statement is a **SELECT** statement. This statement is described in more detail later in this chapter.

WITH CHECK OPTION
This option checks all inserts and updates against view definitions.

WITH *common-table-expression*
This parameter is to list one or more common table expressions used in the subselect that follows.

● Usage

Embedded in an application program, dynamically prepared and executed, and issued interactively.

● Example

The following example creates a view called CUSTNAME through a **SELECT** statement. The view consists of two columns, SOC_SEC and FIRST_AND_LAST, from the CUSTOMER table. The WITH CHECK OPTION verifies all inserts and updates against view definitions.

```
CREATE VIEW CUSTNAME
   (SOC_SEC,FIRST_AND_LAST)
   AS SELECT CUST_SOC_SEC, CUST_NAME
       FROM CUSTOMER
       WHERE CUST_SOC_SEC < 7000000
       WITH CHECK OPTION
```

■■■ Remove Database Objects

The **DROP** statement deletes a specific DB2 object, such as a particular view, index, or tables. It removes from the DB2 catalog the named object entry and any associated objects below it. It also deletes any packages that reference the object.

● Syntax

```
DROP <ALIAS alias-name
       or
     DISTINCT TYPE distinct-type-name
       or
     EVENT MONITOR event-monitor-name
       or
     FUNCTION function-name [(data-type,...)]
       or
     INDEX   index-name
       or
     PACKAGE package-name
       or
     TABLE table-name
       or
     TABLESPACE tablespace-name
       or
```

```
TRIGGER trigger-name
   or
VIEW view-name
```

Note:

```
SYNONYM can be used instead of ALIAS
DATA can be used instead of DISTINCT
ROUTINE can be used instead of FUNCTION
PROGRAM can be used instead of PACKAGE
```

- Parameters

    ALIAS *alias-name*
    This specifies an alias to be deleted from the database. *alias-name* is a qualified or unqualified alias already described in the database catalog.

    DISTINCT TYPE *distinct-type-name*
    This specifies a distinct type to be dropped from the database.

    distinct-type-name is a user-defined distinct type defined in the database catalog. The name can be qualified or unqualified.

    EVENT MONITOR *event-monitor-name*
    This specifies an event monitor to be removed from the database.

    event-monitor-name is the name of an event monitor already defined in the database catalog.

    FUNCTION *function-name*
    This specifies a function to be deleted from the database.

    function-name is a user-defined function already defined in the database catalog.

    INDEX *index-name*
    This specifies the index to be deleted. *index-name* is a name of an unpartitioned and user-created index already defined in the DB2 catalog.

    PACKAGE *package-name*
    This specifies the package to be invalidated. *package-name* is the name of a package already defined in the DB2 catalog.

TABLE *table-name*
This specifies the table to be removed from a database. This will also drop all the indexes and primary keys associated with the table. *table-name* is the name of a table already defined in the DB2 catalog. You cannot enter a catalog table that belongs to DB2.

TABLESPACE *tablespace-name*
This specifies a tablespace to be dropped from the database.

tablespace-name is the name of tablespace already described in the database catalog.

TRIGGER *trigger-name*
This specifies a trigger to be dropped from the database.

trigger-name is the name of a trigger already defined in the database catalog.

VIEW *view-name*
This specifies the view to be deleted. *view-name* is the name of a view already defined.

- Usage

Embedded in an application program, dynamically prepared and executed, and issued interactively.

- Example

The following example drops table RBA.CLIENTS.

```
DROP TABLE RBA.CLIENTS
```

■■■ Conditional Processing

The **WHENEVER** statement causes the DB2 translator to generate the code needed to check **SQLCODE** and/or **SQLWARN0** after each SQL statement is executed. If a certain condition is met, a specific action is taken. The condition may be an error, an exception, or a warning that exists in **SQLCA**. The following describes the conditions triggered after a statement is executed and the actions that can be taken.

- Syntax

```
WHENEVER <NOT FOUND
         or
         SQLERROR
         or
         SQLWARNING
      >
      <CONTINUE
       or
       GOTO[:]host-label
      >
```

- Parameters

    NOT FOUND is a condition where **SQLCODE** is +100 or with a **SQLSTATE** of '02000'.

    SQLERROR is a condition where **SQLCODE** is negative.

    SQLWARNING is a condition where **SQLCODE** is greater than zero but not equal to 100 or where **SQLWARN0** is `W'.

    CONTINUE means to ignore the exception and continue processing.

    GOTO *host-label*
    This means to branch to a label in a program and begin processing the statements found there. In COBOL it is a paragraph or section, and a function in C.

    host-label is a paragraph or section.

- Usage

    Embedded in an application program, dynamically prepared and executed, and issued interactively.

● Example

The following is part of a COBOL program. It causes control to branch to paragraph 9999-SEVERE-ERROR if the condition SQLERROR occurs after any SQL statement is executed.

```
PROCEDURE DIVISION.

MAINLINE.
   EXEC SQL
      WHENEVER SQLERROR GOTO 9999-SEVERE-ERROR
   END-EXEC.
   .
   .
   .

STOP RUN.

9999-SEVERE-ERROR.
   DISPLAY "SEVERE ERROR ENCOUNTERED, SQLCODE = " AT 2001
   DISPLAY SQLCODE AT 2035
   DISPLAY SQLERRMC AT 2101
     END PROGRAM

9999-EXIT. EXIT.
```

In the following **RowExists** function of a C program, the **WHENEVER** statement establishes a jump to the **_sql_error** label in case of an sequel error.

```
/*
 ************************************************************
 * Name      : RowExists
 * Purpose   : To check if a row exists
 * Params    : table name, Column name, and Column value
 ************************************************************
 */
int RowExists( char *TableName, char *ColumnName,
         char *ColumnValue  )
{

EXEC SQL BEGIN DECLARE SECTION;
    char sql[ 2048 ];
    int DoesRowExists = 0;
EXEC SQL END DECLARE SECTION;

EXEC WHENEVER SQLERROR GOTO _sql_error;

  sprintf( sql, "SELECT 1 "
    "FROM %s p \n"
```

```
        "WHERE p.%s = %s \n",
         TableName, ColumnName, ColumnValue);

     EXEC SQL PREPARE C FROM :sql;
     EXEC SQL DECLARE exist_c CURSOR FOR C;
     EXEC SQL OPEN exist_c ;
     EXEC SQL FETCH exist_c INTO :DoesRowExists;
     EXEC SQL CLOSE exist_c ;

     return (DoesRowExists);

_sql_error:
   strcpy(g_function,"RowExists");
   return (FAIL);

}
```

Chapter 8
Distributed Databases

So far, we have seen DB2 clients and servers where they are on PC or UNIX computers. But with a computing world where anything goes — like the Wild Wild West, it begs the question of how to get data when databases are scattered all over the globe in many different platforms. For example, can a DB2 client access Lotus 1-2-3, Microsoft Excel, or DB2 database on the mainframe? This chapter addresses this and many more questions by describing standards and products that are available which make distributed databases possible.

▮▮▮ DRDA and DDCS

Distributed Relational Database Architecture (DRDA) is IBM's standard for distributed databases. It is promoting DRDA among many vendors to accomplish federated database interoperability. So many database and gateway vendors, the likes of Oracle, Sybase, Micro Decisionware, IBI, XDB, and Borland, now support DRDA. But DRDA is most popular among DB2 family members; it is the glue that ties them together. As a standard, it defines a set of protocols that is the vehicle for data to flow among multiple databases, allowing software from many vendors to work together.

Distribution Database Connection Services (DDCS) is a software product from IBM that implements the DRDA standards. It comes with DB2 Universal Database. For a distributed database system to work, one needs many facilities and utilities and DDCS provides them. In this section we will look at some of the key features of DDCS.

DDCS connectivity

Figure 8.1 show the connectivity of DB2 servers and clients through DDCS in OS/2 platform.

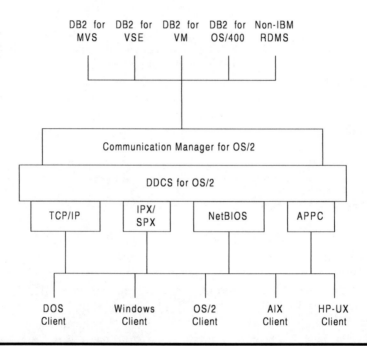

Figure 8.1 DB2 Servers and Clients connectivity through DDCS

DRDA data flow

In a distributed environment, it is important to understand the flow of data, including the responsibility of requesting and executing requests. In DRDA terminology, an *application requester* is the code that interfaces with the application programs requesting database services. This requester code resides in the workstation where DDCS is installed. An *application server* is the code that receives the requester's orders and passes them to the database. The application server and target RDBMS resides in what is known as the DRDA server. Figure 8.2 shows the connection between a DDCS workstation and DRDA server, indicating the flow of data between a client and a DB2 database server.

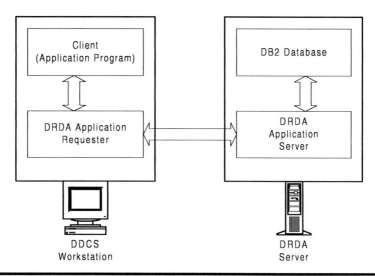

Figure 8.2 DRDA flow of service

In a distributed computing world, where many databases are possible and a client is allowed to use all of them, a request is routed to the correct destination by means of directories that contain communication information and names of DRDA server databases in the network.

Unit of work

In a distributed database, the question arises of how to define *unit of work*, a sequence of SQL statements that are part of a single logical transaction. All the statements have to be successful for the unit of work to be successful. If one fails, then the transaction is not successful.

In a distributed database system, there are two kinds of units of work: remote and distributed. A remote unit of work allows a user or application program to read or update only one remote database per unit of work. Although the client may have access to several databases, it is allowed to read from or change one within a transaction.

A distributed unit of work allows a user or application to read or change one or more databases within a single unit of work. For example, an application can read from a local DB2 database and make changes to many remote databases, or vice versa.

Database directories

One of the major challenges for DDCS is to keep track of all the addresses of the different components spread near and far in a network. It maintains all its information in three database directories using the CATALOG commands of Command Line Processor described in Chapter 11.

Node directory. This contains network address and communication protocol information for every DRDA server accessed by DDCS. It maintains the following information using the CATALOG node commands for IPX/SPX, TCP/IP, Netbios and APPC. These commands were discussed in Chapter 3.

Parameter	Description
Node name	A nickname for the DRDA server system on the remote database, chosen by the user.
Symbolic destination name	The symbolic destination name specified in CPI Communication Side Information.
Security type	The type of security checking that will done.

Database connection services (DCS) directory. It contains data specific to the DRDA server database. It maintains the following information using the CATALOG DCS DATABASE command. The general format is:

```
CATALOG DCS DATABASE database-name
    [AS tdb-name]
    [AR dll-name]
    [PARMS "parameter-string"]
    [IN codepage]
    [WITH "comment-string"]
```

● Parameters
database-name is used to specify the alias of the database that is being cataloged.

tdb-name is used to specify the name of the database that is being cataloged.

dll-name is used to specify the name of the dynamic link library program to be used. It is one of the following:

SQLJRDR1	DRDA-1 database connections for Distributed Relational Database Architecture; this is the default program.
SQL_AR0	ASP-0 or OS/2 database connections
SQLESRVR	Local server

parameter-string is used to specify parameters used by the program named in the AR parameter. This is a string, enclosed in quotes, that contains the connection and operating environment information. The parameters that you can list in this string are:

TPP Transaction program prefix. This is a hex (hexidecimal) value that identifies the first byte of the transaction program name. The default is 07.

TPN Transaction program name. This is a character string that is used as the name of the transaction program, run on the host.

MAPSQLCODE mapping file. This is a character string to specify the name of the file that converts host SQL return codes to DCS return codes. It can be one of the following:

DCS0DSNEE database and DB2 database
DCS1DSNEE database or DB2 database
DCS0ARI EE database and SQL/DS database
DCS0QSQEE database and OS/400 database
DCS1QSQES or DB2 database and OS/400 database

D Disconnect option; this is used to disconnect the host when -300xx is encountered.

V Verify option; this is used to verify a user ID and password before connecting the host.

codepage is used to specify the code page of the characters found in the comment string.

comment-string is used to describe the entry found in the DCS directory. It must be enclosed in quotes (").

System database directory. It contains name and location for every database accessed by DDCS. It maintains the following information using the CATALOG DATABASE command. The general format is:

```
CATALOG DATABASE database-name
   [AS alias]
   <ON drive or AT NODE nodename>
   [IN codepage] [WITH "comment-string"]
```

● Parameters

database-name is used to specify the name of the database being cataloged to the directory.

alias is used to specify an alternate name of the database being cataloged.

drive is used to specify the drive where the database being cataloged is found. This should consist of one character without the colon.

nodename is used to specify the name of the remote workstation where the database is found.

codepage is used to specify the code page of the characters found in the comment string.

comment-string is used to describe the entry found in the database directory. It must be enclosed in quotes (").

● Example

The following statement is used to catalog the CLIENTS database which resides in the NODEXYZ remote workstation.

```
CATALOG DATABASE CLIENTS AT NODE \
    NODEXYZ WITH "CLIENTS database"
```

Binding applications and utilities

DDCS and DRDA servers come with many utility programs that do many useful chores. During the installation program, you must bind these programs. *What is bind?* During the bind process, database access plans are stored for each SQL statement and used during the execution time. These utility programs come with many SQL statements. The access plans for each program are determined during the precompile process and are contained in a "bind file". Each DB2 for DRDA server has many utility programs and they are listed in the following files:

ddcsmvs.lst	for MVS
ddcsvse.lst	for VSE
ddcsvm.lst	for VM
ddcs400.lst	for OS/400

The bind process must be done at these systems:

● DRDS servers where DB2 databases are accessed
● DDCS workstation where DDCS is installed
● DB2 Client Application Enabler for Windows
● DB2 Client Application Enabler for OS/2
● DB2 Client Application Enabler for UNIX
● DB2 Client Application Enabler for DOS

The same bind process is necessary for any application programs that access DB2 databases on a DRDA server. The Syntax for the BIND command is given in Chapter 11.

Administrative Chores

After the bind process is complete, you can use some of the utilities that come with DDCS.

Command Line Processor. You can issue SQL commands, interactively or in batch mode, against a remote database. The interface between you and the DRDA server is the **db2** command executed where DDCS is installed on the client workstation. This command is explained in Chapter 3. One point to remember when executing SQL commands is that they are not the same in all platforms even though they all come from IBM or other vendors. For example, some SQL statements for DB2 on OS/2 differ from the ones on MVS. IBM is trying to rectify this problem, by making all statements consistent across all platforms. For the correct syntax of the target database of the DRDA server, refer to its SQL reference manual.

Database System Monitor. It is possible to monitor the connections for remote client. When an error occurs at the DRDA server, the system administrator can determine if the problem was on the DDCS workstation. If it is, then it will show the information about the DDCS connection that is the cause of the problem. This allows the system administrator to disconnect individual client applications without disrupting other clients using the same DDCS connection.

The information is retrieved from DB2 through the LIST DCS APPLICATIONS command, discussed in Chapter 11. This command will show the following information:

- Authorization ID
- Application Name
- Agent ID
- Outbound Application ID

By giving the SHOW DETAIL option to the LIST DCS command, you can receive additional data that is useful in resolving problems. It includes:

- Client Application ID
- Client Sequence number
- Client DB alias

- Client NNAME
- Client Product ID (client)
- Code Page ID
- Outbound Sequence Number
- Host Database Name
- Host Product ID

Exchange Data. The data is moved between the DRDA server and DDCS workstation using the EXPORT and IMPORT commands. Both have been discussed in Chapter 11. In this process, both are like two sides of the same coin. For example, to move data from a workstation to a DRDA server, you do the following:

- Export data from DB2 table in the workstation into a PC/IXF file.
- Import the PC/IXF file to a table in a DRDA server database.

For moving the data from a DRDA server to a workstation, you do the following:

- Export from data DB2 table in the DRDA server database into a PC/IXF file.
- Import the PC/IXF file to a table in a workstation database.

However, the task is not always simple. All DB2 databases not being the same, you have to be aware of the fact that the data to be moved from one database may not comply with the size and data type restrictions of the other database. The file type must be PC/IXF. One must note that index definitions are not transferred with the data. Finally, the table definitions on both sides must be compatible.

Trace Utility. In a distributed database, where multiple heterogeneous systems interact with each other, one of the most challenging tasks is to resolve problems when links between them break down. DB2 comes with **ddcstrc** utility that traces the data interchange between the DDCS workstation (on behalf of the clients) and the DRDA server DB2 database.

This is a useful tool for both developers of software and administrators to understand the flow of data. This knowledge will help you tremendously in determining the source of a problem when it occurs. For example, you issue a CONNECT TO command to a DRDA server database and you receive an unsuccessful return code. By understanding how commands are conveyed to a DRDA server database, you will be able to determine the cause of the problem.

The output from **ddcstrc** shows the data streams exchanged between the DDCS workstation and the DRDA server database. For example, data sent to the DRDA server is labeled SEND BUFFER and data received from DRDA server RECEIVE BUFFER.

▮▮▮ ODBC

Open Database Connectivity (ODBC) is from Microsoft. It is a Windows API standard to access SQL databases. In 1992, when it was released, its original objective was to access database through Windows application. Since then, it has made wider appeal and now is available in many platforms, including Windows 3.11, Windows 95, Windows NT, OS/2, Mac, and Unixes. Many database vendors, such as Microsoft, IBM, Oracle, Sybase, Tandem, and Informix, all support ODBC in their products.

Why ODBC?

The 80s and early 90s was a time when windows "shrink-wrapped" software for accounting, investment, spreadsheets, etc. and so on, flourished beyond anybody's imagination. In the same period, many database products, such as dBase, FoxBase, DB2, WATCOM, and ORACLE were available on PCs. These two trends combined with client/server environment created a few problems for the software vendors. Should they add an interface into their product for each database? If yes, how many? As databases were multiplying — each having a unique way of accessing the data — combining all database access software with all the software was not a good solution. When using "shrink-wrapped" package, it must be-re-compiled or bound to a particular database. It is not a favorable idea in an age of mass production and easy use of PC sofware. It also meant spending huge amounts of resources on writing and maintaining codes for data access rather than application. Microsoft response to the situation is ODBC drivers, one for each database. The idea is very similar to printer drivers installed on your PC that could be used by any product.

Since ODBC drivers are designed with interoperability — the ability for a single application to access different databases — it became important glue in distributed database computing. Since enterprise data is found on many different platforms, from PC to mainframe, ODBC drivers expanded their horizon to UNIX, OS/400 and mainframe, as shown in Figure 8.3. In a client/server environment, ODBC drivers became extensions of clients, especially for Windows. One of the main advantages of using ODBC drivers is that programmers need not be concerned about the nuances of SQL for different databases.

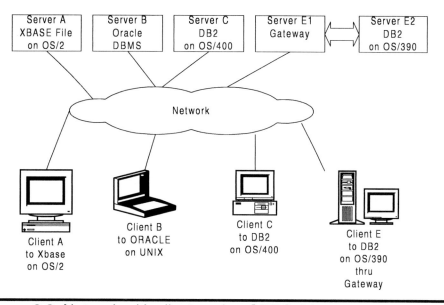

Figure 8.3 Network with clients using ODBC drivers

What is ODBC?

ODBC is a specification for a database API, one that is independent of any one RDBMS or operating system. This means that to a program, a DB2 ODBC driver looks the same as ORACLE ODBC driver. ODBC provides a set of routines that an application can call to maintain a remote or local database. The ODBC API is based on the CLI (Call Level Interface) specification from X/Open and ISO/IEC. Only ODBC 3.0 fully implements these standards; however, earlier versions of ODBC are partially compliant. DB2 comes with CLI libraries, which include c-like functions to main relational databases, just like SQL. There is also an ODBC driver that accompanies DB2 Universal Database.

What are the ODBC parts?

According to the ODBC architecture, there four main components: application, driver manager, driver, and data source. Figure 8.4 shows the relationship among all these different parts.

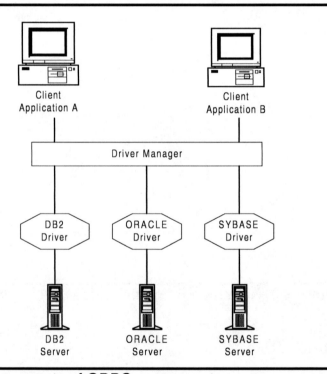

Figure 8.4 Components of ODBC components

Application. The application program is the user of the ODBC API. It calls the appropriate function to all the chores of a relational database such as DB2. Some of them are:

- Select a data source and connect to it.
- Submit an SQL statement for execution.

- Retrieve results.
- Process database errors.
- Commit or rollback a transaction.
- Disconnect from the data source.

Some of the most common applications are the shrinked-wrapped ones developed in environments such as PowerBuilder, Visual Basic, Visual Age, Delphi and the likes. These are designed to access any data source using ODBC drivers. Another type is custom application which is built to process data from many sources in a company. Spreadsheet applications, such as Lotus-1-2-3 and Excel, also use ODBC drivers to get data from common databases.

Driver Manager. Given the distributed database environments, the process may require switching to two or more databases. The driver manager loads and unloads appropriate drivers on behalf of an application. In fact, the driver manager is the first contact between an application and an ODBC software. The manager processes the ODBC function calls or passes them to a driver. The driver manager is a dynamic-link library (DLL) written by Microsoft and can be redistributed by users of the Microsoft ODBC Software Development Kit (SDK).

Driver. The driver processes an ODBC function call, and after checking its validity, submits an SQL statement to a specified data source. Not all databases accept SQL statements in the same syntax; ODBC may modify the statements to conform to the requirements of the associated DBMS. Then ODBC waits for the response from the database and passes data, if any, and status to the application. Some of the drivers tasks are:

- Connecting to and disconnecting from a database
- Validating requests not checked by the Driver Manager.
- Submitting SQL statements to the target database.
- Passing data between application and database.
- Passing status of every request to the application.

Data source. The data source is where the data for application is to be found. It can be a relational DBMS like DB2, ORACLE, or SYBASE. At the data source, there is no need to do anything special, as it sees the ODBC driver as another client. This database could be on any platform, such as mainframe, UNIX, Windows or OS/2, either standalone or on a network.

Who Writes ODBC Drivers?

There are numerous ODBC drivers for various data sources. Initially, Microsoft wrote a dozen of them. Anyone can develop one using the Microsoft ODBC Software Development Kit (SDK), which can be downloaded from Microsoft's Web site. This site contains many other information such as white papers, ODBC architecture documents, and other reference materials. Currently, database vendors like IBM, Oracle, and Sybase, supply their own ODBC drivers.

▮▮▮ JDBC

Java Database Connection (JDBC) was first released in March 1996, jointly prepared by Oracle, Sybase, Informix, Sun, and many others. It is a set of Java classes that interfaces to an SQL database, very much like ODBC. The 90s has made Internet a household name as popular as TV, Telephone, PC, VCR, and other common appliances. Internet is attractive not only for allowing its user to access depots of information scattered all over the world, but for its interactive approach with pictures, colors, sound, and video. This trend led to an opportunity to develop a language to create visually appealing applications. In addition to multimedia, it must lend itself to client/server environment as a simple to use, object-oriented, network-savvy, and dynamic language. In the early 90s, a team of six from Sun Microsystems went into a self-imposed exile, and after nine months of labor, gave birth to a beautiful language named Java. It is very much like C++, but without some of the programming pitfalls.

Java is very popular among Internet users and is whole-heartedly supported by database vendors. Programs written in Java need to access databases distributed in a network. This led to the development of JDBC. It consists of a set of classes and interfaces written in Java. Therefore, it establishes a standard API for tool/database developers to write database applications using a pure Java API. Although JDBC is modelled after ODBC, there are some fundamental differences between the two. ODBC is an architecture for any program and its driver code is machine dependent. While JDBC is strictly for application clients written in Java, the final code for the driver code is platform independent; in other words, a developer writes a Java and JDBC application only once and it can run on any system, for example OS/2, UNIX or Windows. Figure 8.5 shows a number of database servers on different platforms, all connected to clients called Java applets that access one or many of these databases through a network. The design of each applet determines how many databases to utilize.

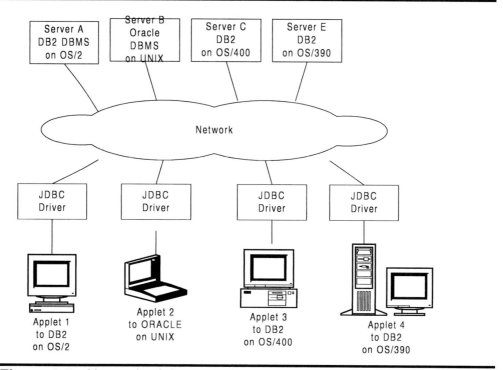

Figure 8.5   Network of Java applets and database servers using JDBC drivers

What Does JDBC Do?

Basically, JDBC does three main tasks:

- Establishes connection on behalf of an application program with a specified database in a network.
- Upon successfully linking to a database, the program can send SQL statements to the database via JDBC.
- JDBC waits for a response from the server and passes results and status to the Java applet.

SQL Conformance

As mentioned earlier, not all the database servers execute SQL statements in the same way. For example, not all of them support stored procedures or outer joins. Even some of the syntax of the basic SQL statements are different. Unlike ODBC, JDBC does not deal with this issue directly; therefore, it passes the statements to the server as is, without any change. It is the responsiblity of the application to resolve the conformance issue. But it does provide an ODBC-like escape clause. The escape syntax provides a standard JDBC syntax for several of the more common areas of SQL divergence.

JDBC Drivers

JavaSoft provides three components as part of the Java Development Kit (JDK):

- Driver manager
- Driver test suite
- JDBC-ODBC bridge

The driver manager is the backbone of the JDBC architecture and its main function is to associate a Java application with the correct ODBC driver.

The driver test suite gives some confidence that JDBC drives will run with your programs. By passing the test, a driver is designated JDBC COMPLIANT.

The JDBC-ODBC bridge allows ODBC drivers to be used as JDBC drivers, a way to get JDBC off the ground in a short period of time. Over the long haul, this bridge will disappear as pure JDBC drivers are more available.

JDBC and DB2

There are many JDBC drivers available and one comes with DB2 Universal Database.

Chapter 9
DB2 Application Development

In the previous chapter, we looked at how client applications access distributed databases in a network. However, we only discussed how the programs are linked to one or many DB2 databases through DDCS, ODBC, and JDBC. They are the "road maps" that show how data moves between application and DB2. We did not discuss what is "under the hood," the kind of stuff that make program use DB2 databases. When building a DB2 application, there are some special considerations and this is exactly what we will cover in this chapter: how to develop database software. We go through the steps to make a program written in C, C++, COBOL, Java, or REXX executable. In the previous chapter, we only talked about client programs, but very often, an application is made of both client and server programs. Usually on the client sides the emphasis is on the user interface, while the server programs do administrative chores. But the principles of writing programs apply to both. The discussion of writing codes is limited to the ways it applies to access DB2. In other words, it covers how to write applications, but only emphasizes the program requirements to manage a DB2 database.

▮▮▮ What Do You Need?

Before you can start development of software in client/server environment using DB2, there are many conditions and a setup that must exist. They are:

- DB2 Universal Database is installed on the server.
- The DB2 *Software Development Kit* (SDK) is installed on the client or server, or both, where development is to take place.
- A compiler for the programming language, such as C, C++, or COBOL, is installed and configured.

- The communication protocol is installed on both the client and server such that they can communicate to each other. The protocol is configured using the DB2 utility program, as discussed in Chapter 3.
- Make sure that you can connect to DB2 using the Command Line Processor (CLP) and your user account is set up in the database. This is important in precompiling or binding.
- The Client Application Enabler (CAE) is installed on the client workstation where application programming is run, but not developed.
- *Java Development Kit* (JDK) and DB2 JDBC is installed if you are developing Java applications or applets.
- The REXX interpreter is installed, if you plan to do any REXX programming.

■■■ Design Considerations

The main object of application programs is to meet users' requirements. But when DB2 database is the repository of information and programs are used for its maintenance, some special considerations must be given in designing and building codes. They are:

- Access methods
- Transaction processing

Access method

There are three main alternatives to writing DB2 applications:

Embedded SQL. This method allows you to manage information of a database using standard SQL statements. These statements are embedded in a *host programming language* and, for DB2, C, C++, or COBOL is commonly used. This method requires precompilation, bind, and link steps before application programs are ready to be run. The choice of a language depends on many things, for example, some shops are biased towards one particular language and would not consider anything else. If you require a lot of GUI programming, then C or C++ is most suitable. For report writing, COBOL is the choice language. Sometimes the existing resources, such as compilers, debuggers, and programming staff, make a compelling case for staying with a current programming language.

CLI. Call Level Interface is made of a set of C language functions that are specifically designed to manage DB2 or any other relational database. Obviously, it can only work with C. The main advantage of CLI is that once an application is developed, it is highly portable and can be used with database from any vendor through the use of ODBC interface.

REXX. REXX is an interpretive language and has facilities to access DB2 databases. The main advantage of these languages is that the application does not require to be precompiled, compiled, or linked. But it may be slower than the previous methods.

Java. Java is a new but popular language. Although it is fashioned after the C++, its programs do not require to be precompiled or linked. Java applications run in a platform without change to the code.

All these methods are described in more detail in the following pages.

Transaction processing

In a database application, processing is generally divided into units of work which we looked at in Chapter 8. Basically, it consists of a sequence of database operations. when all of them are successful, they are permanently stored. For example, a bank transaction may consist of debiting one account and crediting another. This transaction can be said to be complete only if both steps are completed, and only then would you make changes in both accounts permanent with a COMMIT command. Otherwise, a transaction is set to a previous state with a ROLLBACK command, although one or more steps have been done. Therefore, a transaction starts when the application connects to the database or a COMMIT command is issued.

▮▮▮ Embedded SQL Programming With C, C++, and COBOL

Embedded SQL simply means that SQL statements are found in a program. These statements, placed anywhere in the source code, must start with keywords EXEC and SQL; for example,

```
EXEC SQL SELECT * FROM DEPT_TABLE;

  or

EXEC SQL SELECT * FROM DEPT_TABLE END-EXEC.
```

For C or C++, the statement should end with a semi-colon (;) and for COBOL, it must end with END-EXEC. During precompile, these SQL statements are translated into the host language functions.

Next, we will look at some of the required parts of a program with embedded SQL. They are:

Communication between application and database

The communication between an application program and DB2 is done in two ways. One way is through predefined data structures. They are SQLCA and SQLDA and you can use them with the INCLUDE statement as follows:

```
For C/C++

    EXEC SQL INCLUDE SQLCA;
    EXEC SQL INCLUDE SQLDA;

or

For COBOL

    EXEC SQL INCLUDE SQLCA END-EXEC;
    EXEC SQL INCLUDE SQLCA END-EXEC;
```

Through **SQLCA**, the SQL communication area, DB2 passes status code, warnings, and error messages to the program after an SQL statement is executed. A program that executes an SQL statement (except **DECLARE**, **INCLUDE**, and **WHENEVER**) must include this structure. More detailed information about this structure is found in appendix A.

The **SQLDA**, the SQL descriptor area, is required when executing the **SQL DESCRIBE** statement. The **SQLDA** contains variables that are used when executing the **PREPARE**, **OPEN**, **FETCH**, and **EXECUTE** statements. If SQLDA is used with a **PREPARE** or **DESCRIBE** statement, it provides information to your program about a prepared statement. If it is used with an **OPEN**, **EXECUTE**, or **FETCH** statement, it describes the host variables. More detailed information about this structure is found in Appendix B.

Host variables in an SQL statement

Another method of passing data between a program and DB2 is through *host variables*. The declaration of these variables is similar to any other variables except that they must be placed between BEGIN and END DECLARE SECTIONs. This way, they are identified as being used in SQL statements. Host variables are used to receive from DB2 and send data to DB2. *Output host variables* receive data from the database and *input host variables* transfer data to it. Two variables **sql** and **DoesRowExists** are placed in the SQL declaration sections:

```
EXEC SQL BEGIN DECLARE SECTION;
   char sql[ 2048 ];
      int DoesRowExists = 0;
EXEC SQL END DECLARE SECTION;
```

Next, **sql** and **DoesRowExists** are used in the PREPARE and FETCH statements in the following C program fragment.

```
sprintf( sql, "SELECT 1 "
   "FROM %s p \n"
   "WHERE p.%s = %s \n",
   TableName, ColumnName, ColumnValue);

EXEC SQL PREPARE C FROM :sql;
EXEC SQL DECLARE exist_c CURSOR FOR C;
EXEC SQL OPEN exist_c ;
EXEC SQL FETCH exist_c INTO :DoesRowExists;
EXEC SQL CLOSE exist_c ;
```

Error Handling

There are two ways of checking if the processing of an SQL statement is successful. One is to check the return code placed by DB2 in both SQLCODE and SQLSTATE fields of SQLDA. SQLSTATE is a character field that provides common error codes and conforms to the ISO/ANSI SQL92 standard. SQLCODE is an integer value and if it is 0, an SQL statement is successful. A negative value means that an error has occurred and the statement has not been processed. If the SQLCODE is greater than zero, it means a warning has been issued and the statement has been processed.

The other method is to let the system do the checking and whenever an error occurs, control is passed to a specified code. To do this, you have to use the WHENEVER statement. For example, we use it to process the above statements.

```
EXEC WHENEVER SQLERROR GOTO _sql_error;
EXEC SQL PREPARE C FROM :sql;
EXEC SQL DECLARE exist_c CURSOR FOR C;
EXEC SQL OPEN exist_c ;
EXEC SQL FETCH exist_c INTO :DoesRowExists;
EXEC SQL CLOSE exist_c ;

return (DoesRowExists);

_sql_error:
    strcpy(g_function,"RowExists");
    return (FAIL);
```

Note that **_sql_error** is the label to which the program jumps to if an error occurs when processing any of the above SQL statements. You can place the WHENEVER statement once or many times in any order, but only the previous one is current.

Connecting to the database server

Before a program can request DB2 for database processing, it must connect to it with the CONNECT statement, for example,

```
EXEC SQL BEGIN DECLARE SECTION;
   char userid[ 50 ];
   char password[ 50 ];
EXEC SQL END DECLARE SECTION;

strcpy( userid, "GOPAULMI");
strcpy( password, "bluejays");

EXEC SQL CONNECT TO
   oneworld USER :userid USING :password;
```

You need a database name, a valid user ID and password.

Ending a program

The termination process of a program should include:

- Ending the current transaction with a COMMIT or ROLLBACK statement.
- Releasing the connection to the database with a CONNECT RESET statement.
- Releasing any resource by the program.

■■■ Building an Application

There are several steps that you have to take to build:

- Create a source file with SQL statements embedded in a host language program.
- Connect to the database and precompile the source file using the PREP command discussed later. The main function of the precompiler is to convert the SQL statement into function calls to the database manager. It also creates an access package and, optionally, a bind file.
- Compile the file generated in the previous step using the host language compiler, such as C, C++, or COBOL.
- Link all object files created in the previous step to DB2 and host language libraries to create an executable file.
- Bind the bind file, using the BIND command discussed later, to create the access package if this was not already done at precompile time, or to access a different database.
- Run the application to access the database.

■■■ Cursors

In embedded SQL, cursors are often used to retrieve one row at a time from a set. This allows the logic of the program to process each row as it is received and then move to the next one. With cursors, there are four statements that must be used: DECLARE, OPEN, FETCH, and CLOSE, discussed next.

Define a cursor

The **DECLARE CURSOR** statement defines a cursor, which points to many rows of a table. It consists of a cursor name and a **SELECT** statement used to define the selection of rows. This statement is used in a program to access many rows in a table. A cursor can be considered a file and should be treated as such. Therefore, a declared cursor must be **OPEN**ed, **FETCH**ed (or read), or **CLOSE**d.

- Syntax

```
DECLARE cursor-name
        CURSOR [WITH HOLD]
           FOR select-statement
```

- Parameters

cursor-name is the name of the cursor you want to define.

select-statement is a **SELECT** statement; this statement is described in detail later in this chapter.

WITH HOLD means to maintain resources across multiple units of work. For units of work ending with **COMMIT**, the cursor is placed before the next logical row of the result table. For **ROLLBACK**, all open cursors are closed.

- Example

In the following C program fragment, CR_PATIENT cursor is declared, followed by an OPEN, FETCH and CLOSE statement.

```
EXEC SQL DECLARE CR_PATIENT CURSOR FOR
   SELECT PATIENT_ID
         ,LAST_NAME
         ,FIRST_NAME
     FROM PATIENT
     WHERE PATIENT_ID = "A1234";

EXEC SQL OPEN CR_PATIENT;

while (SQLCODE==0)
{
```

```
EXEC SQL FETCH CR_PATIENT
            INTO :patient_id,
                 :l_name,
                 :f_name;
}

EXEC SQL CLOSE CR_PATIENT;
```

Open a cursor

The **OPEN** statement is used after a cursor has been declared. This statement executes the **SELECT** statement associated with the **DECLARE CURSOR** statement; it creates the result table to which the cursor points. Subsequent to the **OPEN** statement, the cursor is initialized to point to a row with a **FETCH** statement.

● Syntax

```
OPEN cursor-name
   [USING host-variable,...
      or
   USING DESCRIPTOR description-name]
```

● Parameters

cursor-name is the name of a cursor already **DECLARE**d.

USING *host-variable,...*
This specifies user-defined variables.

host-variable is the name of a structure or variable that follows the rules of the host program.

USING DESCRIPTION *description-name*
This parameter is used to name a **SQLDA** structure that holds a valid description of host variables. Before executing the **OPEN** statement, you must initialize the following fields of **SQLDA**:

SQLN   The number of **SQLVAR** occurrences provided in the **SQLDA**.

SQLDABC   The number of bytes of storage allocated for this **SQLDA.**

SQLD   The number of variables used in the **SQLDA** while processing the **OPEN** statement.

SQLVAR   The number of occurrences to indicate the attributes of variables.

description-name is the name of a **SQLDA** structure.

● Example

In the following fragment program, there is an **OPEN** statement to open the BRANCH_C. This statement is preceded by a statement to declare the cursor. After the cursor is opened, data is retrieved from the CLIENTS table using a **FETCH** statement. Finally, the cursor is closed.

```
EXEC SQL INCLUDE SQLCA;
EXEC SQL INCLUDE clients.tbl;

EXEC SQL DECLARE BRANCH_C CURSOR FOR
   SELECT NAME
        ,ADDRESS
     FROM CLIENTS
    WHERE BRANCH='E101';

EXEC SQL OPEN BRANCH_C;

while (SQLCODE==0)
{
   EXEC SQL FETCH BRANCH_C
            INTO :clients.name,
                 :clients.address;
   .
   .
   .

}

EXEC SQL CLOSE BRANCH_C;
```

Get a row using the cursor

The **FETCH** statement positions the cursor on the next row of its results table and assigns the column values to variables of your program.

- Syntax

```
FETCH cursor-name < INTO host-variable,...
                            or
                  USING DESCRIPTION description-name >
```

- Parameters

cursor-name is the name of the cursor, which must be **DECLARE**d and **OPEN**ed before use.

INTO *host-variable*
> This specifies the variables of your program. The INTO clause follows the same rules as the INTO clause of the **SELECT** statement. You can have one or more variables. The first value of the row is placed in the first variable, the second value of the row in the second variable, and so on.

host-variable is the name of a structure or variable.

USING DESCRIPTION *description-name*
> This parameter is used to name a **SQLDA** structure that holds a valid description of host variables. Before executing the **FETCH** statement you must initialize the following fields of **SQLDA**:

SQLN	The number of **SQLVAR** occurrences provided in the SQLDA.
SQLDABC	The number of bytes of storage allocated for this SQLDA.
SQLD	The number of variables used in the **SQLDA** while processing the **FETCH** statement.
SQLVAR	The number of occurrences to indicate the attributes of variables.

description-name is the name of a SQLDA structure.

● Example

In the following example, a CR_PATIENT cursor is first declared, followed by an **OPEN** statement to open the cursor. The next data from each row is fetched from the **PATIENT** table into *patient_id*, *l_name*, and *f_name* host variables, until all the rows from the result table are processed. Finally, the cursor is closed.

```
EXEC SQL DECLARE CR_PATIENT CURSOR FOR
   SELECT PATIENT_ID,
          LAST_NAME,
          FIRST_NAME
     FROM PATIENT
    WHERE PATIENT_ID = "A1234";

EXEC SQL OPEN CR_PATIENT;

while (SQLCODE==0)
{
   EXEC SQL FETCH CR_PATIENT
               INTO :patient_id,
                    :l_name,
                    :f_name;
}

EXEC SQL CLOSE CR_PATIENT;
```

Close a cursor

A cursor is a pointer to the current row of a result table. After you have completed processing a result table, the cursor must be **CLOSE**d. But a cursor must first be **DECLARE**d and **OPEN**ed before it is used or closed. A **COMMIT** statement automatically closes all cursors.

● Syntax

```
CLOSE cursor-name
```

● Parameters

cursor-name is the name of a cursor that was previously used in the **DECLARE CURSOR** statement.

● Example

In the following C program fragment, a cursor called BRANCH_C is first declared, followed by an **OPEN** statement to open the cursor. Subsequently, this cursor is used to retrieve data from the database using the **FETCH** statement. Finally, the cursor is closed with the **CLOSE** statement.

```
EXEC SQL DECLARE BRANCH_C CURSOR FOR
   SELECT NAME
         ,ADDRESS
      FROM CLIENTS
   WHERE BRANCH='E101';

EXEC SQL OPEN BRANCH_C;

while (SQLCODE==0)
{
   EXEC SQL FETCH BRANCH_C
            INTO :name
                ,:address;

      .
      .
      .

}

EXEC SQL CLOSE BRANCH_C;
```

Dynamic SQL

In a program it is possible to build SQL statements and execute them, rather than hard-coding them. Usually, an application program will dynamically build an SQL statement in a host variable using data fed to it (e.g., input from a user). Once the statement is constructed with a character string, it is executed with an embedded statement, namely, **PREPARE** and **EXECUTE**.

Prepare an SQL statement for execution

This **PREPARE** statement is used to dynamically prepare an SQL statement for execution. This statement takes a string statement, which contains an

SQL statement and converts it into an executable form, called a *prepared statement*. As seen earlier, the prepared statement is used before issuing an **EXECUTE** statement.

With the PREPARE statement you can use only the following statements: **ALTER TABLE, COMMENT ON, COMMIT, CREATE INDEX, CREATE TABLE, CREATE VIEW, DELETE, DROP, GRANT, INSERT, LOCK TABLE, REVOKE, ROLLBACK, SELECT** statement, and **UPDATE**.

Also, when composing the string statement, you have to keep in mind the following restrictions:

- A **SELECT** statement must not have the **INTO** clause; instead use a cursor and **FETCH** statement.
- The statement should not have the EXEC SQL keywords and a statement termination.
- The statement must not have host variables; instead you use parameter markers (?) and place corresponding host variables in the **EXECUTE** statement.
- The statement should not have any comments.

- **Syntax**

```
PREPARE statement-name
   [INTO descriptor-name]
   FROM host-variable
```

- **Parameters**

statement-name is the name of the prepared statement.

INTO *descriptor-name*
  This parameter is used to identify a descriptor name where information is written after a successful execution of the **PREPARE** statement. As we saw earlier, the **DESCRIBE** statement can be used to accomplish the same function.

  description-name is the name of a **SQLDA** structure.

FROM *host-variable*

This parameter is used to supply a statement string to the SQL statement.

host-variable contains the statement string and is defined in a program according to the rules of the host language.

● Example

In the following example, there are three C statements. The first one is to copy a statement string into a string variable *s*. The second one contains a **PREPARE** statement. Next is a **DESCRIBE** statement that obtains the information about this **SELECT** prepared statement and places it into the data structure **sqlda**.

```
strcpy(s,"SELECT CLIENTS_ID FROM CLIENTS");
EXEC SQL PREPARE select_clients FROM :s;
EXEC SQL DESCRIBE select_clients INTO :sqlda;
```

In the following **RowExists** function, a dynamic SELECT statment is first parsed using the PREPARE statement. Subsequently, an **exist_c** cursor, associated with this SELECT, is DECLAREed, OPENed, FETCHed, and CLOSEd.

```
/*
 ************************************************************
 * Name      : RowExists
 * Purpose   : To check if a row exists
 * Params    : table name, Column name, and Column value
 ************************************************************
 */
int RowExists( char *TableName,
               char *ColumnName,
               char *ColumnValue )
{

EXEC SQL BEGIN DECLARE SECTION;
    char sql[ 2048 ];
    int DoesRowExists = 0;
EXEC SQL END DECLARE SECTION;

EXEC WHENEVER SQLERROR GOTO _sql_error;

  sprintf( sql, "SELECT 1 "
    "FROM %s p \n"
    "WHERE p.%s = %s \n",
```

```
          TableName, ColumnName, ColumnValue);

      EXEC SQL PREPARE C FROM :sql;
      EXEC SQL DECLARE exist_c CURSOR FOR C;
      EXEC SQL OPEN exist_c ;
      EXEC SQL FETCH exist_c INTO :DoesRowExists;
      EXEC SQL CLOSE exist_c ;

      return (DoesRowExists);

_sql_error:
    strcpy(g_function,"RowExists");
    return (FAIL);
}
```

Execute a prepared SQL statement

The EXECUTE statement is to execute a dynamic SQL statement. A
dynamic statement must be first parsed using the PREPARE statement,
before it can be executed with the EXECUTE statement.

● Syntax

```
EXECUTE statement-name
    < USING host-variable,...
         or
      USING DESCRIPTOR descriptor-name
    >
```

● Parameters

statement-name is the name of a dynamic statement that has been
previously assigned in a PREPARE statement. This prepared statement
cannot be a SELECT statement.

USING *host-variable*,...
  This parameter is used to list host variables that hold values used
  during the execution of a dynamic SQL statement. For each such
  value, a marker (question mark ?) is placed in the SQL statement.
  During execution, the mark is substituted with a corresponding value
  of the host variable.

host-variable is the name of a structure or variable defined in the program.

USING DESCRIPTOR *descriptor-name*
This parameter is used to name an SQLDA structure that holds a valid description of host variables. Before executing the EXECUTE statement, you must initialize the following fields of SQLDA:

SQLN   The number of **SQLVAR** occurrences provided in the SQLDA.

SQLDABC   The number of bytes of storage allocated for this SQLDA.

SQLD   The number of variables used in the **SQLDA** while processing the **FETCH** statement.

SQLVAR   The number of occurrences to indicate the attributes of variables.

description-name is the name of an SQLDA structure.

● Example

In the following C program fragment, we illustrates how an INSERT statement is dynamically prepared and executed. The INSERT statement, with three markers where values will be supplied during execution, is first placed in a sql_statement variable. Next, the PREPARE statement parses this INSERT statement assigns a doit name to it. We initialize the d_num, d_name, and d_loc variables with values that are passed to the SQL statement. Finally, we execute the prepared statement.

```
sprintf(sql_statement, "INSERT INTO DEPARTMENTS\n"
        "(DEPARTMENT_NUM,DEPT_NAME,LOCATION) \n"
        "VALUES (?,?,?)");
EXEC SQL PREPARE doit FROM :sql_statement;
d_num = 1000;
strcpy(d_name,"Tex-Mex Restaurant");
strcpy(d_loc,"Rodeo Circle");
EXEC SQL EXECUTE doit USING :d_num, :d_name, :d_loc;
```

Prepare and execute an SQL statement

The EXECUTE IMMEDIATE statement is used to both prepare and execute a dynamic statement in one step.

- Syntax

```
EXECUTE IMMEDIATE host-variable
```

- Parameters

  host-variable is a host variable in a program that contains the SQL statement to be prepared and executed. You cannot have markers in such a SQL statement. It can one of the following SQL statements:

```
ALTER   COMMENT ON       COMMIT
CREATE  DELETE           DROP
GRANT   INSERT           LOCK TABLE
REVOKE  ROLLBACK
SET CONSTRAINTS
SET CURRENT EXPLAIN SNAPSHOT
SET CURRENT CURRENT FUNCTION PATH
SET CURRENT QUERY OPTIMIZATION
SET EVENT MONITOR STATE
SIGNAL SQLSTATE
UPDATE
```

- Example

  In the following C program, an INSERT is first placed in an **sql_statement** variable, followed by EXECUTE IMMEDIATE, which prepares and executes the insert statement.

```
sprint(sql_statement, "INSERT INTO DEPARTMENTS\n"
    "(DEPARTMENT_NUM,DEPT_NAME,LOCATION) \n"
    "VALUES (1000,'Tex-Mex Restaurant','Rodeo Circle')");
EXEC SQL EXECUTE IMMEDIATE :sql_statement;
```

▐▐▐▐ Using CLI

In the previous chapter, CLI (Call Level Interface) was mentioned when discussing ODBC. Both go together; in a client/server environment, the client

application that manages DB2 database is written using CLI while ODBC connects the application to the database server. CLI is a collection of C language functions specially written to do many database chores, such as connecting to it, and selecting, inserting, deleting or updating data in tables. Therefore, application using CLI can only be written in C or C++.

Why CLI?

CLI, is often compared to embedded SQL. We will do that here, too. The SQL statements are passed to function as arguments and at run time, each statement is interpreted and executed. It does not require a precompiler to convert each SQL statement into functions before the compile time as in embedded SQL. CLI application does not need binding step before running it, which does not tie it to any particular database.

CLI applications are compiled once and shipped as "shrink-wrapped" software, for accounting, investment, spreadsheets, etc. The database access is done through ODBC drivers.

Another advantage over embedded SQL is that CLI application does not require declaration of global data areas such as SQLDA and SQLCA, as we saw previously in embedded SQL.

Why not CLI?

The main disadvatage of CLI is that the SQL statements can only be validated dynamically at run-time. This slows down the processing and prevents encapsulation. DB2 provides a method of CLI applications to use static SQL, but this involves creating stored procedures. Stored procedures are coded with SQL statements and placed in the DB2 server to be used by the CLI application.

DB2 CLI application

Now let's look at what an application needs to comply to the CLI standard and enable it to access a database.

Initialization.

- Allocate environement and connection handles. A handle is a variable that refers to a data object controlled by DB2 CLI. There are four kinds of handles: environment, connection, statement, and descriptors.
- Connect the application to the database.

Transaction Processing.

- Allocate statement handles before any SQL can be executed, using **SQLAllocStmt()**.
- Prepare and execute SQL statement in one of the two ways.
- Prepare then execute, with **SQLPrepare()** and **SQLExecute()**, respectively. This method is used when the statement is executed repeatedly, usually with different parameter values.
- Execute directly, using **SQLExecDirect()**, which combines the prepare and execute into one step.
- Process the results of the SQL statement, depending on the requirements. The following list gives some possible database activities and their associated functions.

Receive Query Results (Select Values)	Update Data (UPDATE, DELETE, INSERT)	Other Alter, Create
SQLNumResiltsCol() ⇓ SQLDescribeCol() or SQLColAttributes() ⇓ SQLBindCol() ⇓ SQLFetch() and SQLGetData()	SQLRowCount()	(no functions Required)

- Free the statement handle, ending processing for that statement.
- Complete (COMMIT) or undo (ROLLBACK) the transaction.

Termination

- Disconnect the application from the database.
- Free the handles.

▌▌▌▌ Using REXX

REXX is a language popular on IBM platforms, namely MVS, CMS, AIX, and OS/2; now it is also available on Windows 95 and Windows NT. With REXX, you write a program and run it without the need to precompile, compile, and link as for C, C++, and COBOL. Since every line of code is parsed and executed at run time, it is generally slower than a compiled language. The main advantage of REXX is that it is easy and fast to write small programs.

REXX application to access DB2 database can be created in three different ways, accomplished by three special routines. They are:

SQLEXEC - issue SQL command.
SQLDBS - issue command-like versions of DB2 APIs.
SQLDB2 - issue CLI commands.

Registering access types

Before using accessing DB2 or SQL commands in a REXX application, the program must register the SQLDBS, SQLDB2 and SQLEXEC routines. This tells the REXX interpreter what is the REXX/SQL entry points. The method you use for registering varies slightly between the OS/2 and AIX platforms. The following examples show the correct syntax for registering each routine:

Sample registration on OS/2 or Windows

```
/* - Register SQLDBS with REXX--*/
If Rxfuncquery('SQLDBS')  <> 0 then
   rcy = Rxfuncadd('SQLDBS','DB2AR','SQLDBS')
If rcy \= 0 then
    do
    say 'SQLDBS was not successfully added to the REXX
    environment'
    signal rxx_exit
  end
```

```
/* -- Register SQLDB2 with REXX  --*/
If Rxfuncquery('SQLDB2')  <> 0 then
   rcy = Rxfuncadd('SQLDB2','DB2AR','SQLDB2')
If rcy \= 0 then
   do
   say 'SQLDB2 was not successfully added to the REXX
   environment'
   signal rxx_exit
   end

/* -- Register SQLEXEC with REXX  --*/
If Rxfuncquery('SQLEXEC') <> 0 then
   rcy = Rxfuncadd('SQLEXEC','DB2AR','SQLEXEC')
If rcy \= 0 then
    do
   say 'SQLEXEC was not successfully added to the REXX
   environment'
   signal rxx_exit
    end
```

Sample registration on AIX

```
/* -- Register SQLDBS, SQLDB2 and SQLEXEC with REXX --*/
rcy = SysAddFuncPkg("db2rexx")
If rcy \= 0 then
   do
   say 'db2rexx was not successfully added to the REXX
   environment'
   signal rxx_exit
   end
```

Executing SQL statements

The SQLEXE routine is to process all SQL statements and its only argument is a character string, enclosed in quotes, that makes up a statement, as follows:

```
CALL SQLEXEC "statement"
```

In the following example, the SQL statement is to count the number of rows in EMPLOYEES table with the SELECT command,

```
CALL SQLEXEC "SELECT count(*) INTO :c from EMPLOYEES"
```

Often SQL statements are long and you may want to break them into several lines for the sake of readability. It is done by separating parts of the same statement with commas, and placing them on separate lines, for example,

```
CALL SQLEXEC "SELECT SURNAME",
             "   INTO :surname",
             "   FROM EMPLOYEES",
             " WHERE DEPARTMENT_NUM = 1000",
             "   AND EMPLOYEE_ID = '1000-JK'"
IF (SQLCA.SQLCODE < 0) THEN
   SAY 'ERROR: SELECT FROM EMPLOYEES, SQLCODE = '
   SQLCA.SQLCODE
```

After a statement is processed a status code is placed in SQLCA.SQLCODE which is checked for any errors.

Only the following SQL statements can be passed to SQLEXEC routine:

```
CALL
CLOSE
COMMIT
CONNECT
CONNECT TO
CONNECT RESET
DECLARE
DESCRIBE
DISCONNECT
EXECUTE
EXECUTE IMMEDIATE
FETCH
FREE LOCATOR
OPEN
PREPARE
RELEASE
ROLLBACK
SET CONNECTION
```

Other SQL statements are executed dynamically using the EXECUTE IMMEDIATE, or PREPARE and EXECUTE statements, using SQLEXEC, which we will discuss shortly.

Host variables

Host variables are REXX variables used in SQL statements to pass data to DB2 or receive data from DB2. In the previous examples, we have already used two variables '*c*' and '*surname*', respectively, to receive the count and surname from the database. Note that a variable in an SQL statement is always prefixed with a colon (:). The host variables are not declared; at run-time, its data type and size is determined. However, LOB locators and LOB file reference variables must be declared.

REXX updates several predefined variables after calling the SQLEXEC, SQLDBS, and SQLDB2. These values are worth considering when writing an application as they can make processing more accurate and robust. They are:

RESULT. The possible values of this variable are:

n	A positive indicates the number of bytes in a formatted message. The GET ERROR MESSAGE API alone returns this value.
0	The API was executed. The variable SQLCA contains the completion status of the API. If SQLCA.SQLCODE is not zero, SQLMSG contains the text message associated with that value.
-1	There is not enough memory available to complete the API. The requested message was not returned.
-2	SQLCA.SQLCODE is set to zero. No message was returned.
-3	SQLCA.SQLCODE contained an invalid SQLCODE. No message was returned.
-6	The SQLCA REXX variable could not be built. This indicates that there was not enough memory available or the REXX variable pool was unavailable for some reason.
-7	The SQLMSG REXX variable could not be built. This indicates that there was not enough memory available or the REXX variable pool was unavailable for some reason.
-8	The SQLCA.SQLCODE REXX variable could not be fetched from the REXX variable pool.
-9	The SQLCA.SQLCODE REXX variable was truncated during the fetch. The maximum length for this variable is 5 bytes.
-10	The SQLCA.SQLCODE REXX variable could not be converted from ASCII to a valid long integer.
-11	The SQLCA.SQLERRML REXX variable could not be fetched from the REXX variable pool.
-12	The SQLCA.SQLERRML REXX variable was truncated during the fetch. The maximum length for this variable is 2 bytes.
-13	The SQLCA.SQLERRML REXX variable could not be converted from ASCII to a valid short integer.

-14   The SQLCA.SQLERRMC REXX variable could not be fetched from the REXX variable pool.

-15   The SQLCA.SQLERRMC REXX variable was truncated during the fetch. The maximum length for this variable is 70 bytes.

-16   The REXX variable specified for the error text could not be set.

-17   The SQLCA.SQLSTATE REXX variable could not be fetched from the REXX variable pool.

-18   The SQLCA.SQLSTATE REXX variable was truncated during the fetch. The maximum length for this variable is 2 bytes.

SQLMSG If SQLCA.SQLCODE is not 0, this variable contains the text message associated with the error code.

SQLISL   The isolation level. Possible values are:
RR Repeatable read.
RS Read stability.
CS Cursor stability. This is the default.
UR Uncommitted read.
NC No commit (NC is only supported by some DRDA servers.)

SQLCA   The SQLCA structure updated after SQL statements are processed and DB2 APIs are called. The entries of this structure are described in the API Reference.

SQLRODA   The input/output SQLDA structure for stored procedures invoked using the CALL statement. It is also the output SQLDA structure for stored procedures invoked using the Database Application Remote Interface (DARI) API. The entries of this structure are described in the API Reference.

SQLRIDA   The input SQLDA structure for stored procedures invoked using the Database Application Remote Interface (DARI) API. The entries of this structure are described in the API Reference.

SQLRDAT   An SQLCHAR structure for server procedures invoked using the Database Application Remote Interface (DARI) API. The entries of this structure are described in the API Reference.

LOB host variables in REXX

When a variable is used with an LOB data type, it is treated differently than other variables. When the data is fetched from a column of LOB data type, the content is stored as a simple (that is, uncounted) string, in the same manner as all-character-based SQL types (such as CHAR, VARCHAR, GRAPHIC, LONG, and so on). There are four LOB types: CLOB, DBCLOB, and BLOB, and the specific type is assigned dynamically by REXX. On input, if the size of the contents of your host variable is larger than 32K, or if it meets other criteria set out below, it will be assigned the appropriate LOB type, as follows:

Resulting LOB Type	Description of content
CLOB	:hv1=ordinary quoted string longer than 32K
CLOB	:hv2=string with embedded delimiting quotes, longer than 32K
DBCLOB	:hv3=GDBCS string with embedded delimiting single, quotes, beginning with G, longer than 32K
BLOB	:hv4=BIN string with embedded delimiting single, quotes, beginning with BIN, any length.

All LOB host variables in your application must be declared as locators so that its values are stored in an internal format. The syntax to declare a LOB Locator Host Variable in REXX is:

```
DECLARE :variable-name,... LANGUAGE TYPE
        <BLOB or CLOB or DBCLOB> LOCATOR
```

For example:

```
CALL SQLEXEC 'DECLARE :hv1, :hv2 LANGUAGE TYPE CLOB
LOCATOR'
```

Data represented by LOB locators returned from the engine can be freed in REXX/SQL using the FREE LOCATOR statement which has the following format:

```
FREE LOCATOR :variable-name,...
```

For example:

```
CALL SQLEXEC 'FREE LOCATOR :hv1, :hv2'
```

It may be necessary to explicitly clear REXX SQL LOB locator and file reference host variable declarations as they remain in effect after your application program ends. This is because the application process does not exit until the session in which it is run is closed. If REXX SQL LOB declarations are not cleared, they may interfere with other applications that are running in the same session after an LOB application has been executed.

The syntax to clear the declaration is:

```
CALL SQLEXEC "CLEAR SQL VARIABLE DECLARATIONS"
```

You can code it anywhere as a precautionary measure to clear declarations which might have been left by previous applications (for example, at the beginning of a REXX SQL application).

Using cursors in REXX

We discussed cursors with embedded SQL earlier; it is possible to use them with REXX. The concept is the same as before, which means you have to use the DECLARE, OPEN, FETCH and CLOSE statements, but the REXX statements are slightly different. Unlike in C, C++, and COBOL, the cursor names are predefined as follows: Cursor names range from c1 to c50 for cursors declared without the WITH HOLD option, and c51 to c100 for cursors declared using the WITH HOLD option. The cursor name is used for DECLARE, OPEN, FETCH, and CLOSE statements. It identifies the cursor used in the SQL request.

s1 to s100   Statement names, which range from s1 to s100.

When a cursor is declared in REXX, the cursor is associated with a query. The query is associated with a statement name assigned in the PREPARE statement. Statement names from S1 to S100 are also predefined and they are used in the PREPARE statement. The following example shows a DECLARE statement associated with a dynamic SELECT statement.

▮▮▮ Using Java

We mentioned Java in Chapter 8 while discussing JDBC. We merely talked about how a Java program can access remote databases through JDBC drivers. Here, we will look at the Java programs and what needs to be coded for them to work with JDBC. Unlike REXX, Java programs have to be compiled to bytecode format, and unlike C, C++ or COBOL, they do not need to be precompiled or linked to an executable file.

Java is a relatively new language, only developed in the 90s, but it has become very popular among internet users and supported by all vendors including IBM.

Before going any further, let's look at a fundamental point. Java programs are divided into two types: application and applet. In the following pages, we will discuss the characteristics of each and the way applications and applets are created and run.

Java applications

A Java application consists only of a Java code which is compiled and run using a Java interpreter, for example, one supplied by Sun Microsystem. We start by creating a sample program to print "Hello World." Let's name the file HelloWorldApp.java which has the following code:

```
/**
 * The HelloWorldApp class implements an application that
 * simply displays "Hello World!" to the standard output.
 */
    class HelloWorldApp {
        public static void main(String[] args) {
            System.out.println("Hello World!"); //Show
            the message.
        }
    }
```

Next, we compile this short program with the DOS command:

```
javac HelloWorldApp.java
```

The result is that the Java compiler **javac** creates a file called bytecodes file **HelloWorldApp.class** which contains bytecodes. Now we are ready to run this application with a Java interpreter with the DOS command:

```
java HelloWorldApp.class
```

You should see "Hello World!". Note that in the **HelloWorldApp** class there is the **main()** method as the entry point for a Java application, which distinguishes it from an applet, the subject of our next discussion.

Java applets

In discussing Java applet, we will compare it to what we have just learned about the application. To start, we create a source file named **HelloWorld.java** with the following code:

```
import java.applet.Applet;
   import java.awt.Graphics;

   public class HelloWorld extends Applet
   {
        public void paint(Graphics g)
        {
             g.drawString("Hello World!", 50, 25);
        }
   }
```

As before, we compile the program with the DOS command:

```
javac HelloWorld.java
```

The result is a file name **HelloWorld.class** which contains Java bytecodes.
    To run an applet, it has to be part of an HTML; we create one named **Hello.htlm** with the following lines:

```
<HTML>
<HEAD>
<TITLE> A Simple Program </TITLE>
</HEAD>
<BODY>
 <APPLET CODE="HelloWorld.class" WIDTH=150 HEIGHT=25>
 </APPLET>
 </BODY>
 </HTML>
```

Note that the compiled file is referenced in the HTML file as an applet code. Next, we run the HTML file using a Java-compatible browser, for example Netscape, which displays:

```
Here is the output of my program:   Hello World!
```

To load this HTML, we need to tell Netscape the URL of the HTML file we have just created, for example,

```
file:/C:/DB2/HTML/hello.html
```

DB2 with Java application and applet

The previous examples are very simple; to make a program work with DB2 database, more tools are needed. Regardless of how you decide to develop your Java software, there are some typical calls to JDBC APIs:

- Import the appropriate Java packages and classes (**java.sql.***).
- Load the appropriate JDBC driver (**COM.ibm.db2.jdbc.app.DB2Driver** for application; **COM.ibm.db2.jdbc.net.DB2Driver** for applets).
- Connect to the database, specifying the location with a URL (as defined in Sun's JDBC specification) and using the **db2** subprotocol. For applets, you must also provide the user ID, password, host name, and the port number for the applet server; for applications, the Client Application Enabler provides the necessary values.
- Pass the SQL statements to the database.
- Receive the result data.
- Close the database connection.

Application. A Java application needs the DB2 Client Enabler (CAE) to connect to DB2. As shown in Figure 9.1, the application interfaces with JDBC driver which uses CAE to communicate with DB2 database.

Figure 9.1 Java Application Connection to Remote Database

A DB2 Java application is same as C; to understand this, let's look at a sample code called **DB2Appl.java**. It does the following:

- Connects to the ONEWORLD database.
- Selects the first name and surname from the EMPLOYEES table.
- Displays each row of data retrieved.
- Updates the EMPLOYEES table.
- Closes the connection to the database.

The code is as follows:

```
//   Source File Name: DB2Appl.java   %I%
//

//   This sample program shows how to write a Java
application using
//   the JDBC application driver to access a ONEWORLD
database.

// Run this sample by the following steps:
// (1) compile this Java source file: javac DB2Appl.java
// (2) run this sample: java DB2Appl

import java.sql.*;

class DB2Appl {

    static {
       try {
          // register the driver with DriverManager
          Class.forName("com.ibm.db2.jdbc.app.DB2Driver");
       } catch (ClassNotFoundException e) {
          e.printStackTrace();
       }
    }

    public static void main(String argv[]) {
       try {
```

```
// URL is jdbc:db2:dbname
String url = "jdbc:db2:ONEWORLD";

// connect with default id/password
Connection con = DriverManager.getConnection(url);

// retrieve data from the database
   System.out.println("Retrieve some data from the
   database...");
Statement stmt = con.createStatement();
   ResultSet rs = stmt.executeQuery("SELECT
   FIRST_NAME, SURNAME from EMPLOYEES");

System.out.println("Receiving data...");

// display the result set
// rs.next() returns false when there are
//no more rows
while (rs.next()) {
    String a = rs.getString(1);
    String str = rs.getString(2);

    System.out.print(" first_name= " + a);
    System.out.print(" surname= " + str);
    System.out.print("\n");
}

rs.close();
stmt.close();

// update the database
System.out.println("\n\nUpdate the database... ");
stmt = con.createStatement();
    int rowsUpdated = stmt.executeUpdate("UPDATE
    EMPLOYEES set FIRST_NAME = 'JANE' where
    EMPLOYEE_ID = '1000-JK'");

System.out.print("Changed "+rowsUpdated);

if (1 == rowsUpdated)
    System.out.println(" row.");
else
    System.out.println(" rows.");

stmt.close();
con.close();
} catch( Exception e ) {
    e.printStackTrace();
}
    }
}
```

Applet. A DB2 Java applet does not use the CAE component to access a remote database as does an application. When loading an HTML file, the browser downloads the applet to the virtual machine, which in turm downloads the java class files and the DB2 JDBC driver. The driver makes the connection directly to the remote database. Figure 9.2 shows the components on both client and server sides to access a local or remote DB2 database with an applet.

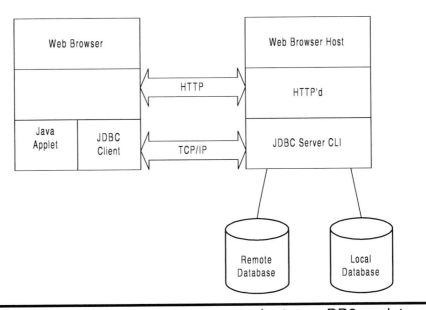

Figure 9.2 The different components require to run DB2 applet

Next, we create a sample program called **DB2Applt.java**. It is very similar to the previous example, except it does one extra step in the beginning:

- Connects to the database server CTS-K460, through port number 8989.
- Connects to the ONEWORLD database using user ID GOPAULMI and password GOPAULMI.
- Selects the first name and surname from the EMPLOYEES table.
- Displays each row of data retrieved.
- Updates the EMPLOYEES table.
- Closes the connection to the database.

The code is as follows:

```
//   Source File Name: DB2Applt.java   %I%
//
// This sample program shows how to write a Java applet
// using the JDBC applet driver to access a DB2
// ONEWORLD database.
//
// Run this sample by the following steps:
// (1) compile this Java source file: javac DB2Applt.java
// (2) start our JDBC applet server on some TCP/IP port:
//     db2jstrt portno
// (3) run this sample: install the applet and the HTML
//     file according to the documentation, run it from a
//     Java-enabled browser.

import java.sql.*;
import java.awt.Graphics;

public class DB2Applt extends java.applet.Applet {

    static {
        try {
            // register the driver with DriverManager
            Class.forName("com.ibm.db2.jdbc.net.DB2Driver");
        } catch (ClassNotFoundException e) {
            e.printStackTrace();
        }
    }

    public void init() {
        resize(150,25);
    }

    public void paint(Graphics g) {
        try {
            // Specify the server the name of the machine your
            // JDBC Server is running on
            String server = "CTS-K460";

            // Specify the port number your JDBC
            // Server is listening on
            String port = "8989";

            // construct the URL ( sample is the database name )
            String url =
                "jdbc:db2://"+server+":"+port+"/ONEWORLD";

            // Set the user id you want to use to access
            // the database
            String userid = "GOPAULMI";
```

```
// Set the password corresponding
// to the above id
String password = "GOPAULMI";

Connection con = DriverManager.getConnection(url,
userid, password );

// retrieve data from database
g.drawString("First, let's retrieve some data from
the database...", 10, 10);

Statement stmt = con.createStatement();
ResultSet rs = stmt.executeQuery("SELECT FIRST_NAME,
SURNAME from EMPLOYEES");
g.drawString("Received results:", 10, 25);

// display the result set
// rs.next() returns false when there
// are no more rows
int y = 50;
int i = 0;
while (rs.next() && (i<2)) {
    i++;
    String a= rs.getString(1);
    String str = rs.getString(2);
      String oneLine = " first_name= " + a + "
      surname= " + str;
    g.drawString(oneLine, 20, y );
    y = y + 15;

}
stmt.close();

// update the database
g.drawString("Now, update the database..."
             , 10, 100);
stmt = con.createStatement();
int rowsUpdated = stmt.executeUpdate("UPDATE
EMPLOYEES set FIRST_NAME = 'JANE' where EMPLOYEE_ID
= '1000-JK'");

// display the number of rows updated
String msg = "Updated " + rowsUpdated;

if (1 == rowsUpdated)
   msg = msg +" row.";
else
   msg = msg +" rows.";
y = y + 40;
g.drawString(msg, 20, y);

stmt.close();
con.close();
```

```
        } catch( Exception e ) {
            e.printStackTrace();
        }
    }
}
```

■■■ Precompiling a Program With Embedded SQL

The **PRECOMPILE or PREP** command is used to process a program source
file that has embedded SQL statements. A modified source file is produced,
which contains host language equivalents to the SQL statements. By default, a
package is created in the database to which a connection has been established.
The name of the package is the same as the filename (minus the extension and
folded to uppercase), up to a maximum of 8 characters. This command is only
for C, C++, FORTRAN, and COBOL.

Following connection to a database, PREP executes under the transaction
that was started. PREP then issues a COMMIT or a ROLLBACK operation to
terminate the current transaction and start another one.

During precompilation, an Explain Snapshot is not taken unless a package is
created. The snapshot is put into the Explain tables of the user creating the
package. Precompiling stops if a fatal error or more than 100 errors occur. If a
fatal error does occur, PREP stops precompiling, attempts to close all files, and
discards the package.

It is run using **db2**, the Command Line Processor, discussed in Chapter 3.
The syntax of the **PRECOMPILE** command is found in Chapter 11.

■■■ Bind and Rebind Application to a Database

The **BIND** command takes a bind created by the precompiler and generates a
package which is used to access DB2 data during the execution of a program.
During a bind processing, the following happens:

- Validation of the rules, structure, and syntax of SQL statements used in a
  program.
- Verification of authority to access DB2 data.
- Choice of an access path to data.
- Creation of a package which is used to allocate resources during program
  execution.

It is run using **db2**, the Command Line Processor. The syntax of the **BIND** command is found in Chapter 11.

Chapter 10
Built-in Functions

This chapter is a reference guide for using built-in functions that come with DB2. DB2 has a number of built-in functions, each are performing a specific operation. They are different from SQL statements, each function name is followed by a pair of parentheses, as in C. These functions take one or more operands called *arguments*, placed within these parentheses. There are two types of functions: *column* and *scalar*.

There are five column functions: **AVG, COUNT, MAX, MIN,** and **SUM**. The argument of each of these functions is a set of values derived from one or more columns. The main distinction of a scalar function is that its argument can be an expression. An expression can include a function (scalar or column), a constant, column names, host variables, and special registers. All these possible components of an expression must conform to the rules of SQL. This chapter gives the description, followed by the format, description of arguments, and examples of the following functions.

■■■ AVG — Calculate the Average of Numbers

The **AVG** function returns the average of a set of numbers. The returned value depends on the data type of the column. The return value for an integer column is integer, for a floating-point column is floating-point, and so on. And of course, the result should be within the range of the data type; otherwise, the operation will result in error.

● Syntax

```
AVG ([DISTINCT] column-name)
```

- Argument

  DISTINCT means that duplicate values are eliminated. If this keyword is omitted, then all values are used to calculate the average.

  column-name is the name of an existing table whose values are used to calculate the average.

- Example

  In the next **SELECT** statement, **AVG** is used to calculate the average of staff in department DX01. By omitting the **DISTINCT** parameter, duplicate values are not ignored. The column STAFF_AGE of the table DEPARTMENT is the argument to the **AVG** function. The result is placed in the AVG_AGE host variable.

  ```
  SELECT AVG(STAFF_AGE)
     INTO :AVE_AGE
     FROM DEPARTMENT
    WHERE DEPNO = 'DX01'
  ```

  In the next statement, the **DISTINCT** keyword is used with STAFF_AGE. This means that the averages of only unique values are used to calculate the average.

  ```
  SELECT AVG(DISTINCT STAFF_AGE)
     INTO :AVE_AGE
     FROM DEPARTMENT
    WHERE DEPNO='DX01'
  ```

  The two previous examples are embedded SQL statements; the next one is an example of AVG() in interactive mode.

  ```
  SELECT AVG(DISTINCT STAFF_AGE)
     FROM DEPARTMENT
    WHERE DEPNO = 'DX01'
  ```

▮▮▮ COUNT — Calculate the Number of Rows

The **COUNT** function returns the number of rows in a table or the number of values in a set of rows.

● Syntax

```
COUNT(*)
    or
COUNT(DISTINCT column-name)
```

● Argument

COUNT(*) returns a number of rows in a table. Rows where all the columns have NULL values are counted.

DISTINCT *column-name*
This parameter is used to specify distinct values of a column.

column-name is the name of a column in a table.

● Example

In the next **SELECT** statement, COUNT( ) returns the number of rows in the DEPARTMENT table, which has the department number 'DX01'. The value is placed in the STAFF_CNT host variable.

```
SELECT COUNT(*)
   INTO :STAFF_CNT
   FROM DEPARTMENT
  WHERE DEPNO = 'DX01'
```

In the next **SELECT** statement, the argument of COUNT is DISTINCT STAFF_LEVEL. DISTINCT means that any duplicate values of STAFF_LEVEL will not be counted. Also, the rows that are counted must have DEPNO = 'DX01'. The count is placed in the STAFF_LVL host variable.

```
SELECT COUNT(DISTINCT STAFF_LEVEL)
   INTO :STAFF_LVL
   FROM DEPARTMENT
  WHERE DEPNO = 'DX01'
```

∎∎∎ MAX — Calculate the Maximum of a Set of Values

The **MAX** function calculates the maximum value in a set of values of a column. The data type of the returned value is the same as that of the argument.

- Syntax

```
MAX (column-name)
```

- Argument

   column-name is the name of a column in a table for which the maximum value is to be calculated.

- Example

   The following **MAX** function within the **SELECT** statement is used to find the maximum value of STAFF_AGE from the DEPARTMENT where DEPNO = 'DX01'.

```
SELECT MAX(STAFF_AGE)
   INTO :MAX_AGE
   FROM DEPARTMENT
  WHERE DEPNO ='DX01'
```

∎∎∎ MIN — Calculate the Minimum of a Set of Values

The **MIN** function calculates the minimum value in a set of values of a column. The data type of the returned value is the same as the data type of the argument.

- Syntax

```
MIN (column-name)
```

- Argument

   column-name is the name of a column in a table for which the minimum value is to be calculated.

● Example

The following **MIN** function within the **SELECT** statement is used to find
the minimum value of STAFF_AGE from the DEPARTMENT where
DEPNO = 'DX01'.

```
SELECT MIN(STAFF_AGE)
  INTO :MAX_AGE
  FROM DEPARTMENT
 WHERE DEPNO = 'DX01'
```

▍▍▍ SUM — Calculate the Sum of a Set of Numbers

The **SUM** function returns the sum of a set of numbers. The returned value
depends on the data type of the column. The return value for an integer column
is integer, for a floating-point column is floating-point, and so on. And, of
course, the result should be within the range of the data type; otherwise, the
operation will result in error.

● Syntax

```
SUM ([DISTINCT] column-name)
```

● Argument

DISTINCT means that duplicate values are eliminated. If this keyword is
omitted, then all values are used to calculate the sum of the numbers.

column-name is the name of an existing table whose values are used to
calculate the sum.

● Example

In the next **SELECT** statement, **SUM** is used to calculate the sum of the
staff in department DX01. By omitting the DISTINCT parameter, duplicate
values are not ignored. The column STAFF_AGE of the table
DEPARTMENT is the argument to the **SUM** function. The result is placed
in SUM_AVG.

```
SELECT AVG(STAFF_AGE)
```

```
INTO :SUM_AGE
FROM DEPARTMENT
WHERE DEPNO='DX01'
```

In the next statement, the DISTINCT keyword is used with STAFF_AGE. This means that only unique values are used to calculate the sum.

```
SELECT SUM(DISTINCT STAFF_AGE)
INTO :SUM_AGE
FROM DEPARTMENT
WHERE DEPNO = 'DX01'
```

▚▚▚ CHAR — Converts a Date or Time Value to a String

The **CHAR** function converts a datetime value into a string.

● Syntax

```
CHAR (expression [,date-format])
```

● Argument

expression must evaluate to a date, time, or a timestamp.

date-format determines the format of the datetime value. If it used, it is one of the following: ISO, USA, EUR, JIS, or LOCAL. These formats are described in Figure 10.1.

Date format	Example	Type
yyyy-mm-dd	1998-12-10	International Standards Organization (ISO)
mm/dd/yyyy	12/10/1998	USA Standard (USA)
dd.mm.yyyy	10.12.1998	European Standard (EUR)
yyyy-mm-dd	1998-12-10	Japanese Industrial Standard (JIS)

Figure 10.1 Data string formats

● Example

In the next example, let's say the host variable CURRENT-DATE has 1994-01-10 in the internal format. The **CHAR** function will return '01/10/1994' in USA format.

```
CHAR (:CURRENT-DATE, USA)
```

In the next example, the expression is a bit more complicated. It adds the time value of the ELAPSE-TIME host variable and START_TIME column. Assume that START_TIME is 10.20.30 and ELAPSE-TIME is 050000 (5 hours). The return value will be be '15:20 PM'.

```
CHAR (START_TIME + :ELAPSE-TIME, USA)
```

▮▮▮ DATE — Convert Value to Date Format

The **DATE** function value returns the date portion of a value.

● Syntax

```
DATE (expression)
```

● Argument

expression must evaluate to a date, timestamp, a positive number less than or equal to 3,652,059, or a string holding a date or a timestamp.

● Example

In the next example, the expression is TIMESTAMP, a register that holds the current time and date. The **DATE** function is used to extract the date portion. Let's say the timestamp is equivalent to '1994-01-11-10.20.30.000000'. The result of

```
DATE(TIMESTAMP)
```

will be '1994-01-11'.

■■■ DAY — Get the Day Part of a Value

The **DAY** function returns the day part of a date or timestamp.

● Syntax

```
DAY(expression)
```

● Argument

expression can be a date, timestamp, date duration, timestamp duration, or a valid string holding a date or a timestamp.

● Example

The following **SELECT** statement is used to retrieve a date from the CLIENT_ID column of the CLIENTS table. The search clause of this statement uses the **DAY** function twice. The first time, it calculates the day of the current date; the next time, the day of the START_DATE column. Both return a day value, and if the difference is greater than 15, the CLIENT_ID for that row is placed into the WS-CLIENT host variable.

```
SELECT CLIENT_ID
   INTO :WS-CLIENT
   FROM CLIENTS
  WHERE DAY(TIMESTAMP) - DAY(START_DATE) > 15
```

In the next **SELECT** statement, the **DAY** function is used to get the day portion of the START_DATE column whose data type is date.

```
SELECT DAY(START_DATE)
   INTO :DATE
   FROM CLIENTS
  WHERE CLIENT_ID = 'ICM'
```

The selected row(s) must have CLIENT_ID = ICM. If START_DATE has '1994-01-30', the 30 will be placed in the DATE host variable.

■■■ DAYS — Get Integer Value of Day From Date

The **DAYS** function returns the integer value of a date.

● Syntax

```
DAYS (expression)
```

● Argument

expression must be a date, timestamp, or a string holding a date or a timestamp.

● Example

The following **SELECT** statement is used to calculate the difference in days between the current day and time, and the value retrieved from the CLIENT_ID column of the CLIENTS table. The returned number of days is placed into the :WS-DAYS host variable.

```
SELECT DAYS(TIMESTAMP) - DAYS(START_DATE)
   INTO :WS-CLIENT
   FROM CLIENTS
  WHERE DEPTNO = 'DEP001'
```

▌▌▌ DECIMAL — Convert a Number to a Decimal

The **DECIMAL** function is used to convert any type of numbers into its decimal representation.

● Syntax

```
DECIMAL (numeric-expression
         [,precision-integer, scale-integer]
        )
```

● Argument

numeric-expression must evaluate to a numeric data type.

precision-integer is an operational integer that specifies the precision of the result. Its value must be in the range of 1 to 31. The default precision integer for a floating-point or decimal value is 15; for large integers, 11; and for small integers, 5.

scale-integer is a value in the range 0 to the value of *precision-integer*.

● Example

In the next interactive **SELECT** command, the decimal representation of SALES is returned. The SALE column is of SMALLINT data type and is converted to DECIMAL data type in this **SELECT** statement, which gets two columns of all rows where DEPNO = `DX01'.

```
SELECT CLIENT_ID, DECIMAL(SALES,5,2)
  FROM CLIENTS
 WHERE DEPNO = 'DX01'
```

▌▌▌▌ FLOAT — Convert a Number to a Floating-point Value

The **FLOAT** function is used to convert any numeric value to a double precision floating-point number.

● Syntax

```
FLOAT (numeric-expression)
```

● Argument

numeric-expression must evaluate to any numeric data type. If this value is null, the result from the **FLOAT** function is null.

● Example

In the next **SELECT** statement, the **FLOAT** function is used to convert the value of the AMOUNT column from decimal to floating-point.

```
SELECT CLIENT_ID
       ,FLOAT(AMOUNT)
  FROM CLIENTS
 WHERE DEPNO = 'DX01'
```

▓▓ HOUR — Get the Hour Part of a Value

The **HOUR** function returns the hour part of a date or timestamp. The return value is in the range of 0 to 24.

- Syntax

```
HOUR(expression)
```

- Argument

  expression can be a date, timestamp, date duration, timestamp duration, or a valid string holding a date or a timestamp.

- Example

  The following **SELECT** statement is used to retrieve a date from the CLIENT_ID column of the CLIENTS table. The search clause of this statement uses the **HOUR** function twice. The first time, it calculates the hour of the current date; the next time the hour of the START_DATE column. Both return an hour value, and if the difference is greater than 15, the value of the CLIENT_ID column for that row is placed into the WS-CLIENT host variable.

```
SELECT CLIENT_ID
  INTO :WS-CLIENT
  FROM CLIENTS
 WHERE HOUR(TIMESTAMP) - HOUR(START_DATE) > 15
```

▓▓ INTEGER — Convert a Number to an Integer

The **INTEGER** function returns the integer part of a number. The result is a large integer.

- Syntax

```
INTEGER(numeric-expression)
```

- Argument

  numeric-expression must evaluate to any numeric data type. If this value is null, then the result from the **INTEGER** function is null.

- Example

  In the next **SELECT** statement, the **INTEGER** function is used to obtain the integer part when AMOUNT is divided by EDLEVEL.

  ```
  SELECT CLIENT_ID
        ,EDLEVEL
        ,(AMOUNT/EDLEVEL)
    FROM CLIENTS
   WHERE DEPNO = 'DX01'
  ```

■■■ LENGTH — Calculate the Length of a Value

The **LENGTH** function calculates the length of a value. This argument can be any data type. The return length is a large integer in the number of bytes. If the argument is graphic, the return value is half the length in bytes of the argument. If the argument is a null, the result is a null value.

The following shows the length in bytes and data types.

Length	Data types
2	Small integer
4	Large integer
$p/2 + 1$	For decimal number with precision p
8	Float
4	Date
3	Time
10	Timestamp
length of string	Character string

- Syntax

  ```
  LENGTH(expression)
  ```

● Argument

expression can evaluate to any data type.

● Example

Let's say the NAME host variable contains 'John Smith'.

```
LENGTH(:NAME)
```

returns 10. And, assuming that the START_DATE column is a DATE data type,

```
LENGTH (START_DATE)
```

returns 4.

▌▌▌▌ MICROSECOND — Get the Microsecond Part of a Time Value

The **MICROSECOND** function returns the microsecond part of a date or timestamp. The return value is in the range of 0 to 999999.

● Syntax

```
MICROSECOND(expression)
```

● Argument

expression can be a date, timestamp, date duration, timestamp duration, or a valid string holding a date or a timestamp.

● Example

The following **SELECT** statement is used to retrieve a date from the CLIENT_ID column of the CLIENTS table. The search clause of this statement uses the **MICROSECOND** function to determine whether the microsecond of the START_DATE column is greater than 0. If this evaluation is valid, the value of the CLIENT_ID column for that row is placed into the WS-CLIENT host variable.

```
SELECT CLIENT_ID
  INTO :WS-CLIENT
  FROM CLIENTS
 WHERE MICROSECOND(START_DATE) > 0
```

■■■ MINUTE — Get the Minute Part of a Time Value

The **MINUTE** function returns the minute part of a date or timestamp. The return value is an integer in the range of 0 to 59.

- Syntax

   MINUTE(*expression*)

- Argument

   expression can be a date, timestamp, date duration, timestamp duration, or a valid string holding a date or a timestamp.

- Example

   The following **SELECT** statement is used to retrieve a date from the CLIENT_ID column of the CLIENTS table. The search clause of this statement uses the MINUTE function to determine whether the minute of the START_DATE column is greater than 0. If this evaluation is valid, the value of the CLIENT_ID column for that row is placed into the WS-CLIENT host variable.

```
SELECT CLIENT_ID
  INTO :WS-CLIENT
  FROM CLIENTS
 WHERE MINUTE(START_DATE) > 0
```

■■■ MONTH — Get the Minute Part of a Time Value

The **MONTH** function returns the month part of a date or timestamp. The return value is an integer in the range of 1 to 12.

● Syntax

```
MONTH(expression)
```

● Argument

expression can be a date, timestamp, date duration, timestamp duration, or a valid string holding a date or a timestamp.

● Example

The following **SELECT** statement is used to retrieve a date from the CLIENT_ID column of the CLIENTS table. The search clause of this statement uses the **MONTH** function to determine whether the month of the START_DATE column is equal to 1. If this evaluation is valid, the value of the CLIENT_ID column for that row is placed into the WS-CLIENT host variable.

```
SELECT CLIENT_ID
  INTO :WS-CLIENT
  FROM CLIENTS
 WHERE MINUTE(START_DATE) = 1
```

■■■ SECOND — Get the Second Part of a Time Value

The **SECOND** function returns the second part of a date or timestamp. The return value is an integer in the range of 0 to 59.

● Syntax

```
SECOND(expression)
```

● Argument

expression can be a date, timestamp, date duration, timestamp duration, or a valid string holding a date or a timestamp.

● Example

The following **SELECT** statement is used to retrieve a date from the CLIENT_ID column of the CLIENTS table. The search clause of this statement uses the **SECOND** function to determine whether the minute of the START_DATE column is greater than 0. If this evaluation is valid, the value of the CLIENT_ID column for that row is placed into the WS-CLIENT host variable.

```
SELECT CLIENT_ID
  INTO :WS-CLIENT
  FROM CLIENTS
 WHERE SECOND(START_DATE) > 0
```

▮▮▮▮ SUBSTR — Get a Substring of a String

The **SUBSTR** function returns a substring of a string.

● Syntax

```
SUBSTR (string, start [,length])
```

● Argument

string is a character or graphic string from which the substring is returned.

start is the starting position of the first byte of the substring.

length is the number of bytes from the starting position.

● Example

In the following example, the SUBSTR(F_NAME,1,1) returns the first character of the F_NAME column.

```
SELECT SUBSTR(F_NAME,1,1)
     ,L_NAME
  FROM CUSTOMER
```

▐▐▐ TIME — Get a Time From a Value

The **TIME** function returns the time from the time value. The return value is the same as the argument; it returns timestamp for timestamp, time for time, string for string, and null for null.

- Syntax

```
TIME(expression)
```

- Argument

expression can be a date, timestamp, date duration, timestamp duration, or a valid string holding a date or a timestamp.

- Example

In the search condition of the following **SELECT** statement, the TIME function is used to extract the time part of the START_TIME column. Next, it is determined whether it is equal to or greater than one hour after the current time.

```
SELECT NAME
  FROM COURSES
 WHERE TIME(START_TIME) >= CURRENTTIME + 1 HOUR
```

▐▐▐ TIMESTAMP — Get a Time Stamp From a Value

The **TIMESTAMP** function returns a timestamp value from one or two arguments. If the arguments are null, then the result is also a null value.

- Syntax

```
TIMESTAMP(expression1 [,expression2])
```

- Argument

expression1 must be a timestamp or a string holding a valid timestamp, if *expression2* is not specified. If both expressions are entered, then *expression1* must be a date or a string holding a valid date.

expression2 is optional, and if specified, it must be a time or a string holding a valid time.

● Example

Assume that START_DATE = 1994-01-12 and START_TIME = 10.20.30.

```
TIMESTAMP(START_DATE,START_TIME)
```

returns '1994-01-12-10.20.30.000000'.

▌▌▌▌ TRANSLATE — Translate Characters

The **TRANSLATE** function is used to convert characters in a character string or a graphic string.

● Syntax

```
Character string format:
    TRANSLATE( char-string-expression
               [,to-string-expression, from-string-expression
               [,' ' or ,pad-char]])
Graphic string format:
    TRANSLATE( graphic-string-expression,
               to-string-expression, from-string-expression
               [,' ' or ,pad-char] )
```

● Argument

char-string-expression or *graphic-string-expression* is the string where the translation occurs.

to-string-expression contains a set of characters that are translated to or from the source string.

from-string-expression is a set of characters that are searched for in *char-string-expression* or *graphic-string-expression*. If found, they are translated to *to-string-expression*.

pad-char is a single character that is used to pad *to-string-expression*, if the length of *to-string-expression* is shorter than *from-string-expression*.

- Example

Let's say that the DISNEY host variable contains 'HANA BARBARA'. The following shows the operands and return values of the TRANSLATE function.

```
TRANSLATE(:DISNEY) returns `HANA BARBARA'.
TRANSLATE(:DISNEY,I,A) returns `HINI BIRBIRI'.
TRANSLATE(:DISNEY,ei,aa) returns `HeNe BeRBeRe'.
TRANSLATE(:DISNEY,'i',ar) returns `HiNi Bi Bi A'.
```

▮▮▮ VARGRAPHIC — Convert to Double-byte Character String

The **VARGRAPHIC** function converts a string that has both single-byte and double-byte characters to pure double-byte character strings.

- Syntax

```
VARGRAPHIC(expression)
```

- Argument

expression must evaluate to the character string data type, except LONG VARCHAR. The length of the string cannot exceed 2000 bytes.

▮▮▮ YEAR — Calculate the Year Part of a Time Value

The **YEAR** function returns the year part of a date or timestamp. The return value is an integer in the range of 1 to 9999.

- Syntax

```
YEAR(expression)
```

- Argument

  expression can be a date, timestamp, date duration, timestamp duration, or a valid string holding a date or a timestamp.

- Example

  The following **SELECT** statement is used to retrieve a date from the CLIENT_ID column of the CLIENTS table. The search clause of this statement uses the YEAR function where the year of the REQUEST_DT column is compared with the year of the timestamp register. If both are equal, then the value of the CLIENT_ID column for that row is placed into the WS-CLIENT host variable.

```
SELECT CLIENT_ID
  INTO :WS-CLIENT
  FROM CLIENTS
 WHERE YEAR(REQUEST_DT) = YEAR(TIMESTAMP)
```

Chapter 11
DB2 Command Line Process Commands

This chapter is a reference guide for users of DB2 command line processor(CLP) commands and utilities. What are CLP commands? They manage the database, server, and client parts of DB2. These commands are issued in a special way. You have to use the DB2 system commands to execute them. We looked at DB2 command, both in interactive and batch mode, in Chapter 3. These CLP commands are used to maintain the operation of the database manager. Some of the operations you can perform are:

- Maintain DB2 databases
- Issue SQL statements
- Request help information

For each command and utility, this chapter provides the description of the function followed by the syntax and its parameters. It also lists privileges and authority needed to execute these commands. In some cases, you will also find examples of how the functions use these parameters.

▮▮▮▮ ACTIVATE DATABASE

The **ACTIVATE DATABASE** command starts up all necessary database services so that the database is available for connection by users and applications.

UNIX	OS/2	NT
X	X	X

- Syntax

```
ACTIVATE DATABASE   database_name
            [USER username USING password]
```

- Parameters

    DATABASE *database*
    This specifies the name of the database to be activated.

    USER *username*
    This specifies a valid user ID that has privileges to do this operation.

    USING *password*
    This specifies the password of the user.

- Authorizations

Authority	Privilege
SYSADM or SYSCTRL or SYSMAINT	None required

■■■ ADD NODE

The **ADD NODE** command must be issued from the node that is being added and it can only be issued on an MPP server. This command only affects the node in which it is executed.

UNIX	OS/2	NT
X		

- Syntax

```
ADD NODE [ LIKE NODE node-number
         [ WITHOUT TABLESPACES] ]
```

- Parameters

LIKE NODE *node-number*
This specifies a number for each database and it must be a node already found in db2nodes.cfg file.

WITHOUT TABLESPACES means that containers for the temporary table spaces are not created for any of the databases.

- Authorizations

Authority	Privilege
SYSADM	None required

▮▮▮ ATTACH

The **ATTACH** command enables a user, such as an application, to name the instance at which instance-level commands, such as **CREATE DATABASE** and **FORCE APPLICATION**, are to be executed. This instance may be the current instance, another instance on the same workstation, or an instance on a remote workstation.

UNIX	OS/2	NT
X	X	X

- Syntax

```
ATTACH [TO nodename]
       [USER username [USING password]]
```

- Parameters

TO *nodename*
This specifies an alias of the instance to which the user wants to attach. This instance must have a matching entry in the local node directory.

USER *username*
This specifies a valid user ID to execute this command.

USING *password*
This specifies the password of the user.

- Authorizations

Authority	Privilege
None required	None required

▌▌▌ BACKUP DATABASE

The **BACKUP DATABASE** command is used to make a backup copy of a database or a table space. This command only affects the node on which it is executed. This command automatically establishes a connection to the specified database.

UNIX	OS/2	NT
X	X	X

- Syntax

```
BACKUP <DATABASE or DB>
       [database-alias  USER   username
       [USING  password]]
       [TABLESPACE  tablespace-name,... ]
       [ [ONLINE] USE ADSM [OPEN  num-sessions  SESSIONS]
                    or
          TO target-area
                    or
          LOAD library-name [OPEN num-sessions SESSIONS]
```

```
]
[WITH  num-buffers  BUFFERS]
[BUFFER  buffer-size]
[PARALLELISM  n ]
[WITHOUT PROMPTING]
```

● Parameters

USER *username*
This specifies the user name under which to back up the database.

USING *password*
This specifies the password used to authenticate the user name. If the password is omitted, the user is prompted to enter it.

TABLESPACE *tablespace-name*
This specifies a list of names used to specify the table spaces to be backed up.

ONLINE
This indicates an online backup. The default is offline backup.

USE ADSM
This indicates that the backup is to use ADSM managed output.

OPEN *num-sessions* SESSIONS
This specifies the number of I/O sessions to be used with ADSM or the vendor product.

TO *target-area*
This specifies a directory or tape device name. The target must reside on the database server.

This parameter may be repeated to specify the target directories and devices that the backup image will span. If more than one target is specified (target1, target2, and target , for example), target1 will be opened first. The media header and special files (including the configuration file, table space table, and history file) are placed in target1. All remaining targets are opened, and are then used in parallel during the backup. Use of tape devices or floppy disks may generate messages and prompts for user input. Valid response options are:

Continue. Continue using the device that generated the warning message (for example, when a new tape has been mounted)
Device terminate. Stop using only the device that generated the warning message (for example, when there are no more tapes)
Terminate. Abort the backup or restore utility. Tape is not supported on OS/2. On OS/2, 0 or 0: can be specified to cause the backup operation to call the user exit program This option is invalid on all other platforms.

LOAD *library-name*
This specifies a name of the shared library (DLL on OS/2) containing the vendor backup and restore I/O functions to be used. It may contain the full path. If the full path is not given, it will default to the path on which the user exit program resides.

WITH *num-buffers* BUFFERS
This specifies the number of buffers to be used.

BUFFER *buffer-size*
This specifies the size, in pages, of the buffer used when building the backup image. The minimum value for this parameter is 16 pages; the default value is 1024 pages. If a buffer-size of 0 is specified, the value of the database manager configuration parameter *backbufsz* is used.

PARALLELISM *n*
This specifies the number of buffer manipulators to be spawned during the restore process. The default value is 1.

WITHOUT PROMPTING
This indicates that the backup will run unattended, and that any actions which normally require user intervention will return an error message.

● Authorizations

Authority	Privilege
SYSADM or DBADM	None required

● Example

In the following command, the CLIENTS database is backed up in drive A
and directory \ONEWORLD\backup

```
BACKUP DATABASE CLIENTS TO A:\ONEWORLD\backup
```

■■■ BIND

The **BIND** command takes a bind created by the precompiler and generates a
package which is used to access DB2 data during the execution of a program.
During a bind processing, the following happens:

● Validation of the rules, structure, and syntax of SQL statements used in a
program

● Verification of authority to access DB2 data

● Choice of an access path to data

● Creation of a package which is used to allocate resources during program
execution

UNIX	OS/2	NT
X	X	X

● Syntax

```
For DB2

    BIND  filename
       [BLOCKING <ALL or NO or UNAMBIG>]
       [COLLECTION  schema-name]
       [DATETIME format]
       [DEGREE <1 or degree-of-I/O-parallelism or ANY>]
       [EXPLAIN <NO or YES>]
       [EXPLSNAP <NO or ALL or YES>]
       [INSERT <BUF or DEF>]
       [ISOLATION isolation]
       [MESSAGES  message-file]
```

```
[QUERYOPT  optimization-level]
[SQLERROR <CHECK or CONTINUE or NOPACKAGE>]
[SQLWARN  <NO  or YES >]
```

For DRDA

```
BIND  filename
[ACTION <ADD or REPLACE> [RETAIN < NO or YES>]]
[REPLVER version-id]
[BLOCKING <ALL or NO or UNAMBIG>]
[COLLECTION schema-name ]
[DATETIME format]
[EXPLAIN <NO or YES>]
[GRANT < authid or PUBLIC >]
[INSERT <BUF or DEF>]
[ISOLATION isolation ]
[MESSAGES message-file]
[SQLERROR <CHECK or CONTINUE or NOPACKAGE>]
```

- Parameters

   BIND *filename*
      This specifies the name of the bind file, generated when the application
      program was precompiled, or a list file containing the names of several
      bind files, for which a binding is to be done. Bind files have the extension
      .bnd. The full path name can be specified.

      For a list file, the @ character must be added before the filename. The list
      file can contain several lines of bind file names. Bind files listed on the
      same line must be separated by plus (+) characters, but a + cannot appear
      in front of the first file listed on each line, or after the last bind file listed.
      For example, /u/smith/sqllib/bnd/@all.lst is a list file that contains the
      following bind files:

         mybind1.bnd + mybind2.bnd + mybind3.bnd+
         mybind4.bnd + mybind5.bnd +
         mybind6.bnd + mybind7.bnd

   ACTION <ADD or REPLACE> [RETAIN < NO or YES>]
      This specifies whether the package can be added or replaced. The options
      are:
         ADD means that the named package does not exist, and that a new
         package is to be created. If the package already exists, execution stops,
         and a diagnostic error message is returned.

REPLACE means that the old package is to be replaced by a new one with the same location, collection, and package name.

RETAIN means whether EXECUTE authorities are to be preserved when a package is replaced.

NO means not to preserve the EXECUTE authorities when a package is replaced.

YES means to preserve the EXECUTE authorities when a package is replaced.

REPLVER *version-id*
This replaces a specific version of a package.

BLOCKING *blocking*
This specifies the type of record blocking and it tells how to deal with ambiguous cursors.

blocking is one of the following:

- ALL means to block for:

  - FETCH-only cursors
  - Cursors not specified as **FOR UPDATE OF**
  - Cursors for which there are no static **DELETE WHERE CURRENT OF** statements
  - Any ambiguous cursors are treated as FETCH-only.

- UNAMBIG means to block for:

  - FETCH-only cursors
  - Cursors not specified as **FOR UPDATE OF**
  - Cursors that do not have static **DELETE WHERE CURRENT OF** statements
  - Cursors that do not have dynamic statements
  - Any ambiguous cursors are treated as UPDATE-only.

- NO means not to block any cursors. Any ambiguous cursors are treated as UPDATE-only.

The default is UNAMBIG.

COLLECTION *schema-name*
This specifies an 8-character collection identifier for the package. If not specified, the authorization identifier for the user processing the package is used.

DATETIME *format*
This specifies the date and time formats used when binding a program.

EXPLAIN <NO or YES>
This stores information in the Explain tables about the access plans chosen for each SQL statement in the package.

NO means not to capture Explain information.

YES means to populate Explain tables with information about the chosen access plan.

EXPLSNAP <NO or YES or ALL>
This stores Explain Snapshot information in the Explain tables.

NO means not to capture Explain Snapshot.

YES indicates an Explain Snapshot for each eligible static SQL statement will be placed in the Explain tables.

ALL indicates an Explain Snapshot for each eligible static SQL statement will be placed in the Explain tables. In addition, Explain Snapshot information will be gathered for eligible dynamic SQL statements at run time, even if the CURRENT EXPLAIN SNAPSHOT register is set to NO.

GRANT < *authid* or PUBLIC >
This specifies who gets the privilege: individual users or all users.

PUBLIC means to grant the privilege to all users.

authid is a user ID or group name. You can specify one or more IDs; they it must not include the user ID that is issuing the command.

INSERT <BUF or DEF>
This allows a program being precompiled or bound from a DB2 V2.1 client to a DATABASE 2 Parallel Edition server to request that data inserts be buffered to increase performance.

BUF means that inserts from an application should be buffered.

DEF means that inserts from an application should not be buffered.

ISOLATION *isolation*
This specifies the isolation level. This tells DB2 how to isolate data in the database from other processing which may occur while the application is accessing the database.

isolation is one of the following:

RR — repeatable read
CS — cursor stability
UR — uncommitted read

MESSAGES *msgfile*
This specifies a destination to which warning or error messages are written.

msgfile can be any one of the filenames. If a message file name is not specified, the messages are written to standard output. If the complete path to the file is not specified, the current directory is used. If the name of an existing file is specified, the contents of the file are overwritten.

QUERYOPT *optimization-level*
This indicates the desired level of optimization for all static SQL statements contained in the package.

optimization-level is an integer. The default value is 3.

SQLERROR <CHECK or CONTINUE or NOPACKAGE>
This indicates whether to create a package or a bind file if an error is encountered.

CHECK means that the target system performs all syntax and semantic checks on the SQL statements being bound. A package will not be created as part of this process. If, while creating a package, an existing package with the same name and version is encountered, the existing package is neither dropped nor replaced if action replace was specified.

CONTINUE means that a package or a bind file is created even when SQL errors are encountered.

NOPACKAGE means a package or a bind file is not created if an error is encountered.

SQLWARN <NO or YES >
This indicates whether warnings will be returned from the compilation of dynamic SQL statements (via PREPARE or EXECUTE IMMEDIATE), or from describe processing (via PREPARE...INTO or DESCRIBE).

NO means warnings will not be returned from the SQL compiler.

YES means warnings will be returned from the SQL compiler.

● Authorizations

Authority	Privilege
SYSADM or DBADM or BIND	BINDADD

● Example

In the following command, TIP.BND is a bind file. This file is generated by the precompiler. The CUSTOMER database is used to validate table and column names found in the SQL statements of the source program.

```
BIND TIP.BND TO DATABASE CUSTOMER \
  MESSAGES=C:\TIP\ERROR.OUT
```

The MESSAGES option is used to write the messages during the bind process to C:\TIP\ERROR.OUT.

▀▀▀ CATALOG APPN NODE

The **CATALOG APPN** command is used to add an entry to the node directory. An entry contains information about a remote workstation that uses APPN (Advanced Peer-to-Peer Network) communication protocols. This information is used by DB2 to connect an application program to a remote database cataloged in this node.

UNIX	OS/2	NT
	X	

● Syntax

```
CATALOG APPN NODE node-name
   [NETWORKID netid]
   REMOTE partner-lu
   [LOCAL local-lu]
   [MODE mode]
   [WITH "comment-string"]
```

● Parameters

NODE *node-name*
This specifies the name of the remote workstation to the catalog. This name is the same as the one used to catalog a database with the **CATALOG DATABASE** command. The node name must conform to DB2 naming conventions.

NETWORKID *netid*
This specifies the SNA (Systems Network Architecture) network ID where the remote LU (logical unit) is to be found. *netid* is a string no longer than eight characters and it must conform to SNA naming conventions.

REMOTE *partner-lu*

This specifies the SNA partner LU (logical unit) that is needed for connection. *partner-lu* is a LU name of the remote node. The length of this name cannot exceed eight characters.

LOCAL *local-lu*

This specifies the alias of the SNA local LU that is used for connection. *local-lu* is a LU name in the local node. The length of this name cannot exceed eight characters.

MODE *mode*

This specifies the SNA transmission mode used in the connection. *node* is the name of the node, and it must be longer than eight characters. If you omit this parameter, DB2 places the default value of eight blank characters.

WITH *comment-string*

This specifies the description of the APPN node entry found in the node directory. It must be enclosed in quotes (").

● Authorizations

Authority	Privilege
SYSADM	None required

● Example

The following command is used to catalog an APPN node called XYZNODE.

```
CATALOG APPN NODE XYZNODE    \
   REMOTE XYZLU              \
   WITH "Catalog APPN NODE XYZNODE"
```

■■■ CATALOG DATABASE

The **CATALOG DATABASE** command is used to add information about a database into the database directory.

UNIX	OS/2	NT
X	X	X

- Syntax

```
CATALOG <DATABASE or DB> database-name
   [AS alias]
   [ON <drive or path>]
   [AT NODE nodename]
   [AUTHENTICATION
      <SERVER or
       CLIENT or
       DCS or
       DCSSERVERPRINCIPAL principalname>]
   [WITH "comment-string"]
```

- Parameters

DATABASE *database-name*
    This specifies the name of the database being cataloged to the directory.

AS *alias*
    This specifies the alias for the database.

ON *<drive or path>*
    This specifies where the database is found.

    drive, for OS/2 only, the letter of the drive on which the database being cataloged resides.

    path, for AIX only, is the directory path on which the database being cataloged resides. On server nodes, the path must exist, or an error will be returned.

AT NODE *nodename*
    This specifies the name of the remote workstation where the database is found.

AUTHENTICATION <SERVER or CLIENT or DCS
        or DCSSERVERPRINCIPAL *principalname*>]
    This specifies the methods of authentication. They are:

SERVER indicates that authentication takes place on the node containing the target database.

CLIENT indicates that authentication takes place on the node where the application is invoked.

DCS indicates that authentication takes place on the node containing the target database, except when using DDCS, when it specifies that authentication takes place at the DRDA AS.

DCE indicates that authentication takes place using DCE Security Services. When authentication is DCE, and an APPC connection is used for access, only SECURITY=NONE is supported.

SERVER PRINCIPAL *principalname*
This specifies a fully qualified DCE principal name for the target server. This value is also recorded in the keytab file at the target server.

WITH *comment-string*
This specifies the description of the entry found in the database directory. It must be enclosed in quotes (").

● Authorizations

Authority	Privilege
SYSADM	None required

● Example

The following statement is used to catalog the ONEWORLD database which resides in the NODEXYZ remote workstation.

```
CATALOG DATABASE ONEWORLD AT NODE NODEXYZ \
        WITH "ONEWORLD database"
```

▄▄▄ CATALOG DCS DATABASE

The **CATALOG DCS DATABASE** command is used to write information about a host database to the Database Connection Services (DCS) directory. This catalog information is needed by a workstation to access the host database using the SAA Distributed Database Connection Series/2 facilities.

UNIX	OS/2	NT
X	X	X

- Syntax

```
CATALOG DCS DATABASE database-name
   [AS tdb-name]
   [AR dll-name]
   [PARMS "parameter-string"]
   [WITH "comment-string"]
```

- Parameters

DATABASE *database-name*
   This specifies the alias of the database that is being cataloged.

AS *tdb-name*
   This specifies the name of the database that is being cataloged.

AR *dll-name*
   This specifies the name of the dynamic link library program to be used. It is one of the following:

   SQLJRDR1   DRDA-1 database connections for Distributed Relational Database Architecture; this is the default program.

   SQL_AR0 ASP-0 or OS/2 database connections
   SQLESRVR   Local server

PARMS *parameter-string*
   This specifies parameters used by the program named in the AR parameter. This is a string, enclosed in quotes, that contains the

connection and operating environment information. The parameters that you can list in this string are:

TPP   Transaction program prefix. This is a hex (hexidecimal) value that identifies the first byte of the transaction program name. The default is 07.

TPN   Transaction program name. This is a character string that is used as the name of the transaction program, run on the host.

MAP   SQLCODE mapping file. This is a character string to specify the name of the file that converts host SQL return codes to DCS return codes. It can be one of the following:

DCS0DSN	EE database and DB2 database
DCS1DSN	EE or DB2 database and DB2 database
DCS0ARI	EE database and SQL/DS database
DCS0QSQ	EE database and OS/400 database
DCS1QSQ	ES or DB2 database and OS/400 database

D   Disconnect option; this is used to disconnect the host when -300xx is encountered.

V   Verify option; this is used to verify a user ID and password before connecting to the host.

WITH *comment-string*
    This specifies a description of the entry found in the DCS directory. It must be enclosed in quotes (").

● Authorizations

Authority	Privilege
SYSADM	None required

■■■ CATALOG GLOBAL DATABASE

The **CATALOG GLOBAL DATABASE** command is used to write information about a host database to the Database Connection Services (DCS) directory. This catalog information is needed by a workstation to access the host database using the SAA Distributed Database Connection facilities.

UNIX	OS/2	NT
X		

- Syntax

```
CATALOG GLOBAL <DATABASE or DB>
  database-global-name
  AS alias USING DIRECTORY DCE
  [WITH "comment-string"]
```

- Parameters

  DATABASE *database-global-name*
  This specifies a fully qualified name that uniquely identifies a database in the DCE name space.

  AS *alias*
  This specifies an alternate name of the database being catalogued.

  WITH *comment-string*
  This specifies the description of the entry found in the system database directory. It must be enclosed in quotes (").

- Authorizations

Authority	Privilege
SYSADM	None required

▉▉▉ CATALOG IPX/SPX NODE

The **CATALOG IPX/SPX NODE** command adds an Internetwork Packet Exchange/Sequenced Packet Exchange (IPX/SPX) node entry to the node directory. The Novell NetWare IPX/SPX communications protocol is used to access the remote node.

UNIX	OS/2	NT
	X	X

- Syntax

```
CATALOG [ADMIN] IPXSPX NODE nodename
        REMOTE  file-server
        SERVER object-name
        [REMOTE_INSTANCE instance-name]
        [SYSTEM system-name]
        [OSTYPE operating-system-type]
        [WITH "comment-string"]
```

- Parameters

ADMIN
   This specifies the administration server node.

NODE *nodename*
   This specifies an alias for the node to be cataloged.

REMOTE *file-server*
   This specifies the name of the NetWare file server where the internetwork address of the database manager instance is registered.

SERVER *object-name*
   This specifies the name of the database manager instance stored in the bindery of the NetWare file server. Each database manager instance registered at one NetWare file server must be represented by a unique *object-name*.

REMOTE_INSTANCE *instance-name*
   This specifies the real name that is used to identify the server machine.

SYSTEM *system-name*
   This specifies the name that is used to identify the server machine.

OSTYPE *operating-system-type*
   This specifies the operating system type; the valid types are OS2, AIX, WIN95, NT, HPUX, SUN, MVS, OS400, VM, VSE, SNI, SCO, and SGI.

WITH *comment-string*
   This specifies the description of the node entry in the node directory.

● Authorizations

Authority	Privilege
SYSADM or SYSCTRL	None required

▮▮▮ CATALOG LOCAL NODE

The **CATALOG LOCAL NODE** command creates an alias name for an instance that resides on the same machine. A local node must be cataloged when there is more than one instance on the same workstation to be accessed from the user's client.

UNIX	OS/2	NT
X	X	X

● Syntax

```
CATALOG [ADMIN] LOCAL NODE nodename
        INSTANCE instancename
        [REMOTE_INSTANCE instance-name]
        [SYSTEM system-name]
        [OSTYPE operating-system-type]
        [WITH "comment-string"]
```

- Parameters

  ADMIN
  This specifies the administration server node.

  LOCAL NODE *nodename*
  This specifies an alias for the node to be cataloged. This arbitrary name on the user's workstation is used to identify the remote node. It should be meaningful such that it is easy to remember. Also the name must conform to the database manager naming conventions.

  INSTANCE *instancename*
  This specifies the user ID of the owner of another instance on the same workstation.

  REMOTE_INSTANCE *instance-name*
  This specifies the real name that is used to identify the server machine.

  SYSTEM *system-name*
  This specifies the name that is used to identify the server machine.

  OSTYPE *operating-system-type*
  This specifies the operating system type; the valid types are OS2, AIX, WIN95, NT, HPUX, SUN, MVS, OS400, VM, VSE, SNI, SCO, and SGI.

  WITH *comment-string*
  This specifies the description of the node entry in the node directory.

- Authorizations

Authority	Privilege
SYSADM or SYSCTRL	None required

▐▐▐ CATALOG NAMED PIPE NODE

The **CATALOG NPIPE NODE** command creates an entry for a named pipe node in the directory. The named pipe (IPC) mechanism) is used to access the remote node.

UNIX	OS/2	NT
X	X	X

● Syntax

```
CATALOG [ADMIN]  NPIPE NODE nodename
        REMOTE computername
        INSTANCE instancename
        [REMOTE_INSTANCE instance-name]
        [SYSTEM system-name]
        [OSTYPE operating-system-type]
        [WITH "comment-string"]
```

● Parameters

ADMIN
  This specifies the administration server node.

NPIPE NODE *nodename*
  This specifies an alias for the node to be cataloged. REMOTE *computername* specifies the computer name of the node where the target database is found. The computer name is known in the domain; its maximum length is 15 characters.

INSTANCE *instancename*
  This specifies a name associated in the instance at the remote node and is the same name as the named pipe in the remote node.

REMOTE_INSTANCE *instance-name*
  This specifies the real name that is used to identify the remote server machine.

SYSTEM *system-name*
  This specifies the name that is used to identify the server machine.

OSTYPE *operating-system-type*
   This specifies the operating system type; the valid types are OS2, AIX, WIN95, NT, HPUX, SUN, MVS, OS400, VM, VSE, SNI, SCO, and SGI.

WITH *comment-string*
   This specifies the description of the node entry in the node directory.

● Authorizations

Authority	Privilege
SYSADM or SYSCTRL	None required

▮▮▮ CATALOG NETBIOS NODE

The **CATALOG NETBIOS NODE** command creates an entry for a NetBIOS node in the directory. This uses NetBIOS communications protocol to access the remote node.

UNIX	OS/2	NT
	X	X

● Syntax

```
CATALOG [ADMIN]  NETBIOS
        NODE nodename
        REMOTE server-name
        ADAPTER adapter-number
        INSTANCE instancename
        [REMOTE_INSTANCE instance-name]
        [SYSTEM system-name]
        [OSTYPE operating-system-type]
        [WITH "comment-string"]
```

● Parameters

   ADMIN

This specifies the administration server node.

NODE *nodename*
This specifies an alias for the node to be cataloged.

REMOTE *server-name*
This specifies the name of the remote workstation where the target database is found.

ADAPTER *adapter-number*
This specifies the local, logical, outgoing LAN adapter. The default is 0.

INSTANCE *instancename*
This specifies the real name of the instance to which an attachment is being made on the remote server machine.

REMOTE_INSTANCE *instance-name*
This specifies the real name that is used to identify the remote server machine.

SYSTEM *system-name*
This specifies the name that is used to identify the server machine.

OSTYPE *operating-system-type*
This specifies the operating system type; the valid types are OS2, AIX, WIN95, NT, HPUX, SUN, MVS, OS400, VM, VSE, SNI, SCO, and SGI.

WITH *comment-string*
This specifies the description of the node entry in the node directory.

● Authorizations

Authority	Privilege
SYSADM or SYSCTRL	None required

■■■ CATALOG TCP/IP NODE

The **CATALOG TCPIP NODE** command is used to write a Transmission Control Protocol/Internet Protocol (TCP/IP) node entry to the node directory. By making this entry, one can use the TCP/IP communications protocol to access the remote node.

UNIX	OS/2	NT
X	X	X

• Syntax

```
CATALOG [ADMIN] TCPIP
        NODE nodename
        REMOTE hostname
        SERVER service-name
        [SECURITY SOCKS]
        [REMOTE_INSTANCE instance-name]
        [SYSTEM system-name]
        [OSTYPE operating-system-type]
        [WITH "comment-string"]
```

• Parameters

ADMIN
This specifies the administration server node.

NODE *nodename*
This specifies an alias of the node to be cataloged. You choose this name on the user's workstation to identify the remote node; it is an arbitrary name. The name should be meaningful so it is easier to remember. The name must conform to database manager naming conventions.

REMOTE *hostname*
This specifies the hostname of the node where the target database resides. This hostname of the node must be known to the TCP/IP network. The maximum length of the hostname is 255 characters.

SERVER *service-name*
  This specifies the service name of the database manager on the remote node, or the port number associated with that service name. This name must be the same service name specified in the database manager configuration file on the remote node, and must be specified in the local and remote TCP/IP services file. The maximum length of the service-name is 14 characters. This parameter is case sensitive.

SECURITY SOCKS
  This specifies that the node will be SOCKS-enabled. This means that the following environment variables must be set:

  SOCKS_NS is set to the Domain Name Server and it should be an IP address.

  SOCKS_SERVER is set to the fully qualified host name or the IP address of the SOCKS server.

REMOTE_INSTANCE *instance-name*
  This specifies the real name that is used to identify the remote server machine.

SYSTEM *system-name*
  This specifies the name that is used to identify the server machine.

OSTYPE *operating-system-type*
  This specifies the operating system type; the valid types are OS2, AIX, WIN95, NT, HPUX, SUN, MVS, OS400, VM, VSE, SNI, SCO, and SGI.

WITH *comment-string*
  This is used to describe the node entry in the node directory.

● Authorizations

Authority	Privilege
SYSADM or SYSCTRL	None required

▐▐▐ CATALOG APPC NODE

The **CATALOG APPC NODE** command is used to add an entry to the node directory. An entry contains information about a remote workstation that uses APPC communication protocols. This information is used by DB2 to connect an application program to a remote database cataloged in this node. The Advanced Program-to-Program Communications protocol is used to access the remote node.

UNIX	OS/2	NT
X	X	X

- Syntax

```
CATALOG [ADMIN] APPC NODE node-name
        REMOTE symbolic-destination-name
        [SECURITY <PROGRAM or NONE or SAME>]
        [REMOTE INSTANCE instance-name]
        [SYSTEM system-name]
        [OSTYPE operating-system-type]
        [WITH "comment-string"]
```

- Parameters

ADMIN means the server nodes are for administration purposes.

NODE *node-name*
   This specifies the name of the remote workstation to be cataloged. This name is the same as the one used to catalog a database with the CATALOG DATABASE command. The node name must conform to the DB2 naming conventions.

REMOTE *symbolic-destination-name*
   This specifies the symbolic destination name of the remote partner node. The name corresponds to an entry in the CPI Communications side information table that contains the necessary information for the client to set up an APPC connection to the server (partner LU name, node name, partner TP name). The maximum length of the name is 8 characters.

SECURITY <PROGRAM or NONE or SAME>

This specifies the level of security.

> PROGRAM means that both a user name and a password are to be included in the allocation request sent to the partner LU.

> NONE means that no security information is to be included in the allocation request sent to the partner LU.

> SAME means that a user name is to be included in the allocation request sent to the partner LU, together with an indicator that the user name has been "already verified". The partner must be configured to accept "already verified" security.

REMOTE_INSTANCE *instance-name*
This specifies the real name of the instance to which an attachment is being made on the remote server machine.

SYSTEM *system-name*
This specifies a name that is used to identify the server machine.

OSTYPE *operating-system-type*
This specifies the operating system type of the server machine. The available systems are OS2, AIX, WIN95, NT, HPUX, SUN, MVS, OS400, VM, VSE, SNI, 2 SCO, and SGI.

comment-string is used to describe the APPC node entry found in the node directory. It must be enclosed in quotes (").

- Authorizations

Authority	Privilege
SYSADM	None required

- Example

The following command is used to catalog an APPC node called XYZNODE.

```
CATALOG APPC NODE xyznode REMOTE db2inst1 \
```

```
SECURITY PROGRAM \
WITH "Catalog APPC NODE xyznode "
```

▉▉▉ CATALOG APPCLU NODE

The **CATALOG APPCLU NODE** command is used to add an entry to the node directory. An entry contains information about a remote workstation that uses APPC communication protocols. This information is used by DB2 to connect an application program to a remote database cataloged in this node.

UNIX	OS/2	NT
X	X	X

- Syntax

```
CATALOG APPCLU NODE node-name
        REMOTE partner-lu
        [LOCAL local-lu]
        [MODE mode]
        [WITH "comment-string"]
```

- Parameters

    NODE *node-name*
        This specifies the name of the remote workstation to be cataloged. This name is the same as the one used to catalog a database with the CATALOG DATABASE command. The node name must conform to the DB2 naming conventions.

    REMOTE *partner-lu*
        This specifies the SNA partner LU that is needed for connection. *partner-lu* is an LU name of the remote node. The length of this name cannot exceed eight characters.

    LOCAL *local-lu*
        This specify the alias of the SNA local LU that is used for connection. *local-lu* is an LU name in the local node. The length of this name cannot exceed eight characters.

MODE *mode*

This specifies the SNA transmission mode used in the connection. *node* is the name of the node, and it must be longer than 8 characters. If you omit this parameter, DB2 places the default value of eight blank characters.

WITH *comment-string*

This specifies a description the APPC node entry found in the node directory. It must be enclosed in quotes (").

- Authorizations

Authority	Privilege
SYSADM	None required

- Example

The following command is used to catalog an APPC node called XYZNODE.

```
CATALOG APPC NODE XYZNODE      \
        REMOTE XYZLU           \
        WITH "Catalog APPCLU NODE XYZNODE"
```

▮▮▮ CHANGE DATABASE COMMENT

The **CHANGE DATABASE COMMENT** command is used to modify a comment in the database directory that is associated with a database.

UNIX	OS/2	NT
X	X	X

- Syntax

```
CHANGE <DATABASE or DB> database-name
       COMMENT
       [ON path or drive]
       [WITH "comment-string"]
```

● Parameters

DATABASE *database-name*
This specifies the alias name of a database already cataloged and whose comment in the directory is to be changed.

ON *path* or *drive*
This specifies the path where the database resides on UNIX or the drive where the database resides on OS/2.

WITH *comment-string*
This is used to describe the node entry in the node directory.

● Authorizations

Authority	Privilege
None required	None required

● Example

The following command is used to change the comment of the CLIENTS database.

```
CHANGE DATABASE CLIENTS COMMENT \
     WITH "Test data loaded"
```

■■■ CHANGE ISOLATION LEVEL

The **CHANGE SQLISL** command is used to modify the method used by DB2 to isolate data accessed by a program while other processes are using the same database.

UNIX	OS/2	NT
X	X	X

- Syntax

```
CHANGE <SQLIST or ISOLATION> TO isolation
```

- Parameters

isolation is one of the following:

> CS — cursor stability at the isolation level
> NC — no commit at the isolation level. Not supported by DB2
> RR — repeatable read
> CS — cursor stability
> UR — uncommitted read

- Authorizations

Authority	Privilege
SYSADM DBADM	None required

▖▖▖ CREATE DATABASE

The **CREATE DATABASE** command is to create a new database at the same time the database is cataloged with an alias. To change the alias name, use the **CATALOG DATABASE** command. The creator of the database automatically receives the **DBADM** authority and **CREATEAB** and **BINDADD** privileges.

UNIX	OS/2	NT
X	X	X

- Syntax

```
CREATE <DATABASE or DB> database-name
   [AT NODE [LIKE NODE node-number or
            WITHOUT TABLESPACES]
   ]
```

```
[ON <drive or path>]
[ALIAS database-alias]
[USING CODESET codeset TERRITORY territory]
[COLLATE USING <SYSTEM or IDENTITY>]
[NUMSEGS numsegs]
[DFT_EXTENT_SZ-dft_extentsize]
[CATALOGTABLESPACE tblspace-defn]
[USERTABLE tblspace-defn]
[TEMPORARYTABLESPACE tblspace-defn]
[WITH "comment-string"]
```

tblspace-defn:

```
MANAGED BY
<SYSTEM USING (container-string,...)    or
 DATABASE USING
  (<FILE or DEVICE> container-string number-of-pages )
>
[EXTENTSIZE number-of-pages]
[PREFETCHSIZE number-of-pages]
[OVERHEAD number-of-milliseconds]
[TRANSFERRATE number-of-milliseconds]
```

● Parameters

DATABASE *database-name*
This specifies the name of the database that you want to create. A database by this name should not already exist in either local or system database directories. The name should also conform to naming conventions for databases.

ON *<drive* or *path>*
This specifies the drive where the database should be created on OS/2. If your operating system is UNIX, the path is where the database is created. If the path is omitted, then the default database path, as indicated in the manager configuration file, is used.

ALIAS *database-alias*
This specifies an alias name for the database and if one is not supplied, then the database name is used.

USING CODESET *codeset*
This specifies the code set to be used for data entered into this database.

TERRITORY *territory*

This specifies the territory to be used for data entered into this database.

COLLATE USING <SYSTEM or IDENTITY>
This indicates the type of collating sequence to be used for the database; there are two options:

SYSTEM means collating sequence is based on the current territory.

IDENTITY means the strings are compared byte for byte.

NUMSEGS *numsegs*
This specifies the numbered segment directories that will be created and used to store DAT, IDX, and LF files.

DFT _EXTENT_SZ *dft_extentsize*
This specifies the default extent size of table spaces in the database.

CATALOGTABLESPACE *tblspace-defn*
This specifies the definition of the tablespace which holds the catalog tables SYSCATSPACE.

USERTABLE *tblspace-defn*
This specifies the definitions of the initial user tablespace, USERSPACE1.

TEMPORARYTABLESPACE *tblspace-defn*
This specifies the definition of the initial user tablespace, TEMPSPACE1.

WITH *comment-string*
This is used to describe the node entry in the node directory.

```
tblspace-defn:

    MANAGED BY
    <SYSTEM USING (container-string,...)     or
     DATABASE USING
     (<FILE or DEVICE> container-string number-of-pages )
    >
    [EXTENTSIZE number-of-pages]
    [PREFETCHSIZE number-of-pages]
    [OVERHEAD number-of-milliseconds]
    [TRANSFERRATE number-of-milliseconds]
```

● Authorizations

Authority	Privilege
SYSADM	None required

● Example

The following example creates the CLIENTS database.

```
CREATE DATABASE CLIENTS
```

■■■ DEACTIVATE DATABASE

The **DEACTIVATE DATABASE** command is used to stop the specified database. In an MPP system, this command deactivates the specified database on all nodes in the system. If one or more of these nodes encounters an error, a warning is issued and it remains active. Those without any errors are deactivated.

UNIX	OS/2	NT
X	X	X

● Syntax

```
DEACTIVATE DATABASE database-alias
   [USER username [USING password]]
```

● Parameters

DEACTIVATE DATABASE *database-alias*
This specifies the alias of the database to be terminated.

USER *username*
This specifies the user starting the database.

USING *password*
This specifies the password of the user.

- Authorizations

Authority	Privilege
SYSADM or SYSCTRL or SYSMAINT	None required

▌▌▌▌ DEREGISTER

The **DEREGISTER** command is used to remove a DB2 server from the network server. The DB2 server's network address is deleted from the network server. This command must be issued locally from the DB2 server. It is not supported remotely.

UNIX	OS/2	NT
X	X	

- Syntax

```
DEREGISTER [DB2 SERVER]
           [IN] registry
           USER userid
           [PASSWORD password]
```

- Parameters

  IN *registry*
  This specifies the network server from which the DB2 server is removed. In this release, the only supported value is "NWBINDERY" (NetWare bindery).

  USER *userid*
  This specifies the User ID needed to log into the network server. Must have SUPERVISOR or Workgroup Manager security equivalence.

  PASSWORD *password*

This specifies a password associated with userid.

● Authorizations

None required

▌▌▌▌ DESCRIBE

The **DESCRIBE** command is used to display one of the following:

● SQLDA information about a select statement
● Columns of a table or view
● Indexes of a table or view

UNIX	OS/2	NT
X	X	X

● Syntax

```
DESCRIBE < select-statement     or
           TABLE table-name
           INDEXES FOR TABLE table-name
         >
         [SHOW DETAIL]
```

● Parameters

select-statement
This specifies the statement about which you want to obtain information.
The select statement is automatically prepared by CLP.

TABLE *table-name*
This specifies the table or view for which information is requested. The
fully qualified name or alias in the form *schema.table-name* must be
used, where the *schema* is the user name under which the table or view
was created. This option displays the following information about each
column:

- column name
- type schema
- type name
- length
- scale
- nulls (yes or no)

INDEXES FOR TABLE *table-name*
This specifies the table or view for which the following information is displayed:
- index schema
- index name
- unique rule
- column count

SHOW DETAIL
This specifies the following information to be displayed:
- where a CHARACTER, VARCHAR or LONG VARCHAR column was defined as FOR BIT DATA
- column number
- partioning key sequence
- codepage
- default

- Authorizations

Authority	Privilege
SYSADM or DBADM	SELECT CONTROL

▌▌▌▌ DETACH

The **DETACH** command is used to remove the logical attachment of a DBMS instance. It also terminates the physical communication connection if there are no other logical connections using this layer.

UNIX	OS/2	NT
X	X	X

- Syntax

  ```
  DETACH
  ```

- Parameters

  None

- Authorizations

  None required

▌▌▌▌ DROP DATABASE

The **DROP DATABASE** command is used to delete a database; all associated data files, user files, and database definitions are removed. DB2 uncatalogs the database from the database directory and the volume directory.

UNIX	OS/2	NT
X	X	X

- Syntax

  ```
  DROP DATABASE database-name
                [AT NODE]
  ```

- Parameters

  DATABASE *database-name*
  This specifies the alias of the database you want to delete.

  AT NODE

This specifies that the database is to be deleted only on the node that issued the DROP DATABASE command. This parameter is used by utilities supplied with the DB2 Universal Database Extended Enterprise edition, and is not intended for general use.

● Authorizations

Authority	Privilege
SYSADM SYSCTRL	None required

● Example

The following command deletes the CLIENTS database from the catalogs.

```
DROP DATABASE CLIENTS
```

▌▌▌▌ DROP NODE VERIFY

The **DROP NODE VERIFY** command is used to check if a node is being used by a database. A message is returned indicating whether a node can be dropped or not.

UNIX	OS/2	NT
X		

● Syntax

```
DROP NODE VERIFY
```

● Parameters

None

- Authorizations

Authority	Privilege
SYSADM	None required

■■■ ECHO

The **ECHO** command is used to write character strings to standard output.

UNIX	OS/2	NT
X	X	X

- Syntax

```
ECHO [string]
```

- Parameters

  string is any character information.

- Authorizations

  None required

■■■ EXPORT

The **EXPORT** command is used to copy the content of one or many tables to a file.

UNIX	OS/2	NT
X	X	X

- Syntax

```
EXPORT TO filename
   OF filetype
   [LOBS TO lob-path,...]
   [LOBFILE filename,...]
   [MODIFIED BY filetype-mod]
   [METHOD N ( column-name,... )]
   [MESSAGES msgfile]
   select-statement
```

- Parameters

TO *filename*
This specifies the name of the file to which data is written from the database.

OF *filetype*
This specifies the format of the output file. The types of files are:

DEL Delimited ASCII format.
WSF Worksheet format. This file can be used by programs such as Lotus 1-2-3 and Lotus Symphony.
IXF DB2 format. This file can be used to import data to a DB2 database.

LOBS TO *lob-path*
This specifies one or many paths to store LOB files. When file space is full on the first path, the second one is used if included.

LOBFILE *filename*
This specifies one or more base file names of the LOB files.

MODIFIED BY *filetype-mod*
This specifies more options when file type is DEL or WSF file. This parameter tells DB2 how to format data written to these files. For the DEL file, the following file type mode can be chosen:

COLDEL	Column delimeter. A character (e.g., ; and :) follows this keyword. This character is placed between columns. The default is comma (,).

CHARDEL	Character string delimiter. A character (such as ', !, or ") follows this keyword. A pair of these characters is used to enclose character strings.
DECPT	Decimal point. A character follows this keyword. This character is used to enclose a character string. The default is period (.).
DECPLUSBLANK	Plus sign character. This option tells EXPORT to prefix positive decimal numbers with a blank space instead of a plus (+) character.

For WSF file format, *filetype-mod* is used to select the generation output of the export file. The generations are

- First generation WSF file is Lotus 1-2-3/1 or 1-2-3/1A. This is the default.
- Second generation WSF file is Lotus Symphony/1.0.

METHOD N (*column-name,...*)
This specifies the column name(s) to be used in the output file.

MESSAGES *msgfile*
This specifies the destination file to which messages, errors, and warnings are written during export.

select-statement is used to specify a **SELECT** statement that retrieves data from one or more tables. For more details on the **SELECT** statement, refer to Chapter 7.

- Authorizations

Authority	Privilege
SYSADM DBADM	CONTROL or SELECT for the chosen tables

● Example

The following **EXPORT** command exports data from the SALES tables of the CLENTS database. The data is written to a DB2 file called SALES.IXF. The error or warning messages are directed to SALES.MSG.

```
EXPORT FROM CLIENTS            \
    TO A:\SALES.IXF OF IXF \
    MESSAGES SALES.MSG         \
    SELECT * FROM SALES
```

▌▌▌ FORCE APPLICATION

The **FORCE APPLICATION** command is used to force local or remote users or applications off the system. One reason to use this command is to allow for maintenance on a server.

UNIX	OS/2	NT
X	X	X

● Syntax

```
FORCE APPLICATION
    < ALL or (application-handle,...) >
    [MODE SYNC]
```

● Parameters

ALL means to disconnect all applications from the database.

application-handle is the agent to be terminated. A list is acquired by issuing the **LIST APPLICATIONS** command.

MODE ASYNC
    This specifies not to wait for all specified agents to be terminated before returning; it returns as soon as the function has been successfully issued or an error (such as invalid syntax) is discovered. This is the only mode currently supported.

● Authorizations

Authority	Privilege
SYSADM or SYSCTRL	None required

● Example

In the following example, two users, with agent-id values of 41234 and 55458, are forced to disconnect from the database:

```
force application ( 41234, 55458 )
```

▌▌▌▌ GET ADMIN CONFIGURATION

The **GET ADMIN CONFIGURATION** command is used to obtain values of individual entries in the database manager configuration file that are relevant to the DB2 Administration Server. The following information is retrieved:

- AGENT_STACK_SZ
- AUTHENTICATION
- DFT_ACCOUNT_STR
- DIAGLEVEL
- DIAGPATH
- FILESERVER
- IPX_SOCKET
- NNAME
- NPIPE (NT only)
- OBJECTNAME
- QUERY_HEAP_SZ
- SVCENAME
- SYSADM_GROUP
- TPNAME
- TRUST_ALLCLNTS
- TRUST_CLNTAUTH

UNIX	OS/2	NT
X	X	X

- Syntax

```
GET ADMIN < CONFIGURATION or
            CONFIG       or
            CFG
         >
```

- Authorizations

None required

IIII GET AUTHORIZATIONS

The **GET AUTHORIZATIONS** command is used to obtain information on authority and privileges granted to a user.

UNIX	OS/2	NT
X	X	X

- Syntax

```
GET AUTHORIZATIONS
```

- Authorizations

None required

IIII GET CONNECTION STATE

The **GET CONNECTION STATE** command is used to show the connection state. The possible states are:

- Connectable and connected
- Connectable and unconnected
- Unconnectable and connected
- Implicitly connectable (if implicit connect is available)

UNIX	OS/2	NT
X	X	X

- Syntax

```
GET CONNECTION STATE
```

- Parameters

  None

- Authorizations

  None required

■■■ GET DATABASE CONFIGURATION

The **GET DATABASE CONFIGURATION** command is used to retrieve information about a database. Normally, the information is shown on the screen, but you can redirect it to a file by using the -R option (see examples).

UNIX	OS/2	NT
X	X	X

- Syntax

```
GET <DATABASE or DB>
    <CONFIGURATION or
     CONFIG          or
     CFG
    >
    FOR database-name
```

- Parameters

  FOR *database-name*
  This specifies the alias of the database for which information is retrieved.

- Authorizations

Authority	Privilege
SYSADM or DBADM	None required

- Example

  In the next example, the configuration data for CLIENTS database is written to the DBM.RPT file.

  ```
  DB2 -RDB2.RPT GET DATABASE CONFIGURATION FOR CLIENTS
  ```

▌▌▌▌ GET DATABASE MANAGER CONFIGURATION

The **GET DATABASE MANAGER CONFIGURATION** command is used to retrieve parameter values from the DB2 configuration file. Normally, this information is shown on the screen, but it can be written to a file (see examples).

UNIX	OS/2	NT
X	X	X

- Syntax

  ```
  GET <DATABASE MANAGER or
       DB MANAGER       or
       DBM
      >
      <CONFIGURATION or
       CONFIG        or
       CFG
      >
  ```

- Authorizations

Authority	Privilege
SYSADM or DBADM	None required

- Example

In the following command, the parameter value from the DB2 configuration file is written to the DBM.RPT file.

```
DBM -R GET DATABASE MANAGER CONFIGURATION
```

In the next example, the information is written to the MANAGER.CFG file.

```
DB2 -RMANAGER.CFG -t GET DATABASE
    MANAGER CONFIGURATION;
```

■■■ GET DBM MONITOR SWITCHES

The GET DATABASE STATUS command is used to retrieve the status of the database system monitor switches. Monitor switches instruct the database system manager to collect database activity information. Each application using the database system monitor interface has its own set of monitor switches.

UNIX	OS/2	NT
X	X	X

- Syntax

```
GET DBM MONITOR SWITCHES
```

- Parameters

None

- Authorizations

Authority	Privilege
SYSADM or SYSCTRL or SYSMAINT	None required

▪▪▪▪ GET INSTANCE

The **GET INSTANCE** command is used to return the current setting of the DB2INSTANCE environment variable.

UNIX	OS/2	NT
X	X	X

- Syntax

```
GET INSTANCE
```

- Parameters

  None

- Authorizations

  None required

▪▪▪▪ GET MONITOR SWITCHES

The **GET MONITOR SWITCHES** command displays the current settings of the database system monitor recording switches.

UNIX	OS/2	NT
X	X	X

- Syntax

```
GET MONITOR SWITCHES
```

- Parameters

  None

- Authorizations

Authority	Privilege
SYSADM or SYSCTRL SYSMAINT	None required

▌▌▌▌ GET SNAPSHOT

The **GET SNAPSHOT** command is used to collect database manager status information and returns it to a data buffer allocated by the user. The information represents a "snapshot" of the database manager operation at the time the command was issued.

UNIX	OS/2	NT
X	X	X

- Syntax

```
GET SNAPSHOT FOR <DATABASE MANAGER               or
                DB MANAGER or  DBM>              or
                ALL APPLICATIONS                 or
                ALL DATABASES                    or
                ALL BUFFERPOOLS                  or
                APPLICATION < APPLID appl-id or
                        GENTID agent-id
                    >                            or
                FCM FOR ALL NODES                or
                LOCKS FOR APPLICATION appl-id    or
                    <  ALL              or
                    <DATABASE or DB > or
```

```
                      APPLICATIONS       or
                      TABLES             or
                      TABLESPACES        or
                      LOCKS              or
                      BUFFERPOOLS
                 >    ON database-alias
            >
```

● Parameters

DATABASE MANAGER
This specifies to collect statistical information for the active database manager instance.

ALL DATABASES
This specifies to collect general statistics for all active databases on the current node.

ALL APPLICATIONS
This specifies to collect information for all active applications that are connected to a database on the current node.

ALL BUFFER SPOOLS
This specifies to get information about buffer pool activity for all active databases.

APPLICATION APPLID *appl_id*
This specifies to collect information for a valid application ID.

APPLICATION AGENTID *agent-id*
This specifies to collect information for an agent. The agent ID is a 32-bit number that uniquely identifies an application that is currently running.

FCM FOR ALL NODES
This specifies FCM statistics for all nodes.

LOCKS FOR APPLICATION *agent-id*
This specifies to collect information for all locks held by the specific application.

ALL ON *database-alias*

This specifies to collect information for all applications, tables and locks for a database.

DATABASE ON *database-alias*
This specifies to collect general statistics for a database.

APPLICATIONS ON *database-alias*
This specifies to collect information for all applications connected to a database.

TABLES ON *database-alias*
This specifies to collect table information on database-alias. This will only include those tables that have been accessed since the table switch was turned on.

TABLESPACES ON *database-alias*
This specifies to collect tablespace information on a database.

LOCKS ON *database-alias*
This specifies to collect lock information for every application on a database. This provides a list of every lock held by each application connected to the database.

BUFFER POOLS ON *database-alias*
This specifies to collect informations about pool activity for a database.

- Authorizations

Authority	Privilege
SYSADM or SYSCTRL or SYSMAINT	None required

▐▐▐▐ HELP

The **HELP** command is to get online information about SQL statements and CLP command.

UNIX	OS/2	NT
X	X	X

- Syntax

```
HELP <db2_command or sql_statement>
```

- Parameters

db2_command is used to specify the DB2 command you want to execute. All these commands are listed and explained in this chapter.

sql_statement is used to specify the SQL statements. These statements are discussed in Chapters 6-7.

- Authorizations

None required

▐▐▐▐ IMPORT

The **IMPORT** command is used to copy the content of a file to one or many tables.

UNIX	OS/2	NT
X	X	X

- Syntax

```
IMPORT FROM filename
     OF filetype
   [LOBS FROM lob-path,...]
   [MODIFIED BY filetype-mod...]
   [METHOD < L (column-start column-end,...) or
            [NULL INDICATORS (n,...)]        or
            N (column-name,...)              or
            P (column-position,...)
          >
```

```
[COMMIT COUNT n]
[RESTART COUNT n]
[MESSAGES msgfile]
< < INSERT or
    INSERT_UPDATE or
    REPLACE or
    CREATE or
    REPLACE_CREATE
  > INTO table-name [(insert-column,...)]
                or
  CREATE INTO table-name
              [ (insert-column,...)] tblspace-specs
  >

tblspace-specs:
    IN tablespace-name
    [INDEX IN tablespace-name]
    [LONG IN tablespace-name]
```

- Parameters

FROM *filename*
   This specifies the name of the file from which data is written to the database.

OF *filetype*
   This specifies the format of the input file. The types of files are:

   ASC Non-delimited ASCII format.
   DEL Delimited ASCII format.
   WSF Worksheet format. This file can be used by programs such as: Lotus 1-2-3 and Lotus Symphony.
   IXF DB2 format. This file can be used to import data to a DB2 database.

LOBS FROM *lob-path*
   This specifies where the LOB files to be found. The names of the LOB files are stored in the main data files (ASC, DEL, or IXF format), in the column that will be imported into the LOC column. If lobsinfile is not specified within the *filetype-mod*, this option is ignored.

MODIFIED BY *filetype-mod*

This is used when file type is DEL or WSF file. This parameter tells DB2 how to format data written to these files. For DEL file format, the following file type mode can be chosen:

COLDEL	Column delimeter. A character (e.g., ; and :) follows this keyword. This character is placed between columns. The default is comma (,).
CHARDEL	Character string delimeter. A character (e.g., ', !, or ") follows this keyword. A pair of these characters is used to enclose character strings.
DECPT	Decimal point. A character follows this keyword. This character is used to enclose a character string. The default is a period (.).
DECPLUSBLANK	Plus sign character. This option tells IMPORT to prefix positive decimal numbers with a blank space instead of a plus (+) character.

For WSF file format, *filetype-mod* is used to select the generation output of the export file. The generations are:

● First generation WSF file is Lotus 1-2-3/1 or 1-2-3/1A. This is the default.

● Second generation WSF file is Lotus Symphony/1.0.

METHOD
This indicates the method by which the data is imported. The options are:

L specifies the start and end column numbers from which to extract data in a non-delimited ASCII file.

N specifies one or more column names for which data is imported.

P specifies the number of columns to be imported.

NULL INDICATORS *n*
This specifies a column by number to be used as a null indicator field.

COMMIT COUNT *n*
This specifies the number of records at which to do a commit.

RESTART COUNT *n*
This specifies the number of records to skip before importing data.

MESSAGES *msgfile*
This specifies a file to which error or warning messages are directed.

INSERT
This specifies to add data to a table without changing the existing rows.

INSERT_UPDATE
This specifies to add data to the table or update rows with matching primary keys.

REPLACE
This specifies to remove all existing rows and add the imported data.

REPLACE_CREATE
This specifies to delete the content of the table, if it exists, and then import the data to the table.

CREATE
This specifies to create a new table and import the data.

INTO *tblname*
This specifies the name of the table to which the data is imported.

insert-column
This specifies the column name within the table or view of the database.

IN *tablespace-name*

This specifies the tablespace in which the table will be created.

INDEX IN *tablespace-name*
This specifies the tablespace in which any indexes of the table are created.

LONG IN *tablespace-name*
This specifies the tablespace in which the values of any long columns, such as LONG, VARCHAR, LONG VARGRAPHIC, and LOB data type, are stored.

● Authorizations

Authority	Privilege
SYSADM	CONTROL
DBADM	INSERT
	SELECT
	CREATETAB

● Example

The following **IMPORT** command imports data to the SALES tables of the CLIENTS database. The data is written from a DB2 file called SALES.IXF. The error or warning messages are directed to SALES.MSG.

```
IMPORT TO CLIENTS  \
   FROM A:\SALES.IXF OF IXF   \
   INTO SALES  \
   MESSAGES SALES.MSG
```

▋▋▋▋ INVOKE STORED PROCEDURE

The **INVOKE** command executes a program or procedure at the location of the database. Usually, an application program has two parts: client and server, and when the program is run at the server side, the result is returned to the client.

UNIX	OS/2	NT
X	X	X

- Syntax

```
INVOKE program
       [USING server-input-data]
```

- Parameters

    INVOKE *program*
    This specifies the procedure to be run at the server.

    USING *server-input-data*
    This specifies any argument to be passed to the procedure that is being
    executed on the database server.

- Authorizations

Authority	Privilege
None	CONNECT

■■■ LIST ACTIVE DATABASE

The **LIST ACTIVE DATABASE** command displays a subset of the
information listed by the **GET SNAPSHOT** command. For each active
database, the following is shown:

- Database name
- Number of applications currently connected to the database
- Database path

UNIX	OS/2	NT
X	X	X

- Syntax

  ```
  LIST ACTIVE DATABASES
  ```

- Parameters

  None

- Authorizations

  None required

■■■■ LIST APPLICATIONS

The **LIST APPLICATIONS** command is used to display the application
program name, application handle, application ID, authority ID, and database
name. The information goes to the standard output, normally the screen. This
command can also optionally display an application's sequence number, status,
status change time, and database path.

UNIX	OS/2	NT
X	X	X

- Syntax

  ```
  LIST APPLICATIONS
        [FOR <DATABASE or DB> database-alias]
        [SHOW DETAIL]
  ```

- Parameters

  FOR DATABASE *database-alias*
      This specifies the name of a database which has the information for each
      application connected to it. Database Name information is not displayed.
      If **FOR DATABASE** is omitted, the command displays the information
      for each application that is currently connected to any database at the
      node to which the user is currently attached.

SHOW DETAIL
This specifies that the output includes the following additional
information:

- Sequence #
- Application Status
- Status Change Time
- Database Path

- Authorizations

Authority	Privilege
SYSADM or SYSCTRL SYSMAINT	None required

▋▋▋▋ LIST BACKUP/HISTORY

The **LIST BACKUP** or **LIST HISTORY** command is to show the restore sets
for full database and table space level backups, or display entries in the
recovery history file.

UNIX	OS/2	NT
X	X	X

- Syntax

```
LIST < BACKUP or HISTORY >
     < ALL               or
       SINCE timestamp    or
       CONTAINING <schema.object-name or object-name >
     >
     FOR <DATABASE or DB> database-alias
```

- Parameters

BACKUP

This specifies to list backups and restores.

HISTORY
This specifies to list backups, restores, and loads.

ALL
This specifies to list all entries in the recovery history file.

SINCE *timestamp*
This specifies the time stamp format *yyymmmddhhnnss* or an initial prefix *yyyy*.

CONTAINING
This specifies the qualified or unqualified name that uniquely identifies a table.

FOR DATABASE *database-alias*
This specifies the name of a database for which the listing of the recovery history file is needed.

● Authorizations

Authority	Privilege
SYSADM or SYSCTRL SYSMAINT	None required

▮▮▮ LIST COMMAND OPTIONS

The **LIST COMMAND OPTIONS** command lists the current setting of the following environment variables:

● DB2BQTIME
● DB2DQTRY
● DB2RQTIME
● DB2IQTIME
● DB2OPTIONS

UNIX	OS/2	NT
X	X	X

- Syntax

  ```
  LIST COMMAND OPTIONS
  ```

- Parameters

  None

- Authorizations

  None required

▮▮▮ LIST DATABASE DIRECTORY

The **LIST DATABASE DIRECTORY** command lists the content of the system database directory.

UNIX	OS/2	NT
X	X	X

- Syntax

  ```
  LIST < DATABASE or DB > DIRECTORY
       [ON path or drive]
  ```

- Parameters

  ON *path* or *drive*
      This specifies the local database directory from which to list information.

- Authorizations

  None required

▌▌▌▌ LIST DCS APPLICATIONS

The **LIST DCS APPLICATIONS** command is used to extract the content of the database services (DCS) directory and sends the information to the standard output device. The information includes:

- username
- program name
- agent ID
- outbound application ID

UNIX	OS/2	NT
X	X	X

- Syntax

```
LIST DCS APPLICATIONS
     [SHOW DETAIL]
```

- Parameters

   SHOW DETAIL
   This specifies to show the following additional information:

   - Application ID
   - Application Sequence Number
   - Client Database Alias
   - Client Node Name (nname)
   - Client Product ID
   - Code Page ID
   - Outbound Sequence Number
   - Host Database Name
   - Host Product ID

- Authorizations

Authority	Privilege
SYSADM or SYSCTRL or SYSMAINT	None required

■■■ LIST DCS DIRECTORY

The LIST DCS DIRECTORY command is used to get the content of the DCS directory. This command shows a list of host databases that a workstation can access. Normally, the information goes to the screen, but if needed, it can be directed to a file (see example).

UNIX	OS/2	NT
X	X	X

- Syntax

```
LIST DCS DIRECTORY
```

- Authorizations

Authority	Privilege
None required	None required

- Example

In the following example, the content of the DCS directory is written to the default DBM.RPT file.

```
DBM LIST DCS DIRECTORY
```

In the next command, the data from the DCS directory goes to a specified DCSXS1.RPT file

```
DB2 -rDCSXS1.RPT LIST DCS DIRECTORY
```

▌▌▌ LIST DRDA INDOUBT TRANSACTIONS

The **LIST DRDA INDOUBT TRANSACTIONS** command lists transactions that are indoubt between partner LUs connected by LU 6.2 protocols.

UNIX	OS/2	NT
X	X	X

● Syntax

```
LIST DRDA INDOUBT TRANSACTIONS
     [WITH PROMPTINGS]
```

● Parameters

WITH PROMPTINGS
This specifies that indoubt transactions are to be processed. If this parameter is specified, an interactive dialo mode is initiated allowing a user to commit or rollback indoubt transactions.

● Authorizations

Authority	Privilege
SYSADM	None required

▌▌▌ LIST INDOUBT TRANSACTIONS

The **LIST INDOUBT TRANSACTIONS** command lists transactions that are in doubt. An indoubt transaction is one which has been prepared, but not yet committed or rolled back. Optionally, you can enter into a dialog to commit, rollback, or forget the indoubt transactions.

The two-phase commit protocol splits the commitment of a transaction into the PREPARE and COMMIT phases:

- **PREPARE**: The resource manager writes the log pages to disk so that it can then respond to either a COMMIT or ROLLBACK primitive.

- **COMMIT (or ROLLBACK):** The transaction is actually committed or rolled back.

UNIX	OS/2	NT
X	X	X

- Syntax

```
LIST INDOUBT TRANSACTIONS
     [WITH PROMPTING]
```

- Parameters

WITH PROMPTING
This specifies that you want to process indoubt transactions, interactively. If this parameter is included, then an interactive dialog of CLP is started which allows you to commit, rollback or forget indoubt transactions. By default, indoubt transactions are written to the standard output device, and you do not enter the interactive dialog mode.

In the interactive dialog mode, you can do the following:
- List all indoubt transactions, using 'l'
- List indoubt transaction number x, using 'l x'
- Quit, using 'q'.
- Commit transaction number x, using 'c x'.
- Rollback transaction number x, using 'r x'
- Forget transaction number x, using 'f x'.

- Authorizations

Authority	Privilege
DBADM	None required

▮▮▮ LIST NODE DIRECTORY

The **LIST NODE DIRECTORY** command is used to get the content of the node directory. The node types may be APPC, APPN, or NetBios. Normally, the information goes to the screen, but if needed, it can be directed to a file (see example).

UNIX	OS/2	NT
X	X	X

- Syntax

  ```
  LIST [ADMIN] NODE DIRECTORY
  ```

- Parameters

  ADMIN
  This specifies the administration server node.

- Authorizations

Authority	Privilege
None required	None required

- Example

  In the following example, the content of the node directory is written to the DBM.RPT.

  ```
  DBM -R LIST NODE DIRECTORY
  ```

  In the next command, the content of the node directory is written to the NODEXYZ.RPT file

  ```
  DB2 -rNODEXYZ.RPT NODE DIRECTORY
  ```

▮▮▮ LIST NODE GROUPS

The **LIST NODE GROUPS** command lists all node groups associated with the current database.

UNIX	OS/2	NT
X	X	X

- Syntax

```
LIST NODEGROUPS
     [SHOW DETAIL]
```

- Parameters

  SHOW DETAIL
  This specifies to show the following additional information:
  - Partitioning map ID
  - Node number
  - In-use flag

- Authorizations

  None required

▮▮▮ LIST NODES

The **LIST NODES** command lists all nodes associated with the current database.

UNIX	OS/2	NT
X	X	X

- Syntax

```
LIST NODES
```

- Parameters

  None

- Authorizations

  None required

▮▮▮ LIST PACKAGES/TABLES

The **LIST PACKAGES or LIST TABLES** command is used to show all the packages or tables associated with the current database.

UNIX	OS/2	NT
X	X	X

- Syntax

```
LIST <PACKAGES or TABLES>
   [FOR <USER   or
   ALL          or
   FOR SCHEMA or
   SYSTEM>
   ]
```

- Parameters

  FOR
  This specifies whose package and table is to be displayed. If this optional parameter is not specified, the default is USER. The options are:

  USER is to list the packages or tables in the database for the current user.

  FOR SCHEMA is to list all the packages or tables in the database for a specific schema.

  ALL is to list all packages or tables of a database.

SYSTEM is to list all system packages or tables in the database.

- Authorizations

Authority	Privilege
SYSADM or DBADM	CONTROL or SELECT

■■■ LIST TABLESPACE CONTAINERS

The **LIST TABLESPACE CONTAINERS** command is used to list all the containers for a tablespace.

UNIX	OS/2	NT
X	X	X

- Syntax

```
LIST TABLESPACE CONTAINERS
    FOR tablespace-id
    [SHOW DETAIL]
```

- Parameters

FOR *tablespace-id*
This is a table space used by the current database. It is a number that uniquely represents a table space. To get a list of all the table spaces used by the current database, use the LIST TABLESPACES command. It returns the following:

- Container ID
- Name
- Type (file, disk, or path)

SHOW DETAIL
This specifies to show the following additional information:

- Total number of pages
- Number of usable pages
- Accessible (yes or no)

- Authorizations

None required

▪▪▪ LIST TABLESPACES

The **LIST TABLESPACES** command is used to list all the table spaces contained within the current database. It returns the following:

- Tablespace ID
- Name
- Type (system managed space or database managed space)
- Contents (any data, long data only, or temporary data)
- State

UNIX	OS/2	NT
X	X	X

- Syntax

```
LIST TABLESPACES [SHOW DETAIL]
```

- Parameters

SHOW DETAIL
This specifies to show the following additional information:

- Total number of pages
- Number of usable pages
- Number of used pages
- Number of free pages
- High watermark
- Page size

- Extent size
- Prefetch size
- Number of containers
- Minimum recovery time
- State change tablespace ID
- State change object ID
- Number of quiescers
- Tablespace ID and Object ID for each quiescer

- Authorizations

  None required

▌▌▌▌ LOAD

The **LOAD** command is used to load data into a DB2 table from files, tapes, or named pipes into a DB2 table.

UNIX	OS/2	NT
X	X	X

- Syntax

```
LOAD FROM <filename or pipe-name or device>...
  OF filetype
  [LOBS FROM lob-path...]
  [MODIFIED BY filetype-mod...]
  [METHOD  <L  (column-start column-end,...)
               [NULL INDICATORS (n,...)]
                  or
            N  (column-name,...)
                  or
            P  (column-position,...)
         >
  ]
  [SAVECOUNT n]
  [RESTARTCOUNT [B or D or n]
  [ROWCOUNT n]
  [WARNINGCOUNT n]
  [MESSAGES message-file]
  [REMOTE FILE remote-file]
```

```
<INSERT or REPLACE or RESTART or TERMINATE>
INTO table-name [(insert-column,...)]
[FOR EXCEPTION table-name]
[STATISTICS < YES [WITH DISTRIBUTION AND or
                 <AND or FOR>] [DETAILED] INDXES ALL
                     or
              NO
           >
]
[COPY < NO
        or
       YES < USE ADSM
            [OPEN num-sess SESSIONS]
                or
            TO device/directory,...
                or
            LOAD lib-name
            [OPEN num-sess SESSIONS]
           >
     >
        or
        NONRECOVERABLE
]
[HOLD QUIESCE]
[WITHOUT PROMPTING]
[USING directory,...]
[DATA BUFFER bufsize]
[SORT BUFFER bufsize]
[PARALLELISM n]
```

- Parameters

    FROM *filename* or *pipe-name* or *device*
        This specifies the source of the data, namely, file, pipe or device. The
        source must be found on the node where the database resides. If multiple
        filenames are provided, they will be processed in the sequence they are
        listed.

    OF *filetype*
        This specifies the format of the source data; the options are:

        - ASC (Non-delimited ASCII format)
        - DEL (Delimited ASCII format)
        - IXF   (Integrated Exchange Format, PC version), exported from
                   the same or another DB2 table.

LOBS FROM *lob-path*
This specifies the path of the data files that have the LOB values to be loaded.

MODIFIED BY *filetype-mod*
This is used when file type is DEL or WSF file. This parameter tells DB2 how to format data written to these files. For DEL file format, the following file type mode can be chosen:

COLDEL	Column delimeter. A character (e.g., ; and :) follows this keyword. This character is placed between columns. The default is comma (,).
CHARDEL	Character string delimeter. A character (e.g., ', !, or ") follows this keyword. A pair of these characters is used to enclose character strings.
DECPT	Decimal point. A character follows this keyword. This character is used to enclose a character string. The default is a period (.).
DECPLUSBLANK	Plus sign character. This option tells IMPORT to prefix positive decimal numbers with a blank space instead of a plus (+) character.

For WSF file format, *filetype-mod* is used to select the generation output of the export file. The generations are:

• First generation WSF file is Lotus 1-2-3/1 or 1-2-3/1A. This is the default.

• Second generation WSF file is Lotus Symphony/1.0.

METHOD
This indiacates the method by which the data is imported. The options are:

L specifies the start and end column numbers from which to extract the data from a non-delimited ASCII file.

N specifies one or more column names for which data is imported.

P specifies the number of columns to be imported.

NULL INDICATORS *n*

This specifies a column (by number) to be used as a null indicator field. A null indicator column for each data column must also be specified. A Zero (0) indicator means that the data column is not nullable; in other words, there will always be data in that column.

While processing each row, a Y indicates that the column data is NULL, while an N indicates that the column data is not null, and that column data specified by the method L parameter will be loaded.

SAVECOUNT *n*

This specifies a number which is used to establish consistency points. This value is approximate and it is converted to a page count and rounded out to intervals of the extent size. The default value is 0. This means that no consistency points are established, except when it is necessary.

RESTARTCOUNT

This specifies the restart phase and is one of the following:
    B means to restart at the build phase.

    D means to restart at the delete phase.

    n is a number specifying that the load is to be started at record n+1. The first n records are skipped.

ROWCOUNT *n*

This specifies the number of records to be loaded. This permits you to load only the first *n* number of rows in a file.

WARNINGCOUNT *n*

This specifies a number of warnings after which the load stops.

MESSAGE *message-file*
> This specifies the name of a file that receives warning and error messages that occurred during the load. If the message file is omitted, the messages are written to the standard output. Without specifying this file, LOAD uses the current directory and the default drive as the destination. If you name a file that already exists, LOAD will append the information to the file.

REMOTE *remote-file*
> This specifies the name of a file, used when creating temporary files during a load.

INSERT
> This specifies to add the loaded data to the table without changing the existing table data.

REPLACE
> This specifies to delete all existing data from the table, and inserts the loaded data. The table definition and index definitions are not changed.

RESTART
> This specifies to restart LOAD after a previous load was interrupted. It is important to keep track of the last 'commit' point. You can get this information from the message file passed to LOAD. You can also use the LOAD QUERY command to get this information if the database connection was lost during the load.

TERMINATE
> This specifies to terminate a previously interrupted load and moves the table spaces in which the table resides from load pending state to recovery pending state.

INTO *table-name*
> This specifies the name of a table where data is loaded.

> *insert-column* is the name of a column within the table into which the data is to be inserted.

FOR EXCEPTION *table-name*

This specifies the exception table within the database to which rows in error are copied.

STATISTICS YES
This specifies that statistics will be gathered for the table and for any existing indexes. This option is not supported if you choose the INSERT or RESTART mode. The options are:

WITH DISTRIBUTION	distribution statistics are requested.
AND INDEXES ALL	update statistics for both the table and its indexes.
FOR INDEXES ALL	update statistics for the indexes only.
DETAILED	extended index statistics are requested.

STATISTICS NO
This specifies that no statistics will be gathered, and that the statistics in the catalogs will not be altered.

COPY NO
This specifies that the table space in which the table resides will be placed in backup pending state if forward recovery is enabled (that is, LOGRETAIN or USEREXIT are "ON"). The data will not be accessible until a table space backup or a full database backup is made.

COPY YES
This specifies that a copy of the changes made will be saved. The options are:

USE ADSM   copy will be stored using ADSM.

OPEN *num-sess* SESSIONS
This specifies the number of I/O sessions to be opened with ADSM or the vendor product.

TO *device/directory*

This specifies the name of the device or directory on which the copy image will be created.

LOAD *lib-name*

This specifies the name of the shared library (DLL on OS/2) containing the vendor backup and restore I/O functions to be used. It may contain the full path. If the full path is not given, it will default to the path where the user exit programs reside.

NONRECOVERABLE

This specifies that the load transaction is to be marked as non-recoverable.

USING *directory*

This specifies a directory where temporary files are used when indexes are created. The default is the **sqllib/tmp** directory of the DB2INSTANCE owner's home directory.

HOLD QUIESCE

This specifies that the LOAD must place the table in quiesced exclusive state after the load operation is complete.

WITHOUT PROMPTING

This specifies that the data files, devices, and directories listed are sufficient for the entire load. However, if the input file is not found, the load will fail, and the table will remain in load pending state.

DATA BUFFER *bufsize*

This specifies the number of 4K pages of memory space for data buffers used during the load.

SORT BUFFER *bufsize*

This specifies the number of 4K pages of memory for sorting the index keys.

PARALLELISM *n*

This specifies the degree of parallelism to be used by the load utility, that is, the number of processes or threads that the load utility will spawn to perform the operations that build the object.

● Authorizations

Authority	Privilege
SYSADM or DBADM	None required

▌▌▌ LOAD QUERY

The **LOAD QUERY** command is to check the status of the LOAD command during processing.

UNIX	OS/2	NT
X	X	X

● Syntax

```
LOAD QUERY remote-file
    [TO local-message-file]
```

● Parameters

LOAD QUERY *remote-file*
This specifies the base name that was used when creating temporary files during a load.

TO *local-message-file*
This specifies the destination to which warning and error messages are written during the load.

● Authorizations
None required

▌▌▌ MIGRATE DATABASE

The **MIGRATE DATABASE** command converts a previous version of DB2 database to current formats. The following releases are supported:

- DB2/2 V1.x and DB2/2 V2.X to DB2/2 V 3.0
- DB2/6000 V1.x and DB2/6000 V 2.x to DB2/6000 V 3.0
- DB2/HP V2.x to DB2/HP V 3.0
- DB2/SUN V 2.x to DB2/SUN V 3.0
- DB2/NT V 2.x to DB2/NT V 3.0
- DB2/PEV 1.x to DB2/PEV V 3.0

UNIX	OS/2	NT
X	X	X

- Syntax

```
MIGRATE <DATABASE or DB> database
  [USER userid [USING password]]
```

- Parameters

  DATABASE *database*
  This specifies the alias of the database to be migrated to DB2.

  USER *userid*
  This specifies the User ID authorized to do database migration.

  USING *password*
  This specifies a password associated with userid.

- Authorizations

Authority	Privilege
SYSADM	None required

- Example

  The following command migrates the CLIENTS database.

  ```
  MIGRATE DATABASE CLIENTS
  ```

∎∎∎ PRECOMPILE PROGRAM

The **PRECOMPILE or PREP** command is used to process a program source file that has embedded SQL statements. A modified source file is produced, which contains host language equivalents to the SQL statements. By default, a package is created in the database to which a connection has been established. The name of the package is the same as the filename (minus the extension and folded to uppercase), up to a maximum of 8 characters. This command is only for C, C++, FORTRAN, and COBOL.

Following connection to a database, PREP executes under the transaction that was started. PREP then issues a COMMIT or a ROLLBACK operation to terminate the current transaction and start another one.

During precompilation, an Explain Snapshot is not taken unless a package is created. The snapshot is put into the Explain tables of the user creating the package. Precompiling stops if a fatal error or more than 100 errors occur. If a fatal error does occur, PREP stops precompiling, attempts to close all files, and discards the package.

UNIX	OS/2	NT
X	X	X

- Syntax

```
<PRECOMPILE or PREP> filename
[BINDFILE [USING bind-file]]
[BLOCKING < UNAMBIG or ALL or NO >]
[COLLECTION schema-name]
[CONNECT < 1 or 2 >]
[DATETIME < format >]
[DISCOUNT < EXPLICIT or AUTOMATIC or CONDITIONAL >]
[EXPLSNAP < NO or ALL or YES >]
[FUNCPATH schema-name,...]
[INSERT  < DEF or BUF >]
[ISOLATION < CS or RR or RS or UR >]
[LANGLEVEL <SAA1 or MIA >]
[MESSAGES message-file]
[NOLINEMACRO]
[OPTLEVEL < 0 or 1 >]
[PACKAGE [USING package-name]]
[QUERYOPT optimization-level]
[SQLC < SAA or NONE >]
[SQLERROR < CHECK or NOPACKAGE >]
[SQLFLAG < MVSDB2V23 or MVSDB2V31 or MVSDB2V41 > SYNTAX]
```

```
[SQLRULES < DB2 or STD >]
[SQLWARN < NO or YES >]
[SYNCPOINT < ONEPHASE or NONE or TWOPHASE >]
[SYNTAX]
[TARGET < IBMCOB or MFCOB16 >]
[WCHARTYPE < CONVERT or NOCONVERT >]
```

● Parameters

PREP *filename*
This parameter is used to name the source file to be precompiled.

filename is a source file. Its extension indicates the language of the source program. It can be one of the following:

Extension	Language
.sqc	C programs (generates a .c file)
.sqx	C++ programs (generates a .cxx file)
.sqb	COBOL programs (generates a .cbl file)
.sqf	FORTRAN programs (generates a .for file)

BINDFILE is used to request a bind file. Supplying just this parameter, PRECOMPILE does not create a package unless the package option is also specified.

USING *bind-file*
This parameter is used to provide the name of the bind file that is to be generated by the precompiler. If this parameter is omitted, the precompiler uses the name of the program (entered as the filename parameter), and adds the .bnd extension. If a path is not provided, the bind file is created in the current directory.

bind-file is a file name and its extension must be .bnd.

BLOCKING *blocking*
This option is used to specify the type of record blocking; it tells how to deal with ambiguous cursors.

blocking is one of the following:

- ALL means to block for

  - FETCH-only cursors
  - Cursors not specified as **FOR UPDATE OF**
  - Cursors for which there are no static **DELETE WHERE CURRENT OF** statements
  - Any ambiguous cursors are treated as FETCH-only.

- UNAMBIG means to block for

  - FETCH-only cursors
  - Cursors not specified as **FOR UPDATE OF**
  - Cursors that do not have static **DELETE WHERE CURRENT OF** statements
  - Cursors that do not have dynamic statements
  - Any ambiguous cursors are treated as UPDATE-only.

- NO means not to block any cursors. Any ambiguous cursors are treated as UPDATE-only.

The default is UNAMBIG.

COLLECTION *collection-id*
> This parameters is used to name a collection identification for a package. If omitted, the authorization ID for the user processing the package is used.
>
> *collection-id* is an 8-character collection identifier for the package.

CONNECT <1 or 2>
> This parameter specifies how to process the CONNECT statement.
>
> 1 means to process as type 1 CONNECT.
> 2 means to process as type 2 CONNECT.

DATETIME *format*
> This option is used to specify the date and time formats used when binding a program.
> *format* is a code listed in Figure 10.1.

DISCONNECT <AUTOMATIC or CONDITIONAL or EXPLICIT>
This parameter is used for the three methods of disconnection from a database:

AUTOMATIC means that all database connections are to be disconnected after the COMMIT statement is executed.

CONDITIONAL means that all database connections that have been marked RELEASE or have no open WITH HOLD cursors are disconnected after the COMMIT statement is executed.

EXPLICIT means that only database connections that have been explicitly marked for release by the RELEASE statement are disconnected after the COMMIT statment is executed.

EXPLSNAP <ALL or NO or YES>
This parameter is used to store Explain Snapshot information in the Explain tables.

ALL means that the Explain Snapshot for each eligible static SQL statement must be placed in the Explain tables.
NO means that the Explain Snapshot information will not be captured.
YES means that the Explain Snapshot information for each eligible static SQL statement will be captured and placed in the Explain tables.

FUNCPATH *schema-name*
This parameter is used to supply the function path to be used in resolving user-defined distinct types and functions in static SQL. If this option is omitted, the default function path is "SYSIBM","SYSFUN",USER where USER is the value of the USER special register.

schema-name is an SQL name, either ordinary or delimited, which is a schema that exists at the application server.

INSERT <BUF or DEF>
This parameter is used to specify whether buffers are used to insert data into the database. Buffering increases the performance of the insert operation.

BUF means that the insert operations from an application should be buffered.

DEF means that the insert operations from an application should not be buffered.

ISOLATION *isolation*
This option is used to specify the isolation level. This tells DB2 how to isolate data in the database from other processing which may occur while the application is accessing the database.

isolation is one of the following:

RR — repeatable read
CS — cursor stability
UR — uncommitted read

LANGLEVEL <MIA or SAA1>
This parameter is used to specify termination of strings.

MIA means compatibility with MIA specifications. C null-terminated strings are padded with blank characters.

SAA1 means compatibility with SAA Level 1 Database CPI only. C null-terminated strings are not padded with blank characters.

MESSAGES *msgfile*
This option is used to specify a destination to which warning or error messages are written.

msgfile can be any one of the following:

- A name of a file
- LPT1 for a printer
- CON for the console
- NUL to suppress messages.

NOLINEMACRO is used to tell the precompiler not to generate the #line macros in the output .c file. This option applies to C/C++ programs only.

OPTLEVEL <0 or 1>
This parameter is used to specify whether the precompiler is to optimize the code to initialize internal SQLDAs when host variables are used in SQL statements. Such optimization may improve performance.

0 tells the precompiler not to optimize the SQLDA initialization

1 tells the precompiler to optimize the SQLDA initialization

PACKAGE is used to create a package. If PACKAGE, BINDFILE, or SYNTAX parameters are omitted, the default is to create a package.

USING *package-name*
This parameter is used to provide a package name.

package-name is the name of the package to be generated by the precompiler. If a name is omitted, the name of the application program source file (minus extension and folded to uppercase) is used. Maximum length is 8 characters.

QUERYOPT *optimization-level*
This parameter is used to tell the optimizer the level of optimization to use for all static SQL statements contained in the package.

optimization-level is a number. The default value is 5.

SQLCA <NONE or SAA>
This parameter is used to indicate whether the modified source code is consistent with the SAA definition. This option only applies to FORTRAN programs and is ignored with other languages.

NONE means that the modified source code is not consistent with the SAA definition.

SAA means that the modified source code is consistent with the SAA definition.

SQLERROR <CHECK or NOPACKAGE>
This parameter is used to tell the precompiler whether to create a package or a bind file if an error occurs.

CHECK means that the target system will check the syntax and semantics on the SQL statements being bound. In this case, a package will not be created as part of this process.

NOPACKAGE means that a package or a bind file is not created if an error is is found.

SQLFLAG <MVSDB2V23 or MVSDB2V31 or MVSDB2V41> SYNTAX
The parameter specifies one of three different versions of MVS DB2 SQL language syntax. Any deviation from the specified syntax is reported in the precompiler listing. Local syntax checking can be performed by the precompiler if one of the following options is specified:

- bindfile
- package
- sqlerror check
- syntax

MVSDB2V23 SYNTAX means the SQL statements will be checked against MVS DB2 Version 2.3 SQL language syntax.

MVSDB2V31 SYNTAX means the SQL statements will be checked against MVS DB2 Version 3.1 SQL language syntax.

MVSDB2V41 SYNTAX means the SQL statements will be checked against MVS DB2 Version 4.1 SQL language syntax.

SQLRULES <DB2 or STD>
This parameter is to specify the rules to process type 2 CONNECTs.

DB2 allows the use of the SQL CONNECT statement to switch the current connection to another established (dormant) connection.

STD allows the use of the SQL CONNECT statement to establish a new connection only. The SQL SET CONNECTION statement must be used to switch to a dormant connection.

SQLWARN < NO or YES >
This parameter is used to tell the precompiler whether warnings will be returned from the SQL compiler for any dynamic SQL statements being

compiled (via PREPARE or EXECUTE IMMEDIATE), or described (by the DESCRIBE statement).

NO means warnings will not be returned from the SQL compiler.

YES means warnings will be returned from the SQL compiler.

SYNCPOINT <NONE or ONEPHASE or TWOPHASE>
This parameter is used to specify the processing methods for commits and rollbacks among multiple database connections.

NONE means that the Transaction Manager (TM) is not used to perform a two-phase commit. A COMMIT is fired to each connected database and the application processes the recovery if the commits fail.

ONEPHASE means that the Transaction Manager (TM) is not used to perform a two-phase commit. A one-phase commit is used to commit work by each participating database.

TWOPHASE means that the Transaction Manager (TM) is used to perform a two-phase commit only among databases that have the TM protocol.

SYNTAX tells the precompiler not to create a package or a bind file during precompilation. This option is used to only check the syntax the source file without change existing packages or bind files. Syntax is the same as sqlerror check.

TARGET < IBMCOB or MFCOB16 >
This parameter is to specify the COBOL compiler for which the modified source file is produced. The modified code is tailored according to the target compiler.

IBMCOB means to generate codes for IBM COBOL VisualSet compiler.

MFCOB16 means to generate codes for Micro Focus COBOL compiler. This is the default.

WCHARTYPE < CONVERT or NOCONVERT >

This parameter is used to tell the precompiler whether to convert data to and from the DBCS format for host variables defined as **w_char_t** type.

CONVERT means to convert the input data of the **wchar_t** type host variables to DBCS format using the **wcstombs ()** function. Similarly, the output data is converted with **mbstowcs ()** function before storing it in the host variable.

NOCONVERT means not to convert the data of a **wchar_t** type host variable between the application and the database. The application must ensure that the data in such a variable is in DBCS format. Not needing for conversion may improve efficiency.

- Authorizations

Authority	Privilege
SYSADM or DBADM	BINDADD or BIND

■■■ PRUNE RECOVERY HISTORY FILE

The **PRUNE RECOVERY HISTORY FILE** command is used to delete entries from the recovery history file.

UNIX	OS/2	NT
X	X	X

- Syntax

```
PRUNE HISTORY timestamp
   [WITH FORCE OPTION]
```

- Parameters

PRUNE *timestamp*

This specifies the time range of entries in the recovery history file that will be deleted. A complete timestamp (in the form "yyyymmddhhnnss"), or an initial prefix (at minimum "yyyy") may be specified. All entries with timestamps equal to or less than the timestamp provided are deleted from the recovery history file.

WITH FORCE OPTION
This means that the entries will be deleted according to the timestamp, even if some entries from the most recent restore set are deleted from the file.

- Authorizations

Authority	Privilege
SYSADM or DBADM or SYSCTRL or SYSMAINT	None required

- Example

The following command removes entries for all restores, loads, table space backups, and full database backups taken before and including December 1, 1993 from the recovery history file.

```
DB2 PRUNE HISTORY 199312
```

▊▊▊ QUERY CLIENT

The **QUERY CLIENT** command is used to give the current connection settings for a client application process.

UNIX	OS/2	NT
X	X	X

- Syntax

```
QUERY CLIENT
```

- Parameters

  None Required

- Authorizations

  None required

▐▐▐▐ QUIESCE TABLESPACES FOR TABLE

The **QUIESCE TABLESPACES FOR TABLE** command is used to quiesce table spaces for a table. There are 3 valid quiesce modes: share, intent to update, and exclusive. The result is one of three possible states, which results from the quiesce function: QUIESCED SHARE, QUIESCED UPDATE, and QUIESCED EXCLUSIVE.

UNIX	OS/2	NT
X	X	X

- Syntax

```
QUIESCE TABLESPACES
   FOR TABLE <tablename
             or
            schema.tablename
          >
   [SHARE or INTENT TO UPDATE or EXCLUSIVE or RESET]
```

- Parameters

  FOR TABLE
     This specifies a qualified or non-qualified table name, where *tablename* must be non-qualified and *schema.tablename* is the qualified table name. If a schema is not provided, the authorization ID used in the database connection will be used as the schema.

SHARE
This means that quiesce is in share mode.

INTENT TO UPDATE
This means that quiesce is in intent to update mode.

EXCLUSIVE
This means that quiesce is in exclusive mode.

RESET
This means that the state of the table spaces is reset to normal.

- Authorizations

Authority	Privilege
SYSADM or SYSCTRL or SYSMAINT or RESET	None required

■■■ QUIT

The **QUIT** command exits the command line processor interactive input mode. This command causes CLP to return to the operating system command prompt. If a batch file is used to input the commands to CLP, commands are processed until QUIT, TERMINATE, or the end-of-file is encountered.

UNIX	OS/2	NT
X	X	X

- Syntax

```
QUIT
```

- Parameters

  None required

- Authorizations

  None required

▐▐▐ REBIND

The **REBIND** command is to recreate a package stored in the database without the need for a bind file. This command will not automatically commit the transaction following a successful rebind. You must explicitly commit the transaction. This enables you do the "what if" analysis, in which the user updates certain statistics, and then tries to rebind the package to see what changes. It also permits multiple rebinds within a Unit of Work.

UNIX	OS/2	NT
X	X	X

- Syntax

```
REBIND [PACKAGE] package-name
```

- Parameters

  PACKAGE *package-name*
    This specifies the name of the package to be rebound. The name can be qualified or unqualified. An unqualified package name is implicitly qualified by the current authorization ID.

- Authorizations

Authority	Privilege
SYSADM or DBADM	BIND

■■■ REDISTRIBUTE NODEGROUP

The **REDISTRIBUTE NODEGROUP** command is to redistribute data across the nodes in a node group. You can indicate the current data distribution, whether it is uniform or skewed.

UNIX	OS/2	NT
X		

- Syntax

```
REDISTRIBUTE NODEGROUP nodegroup
          < <UNIFORM      or
             USING DISTFILE   distfile
           > [add-node-clause]   [drop-node-clause]
               or
             USING TARGETMAP targetmap
               or
             CONTINUE
               or
             ROLLBACK
           >
```

add-node-clause:

```
   ADD <NODE or NODES> ( node-number1  [TO node-number2] ),...
```

drop-node-clause]

```
   DROP <NODE or NODES> ( node-number1  [TO node-number2] ),...
```

- Parameters

NODEGROUP *nodegroup*
This specifies the name of the nodegroup described in the SYSNODEGROUPS catalog table.

UNIFORM
This specifies that the data is uniformly distributed across hash partitions (that is, every hash partition is assumed to have the same number of rows), but the same number of hash partitions do not map to each node.

After redistribution, all nodes in the nodegroup have approximately the same number of hash partitions.

USING DISTFILE *distfile*
This specifies that there is a skew in the distribution of partitioning key values. Use this option to achieve a uniform redistribution of data across the nodes of a nodegroup.

ADD NODES (*node-number1* [TO *node-number2*]),...
This specifies the nodes to be added to the nodegroup. The nodes should be defined in the db2nodes.cfg file. Nodes listed must be unique and cannot appear in the DROP clause. For each node, a row is inserted in the SYSNODEGROUPDEF catalog table.

DROP NODE (*node-number1* [TO *node-number2*]),...
This specifies nodes to be deleted from the node group, which must be members of the node group.

USING TARGETMAP *targetmap*
This specifies a file as the target partitioning map. Data redistribution is done according to this file.
CONTINUE
This specifies to continue a previously failed REDISTRIBUTE NODE GROUP command.

ROLLBACK
This specifies a rollback to the previously failed REDISTRIBUTE NODE GROUP command. If none occurred, an error is returned.

● Authorizations

Authority	Privilege
SYSADM or SYSCTRL or SYSMAINT or DBADM	None required

▌▌▌▌ REGISTER

The **REGISTER** command is used to register a DB2 server on the network server. This command adds the DB2 server's network address in a given location on the network server.

UNIX	OS/2	NT
X	X	

- Syntax

```
REGISTER [DB2 SERVER]
      [IN] registry
      USER userid
      [PASSWORD password]
```

- Parameters

    IN *registry*
    This specifies the network server where the DB2 server is registered. In this release, the only supported value is "NWBINDERY" (NetWare bindery).

    USER *userid*
    This specifies the user ID needed to log into the network server. This user must have SUPERVISOR or Workgroup Manager security equivalence.

    PASSWORD *password*
    This specifies a password associated with the user ID.

- Authorizations

    None required

▌▌▌ REORGANIZE TABLE

The **REORG TABLE** command is used to improve the efficiency of a DB2 table. This command reconstructs the rows so that the data is compact and not fragmented.

UNIX	OS/2	NT
X	X	X

● Syntax

```
REORG TABLE table
   [INDEX index-name]
   [USE tablespace-name]
```

● Parameters
   TABLE *table*
   This specifies the name of the table that needs to be reorganized. This table can belong to either a local or a remote database.

   INDEX *index-name*
   This specifies the index that is used by the table to be reorganized.

   USE *tablespace-name*
   This specifies the name of a temporary tablespace where DB2 can temporarily store the table being reconstructed.

● Authorizations

Authority	Privilege
SYSADM or DBADM or SYSCTRL or SYSMAINT	CONTROL

▋▋▋▋ REORGCHK

The REORGCHK command is used to check whether a database needs a reorganization.

UNIX	OS/2	NT
X	X	X

- Syntax

```
REORGCHK
   [UPDATE STATISTICS or
   CURRENT STATISTICS]
   [ON TABLE <USER or
            SYSTEM or
            ALL or
            table-name
         >
```

- Parameters

    UPDATE STATISTICS
    This specifies to issue the **RUNSTATS** command to update the statistical information. The statistic is used to determine whether a **REORG** command must be issued. This is the default.

    CURRENT STATISTICS
    This specifies to use the current statistics to determine whether the tables need to be reorganized.

    ON TABLE <USER or SYSTEM or ALL or *table-name*>
    This specifies one or a group of tables. The options are:

      USER means to check the tables created by the users. This is the default.

      SYSTEM means to check the tables created for system maintenance, such as catalog and tables.

      ALL means to check all tables.

table-name specifies the name of a table to be checked.

● Authorizations

Authority	Privilege
SYSADM or DBADM	CONTROL

● Example

The following command is used to check whether all users of the PRESCRIBER database need reorganization. The output goes to the DBM.RPT.

```
DBM -R REORGCHK PRESCRIBER
```

In the next command, the output information is written to the REORGPRES.RPT file.

```
DB2 -r REORGPRES.RPT REORGCHK PRESCRIBER
```

▮▮▮ RESET ADMIN CONFIGURATION

The **RESET ADMIN CONFIGURATION** command resets the parameters in the database manager configuration file that apply to the administration server to the system default values. These values are by node type, which is always a server with remote clients. The parameters are:

● AGENT_STATCK_SZ
● AUTHENTICATION
● DFT_ACCOUNT_STR
● DIAGLEVEL
● FILESERVER
● IPX_SOCKET
● NNAME
● NPIPE (NT only)
● OBJECT NAME
● QUERY_HEAP_SZ

- SVCENAME
- SYSADM_GROUP
- TPNAME
- TRUST_ALLCLNTS
- TRUST_CLNTAUTH

UNIX	OS/2	NT
X	X	X

- Syntax

```
RESET <CONFIGURATION   or
        CONFIG         or
        CFG
     >
```

- Parameters

  None required

- Authorizations

Authority	Privilege
SYSADM	None required

■■■ RESET DATABASE CONFIGURATION

The **RESET DATABASE MANAGER CONFIGURATION** command is issued to set the parameters in the configuration file to default values used when the system was configured.

UNIX	OS/2	NT
X	X	X

● Syntax

```
RESET <DATABASE   or DB>
        <CONFIGURATION   or
         CONFIG          or
         CFG
        >
     FOR database
```

● Parameters

FOR *database*
This specifies the alias of the database for which the configuration parameters are reset.

● Authorizations

Authority	Privilege
SYSADM	None required

▮▮▮ RESET DATABASE MANAGER CONFIGURATION

The **RESET DATABASE MANAGER CONFIGURATION** command is used to set the parameters in the DB2 configuration to the defaults values shipped with the product. The parameters are:

COMHEAPSZ	Size of the communications heap
NUMRC	Maximum number of remote connections active at one time to or from this workstation
SHEAPTHRES	Amount of memory available for sorts, in 4k-byte pages
INDEXREC	Invalid indexes will be created and will be either ACCESS or RESTART
RQRIOBLK	Storage allocated from communication heap to the I/O block on the database client, in number of segments
RSHEAPSZ	The size of the remote data services heap, in segments
SQLENSEG	Maximum amount of shared storage, in segments
SVRIOBLK	Amount of storage allocated from the communication heap to the I/O block on the database server, in kilobyte segments

NNAME   The workstation name

UNIX	OS/2	NT
X	X	X

- Syntax

```
RESET  <DATABASE MANAGER   or
        DB MANAGER        or
        DBM
        >
       <CONFIGURATION    or
        CONFIG           or
        CFG
        >
```

- Authorizations

Authority	Privilege
SYSADM	None required

▐▐▐▐ RESET MONITOR

The **RESET MONITOR** command is used to reset the internal Database System Monitor data areas of active database(s) to zero. These data areas include all applications connected to the database, as well as the database itself.

UNIX	OS/2	NT
X	X	X

- Syntax

```
RESET MONITOR <ALL
              or
              FOR <DATABASE or DB> database-alias
              >
```

● Parameters

ALL
This specifies that the internal counters for all databases be reset.

FOR DATABASE
This specifies the alias of a database for which to reset internal counters.

● Authorizations

Authority	Privilege
SYSADM or SYSCTRL or SYSMAINT	None required

▮▮▮ RESTART DATABASE

The **RESTART DATABASE** command is used to restart a database that is in an uncommitted state. After you issue this command, a reconnect to the database is necessary.

UNIX	OS/2	NT
X	X	X

● Syntax

```
RESTART <DATABASE or DB> database
    [USER username
    [USING password]
```

● Parameters

DATABASE *database*
This specifies an alias of the database to be restarted.

USER *username*

This specifies the username that is allowed to restart the database.

USING *password*
This specifies a password associated with userid.

● Authorizations

None required

■■■ RESTORE DATABASE

The **RESTORE DATABASE** command is used to rebuild a database from a copy previously created by the **BACKUP DATABASE** command. This operation is needed if a local database is corrupted or damaged; the restored database is in the same state as when the previous backup was done.

UNIX	OS/2	NT
X	X	X

● Syntax

```
RESTORE <DATABASE or DB> source-database-alias
   < restore-options or CONTINUE or ABORT >

restore-options:

   [USER username [USING password]]
   [ TABLESPACE ONLINE   or
     < TABLESPACE tablespace-name >, [ONLINE]   or
     HISTORY FILE        or
     ONLINE
   ]
   [USE ADSM [OPEN num-sessions SESSIONS]    or
    FROM <directory or device>               or
    LOAD shared-library  [OPEN num-sessions SESSIONS]
   ]
   [ TAKEN AT date-time ]
   [ TO target-directory ]
   [ INTO target-database-alias ]
   [ WITH num-buffers BUFFERS ]
   [ BUFFER buffer-size ]
   [ REPLACE EXISTING ]
```

```
[ REDIRECT ]
[ WITHOUT ROLLING FORWARD]
[ PARALLELISM n ]
[ WITHOUT PROMPTING ]
```

● Parameters

DATABASE *source-database-alias*
This specifies the alias of the source database from which the database was taken.

CONTINUE
This indicates that the containers have been redefined, and that the final step in the redirected restore should be performed.

ABORT
This specifies to stop the redirected restore. Useful when an error has occurred that would require one or more steps to be repeated. After RESTORE DATABASE with the ABORT option has been issued, each step of a redirected restore must be repeated, including RESTORE DATABASE with the REDIRECT option.

USER *username*
This specifies the user ID under which the database is to be restored.

USING *password*
This specifies a password for the user ID.

TABLESPACE *tablespace-name*
This specifies a list of names used to specify the table spaces that are to be restored.

ONLINE
This specifies to allow a backup to be restored online and is only applicable when restoring from a table space level backup. It also means that other agents can connect while the backup is being restored.

HISTORY FILE
This specifies to restore the history file from the backup only.

USE ADSM
This indicates that the database is to be restored from ADSM-managed output.

OPEN *num-sessions* SESSIONS
This specifies the number of I/O sessions to be used with ADSM or the vendor product.

FROM *directory* or *device*
This specifies the directory or device on which the backup images reside.

LOAD *shared-library*
This specifies the name of the shared library (DLL on OS/2) containing the vendor backup and restore I/O functions to be used. It may contain the full path. If the full path is not given, it will default to the path where the user exit programs reside.

TAKEN AT *date-time*
This specifies the time stamp of the database backup. The backup image filename includes the timestamp.

TO *target-directory*
This specifies the directory of the target database. This parameter is ignored if the utility is restoring to an existing database.

INTO *target-database-alias*
This specifies the alias of the target database. If the target database does not exist, it will be created.

WITH *num-buffers* BUFFERS
This specifies the number of buffers to be used.

BUFFER *buffer-size*
This specifies the size, in pages, of the buffer used for the restore. The minimum value for this parameter is 16 pages; the default value is 1024 pages.

REPLACE EXISTING

This specifies that if a database with the same alias as the target database alias already exists, this parameter tells the restore utility to replace the existing database with the restored database.

REDIRECT

This specifies a redirected restore. To complete a redirected restore, this command should be followed by one or more SET TABLESPACE CONTAINERS commands, and then by a RESTORE DATABASE command with the CONTINUE option.

WITHOUT ROLLING FORWARD

This specifies not to place the database in roll-forward pending state after it has been successfully restored.

PARALLELISM *n*

This specifies the number of buffer manipulators to be spawned during the restore process. The default value is 1.

WITHOUT PROMPTING

This specifies that the restore will run unattended, and that any actions which normally require user intervention will instead return an error message.

- Authorizations

Authority	Privilege
SYSADM or SYSCTRL or SYSMAINT	None required

▌▌▌▌ ROLLFORWARD DATABASE

The **ROLLFORWARD DATABASE** command is used after a database is restored. After a successful restoration, the database is in the roll-forward pending state. This command recovers a database from its last backup state. As well, all the transactions processed since the backup are reapplied.

UNIX	OS/2	NT
X	X	X

● Syntax

```
ROLLFORWARD <DATABASE or DB> database
   [USER username [USING password]]
   [TO < <isotime or END OF LOGS> [AND CONTINUE or AND STOP]
                 or
           COMPLETE   or
           CANCEL     or
           STOP       or
           QUERY STATUS [ on-node-clause ]
        >
   ]
   [ TABLESPACE < ONLINE or
                   tablespace-name,... [ONLINE]
                  >
   ]
   [OVERFLOW LOG PATH (log-directory,log-over-flow-clause)]

log-over-flow-clause:

   < log-directory ON NODE node-number >,...

on-node-clause:

   ON < node-list-clause  or
       ALL NODES [EXCEPT node-list-clause]
      >

node-list-clause:

   <NODE or NODES> ( node-number1 [TO node-number2] )
```

● Parameters

DATABASE *database*
   This specifies the alias of the database to roll forward.

USER *username*
   This specifies the user ID under which the database is rolled forward.

USING *password*
   This specifies a password for the user ID.

TO
    This specifies how to roll forward.

isotime
    This specifies the point to which all committed transactions are to be
    rolled forward. The format of this parameter is the timestamp (yyyy-
    mmm-ddd.hh.mm.ss.nnnnnn).

END OF LOGS
    This means to apply all committed transactions from all online archive
    log files. These files are listed in the logpath directory.

ALL NODES
    This specifies that transactions are to be rolled forward on all nodes
    specified in the **db2nodes.cfg** file.

EXCEPT
    This specifies that transactions are to be rolled forward on all nodes
    specified in the **db2nodes.cfg** file, except those specified in the node
    list.

ON NODE or ON NODES
    This indicates to recover the database on a set of nodes.

node-number1
    This specifies a node number in the node list.

node-number2
    This specifies the second node number, so that all nodes from
    node-number1 up to and including *node-number2* are included in the
    node list.

AND COMPLETE or AND STOP
    This specifies to complete the roll-forward recovery process by rolling
    back any incomplete transactions and turning off the roll-forward
    pending state of the database.

COMPLETE STOP
: This specifies not to roll forward any more log records, and completes the roll-forward recovery process by rolling back any incomplete transactions and allowing access to the database once again.

CANCEL
: This cancels the roll-forward recovery process. This leaves the database or tablespace(s) on all nodes on which forward recovery has been started in the restore-pending state.

QUERY STATUS
: This obtains the following information about the roll-forward state:
  - Next archive log file
  - Log files processed
  - Last committed transactions

TABLESPACE *tablespace-name*
This specifies the table space level roll-forward.

ONLINE
This allows the table space level roll-forward recovery to be done online. This means that other agents are allowed to connect while roll-forward recovery is in progress.

OVERFLOW LOG PATH (*log-directory*)
This specifies an alternate log path to be searched for archived logs during recovery. In a multi-node environment, this is the default overflow log path for all nodes.

log-directory ON NODE
: In a multi-node environment, allows a different log path to override the default overflow log path for a specific node.

- Authorizations

Authority	Privilege
SYSADM or SYSCTRL or SYSMAINT	None required

▉▉▉ RUN STATISTICS

The **RUNSTATS** command is used to update statistical information on tables and indexes. The affected statistics are:

- Number of records
- Number of pages
- Average record length

This information is used by DB2 to determine the optimal access path to the database.

UNIX	OS/2	NT
X	X	X

- Syntax

```
RUNSTATS ON TABLE table-name
  [WITH DISTRIBUTION
  [AND [DETAILED] < INDEXES ALL or
        INDEX   index-name >
      ]
  ]
  [ <AND or FOR> [DETAILED]
    < INDEXES ALL   or
      INDEX   index-name
    >
  ]
  [SHRLEVEL <REFERENCE or CHANGE>]
```

- Parameters

TABLE *table-name*
This specifies a table on which to update statistics.

WITH DISTRIBUTION
This specifies that distribution statistics are requested. The number of most frequent values collected is defined by the num_freqvalues database configuration parameter. The number of quantiles collected is defined by the num_quantiles database configuration parameter.

AND INDEXES ALL
This updates statistics on both the table and its indexes.

AND INDEX *index-name*
This updates statistics on both the table and the specified index.

FOR INDEXES ALL
This updates statistics on the indexes only. If statistics on the table have never been generated, the database manager calculates statistics on the table as well as on the indexes.

FOR INDEX *index-name*
This updates statistics on the specified index only. If table statistics have never been generated, the database manager calculates statistics on the table as well as on the index.

DETAILED
This calculates extended index statistics.

SHRLEVEL
This specifies the share level of objects while statistics are collected.

CHANGE
This means that other users can read from and write to the table while statistics are calculated.

REFERENCE
This means that other users can have read-only access to the table while statistics are calculated.

● Authorizations

Authority	Privilege
SYSADM or DBADM or SYSCTRL or SYSMAINT	CONTROL

▐▐▐▐ SET CLIENT

The **SET CLIENT** command is used to change the connection settings for a client application process.

UNIX	OS/2	NT
X	X	X

● Syntax

```
SET CLIENT
   [CONNECT <1 or 2>]
   [DISCONNECT
    <EXPLICIT or CONDITIONAL or AUTOMATIC>
   ]
   [MAX_NETBIOS_CONNECTIONS value]
   [SQLRULES <DB2 or STD>]
   [SYNCPOINT <ONEPHASE or TWOPHASE or NONE>]
```

● Parameters

CONNECT
    This specifies the connection type: 1 or 2.
    1 means that a CONNECT command is processed as a type 1
    CONNECT.

    2 means that a CONNECT command is processed as a type 2
    CONNECT.

SQLRULES
    This sets the rules: DB2 or STD.

    DB2 means that the type 2 CONNECT is processed according to the DB2
    rules.

    STD means that the type 2 CONNECT is processed according to the
    Standard (STD) rules.

DISCONNECT <EXPLICIT or CONDITIONAL or AUTOMATIC>

This sets the mode when a disconnect happens. They are: EXPLICIT, CONDITIONAL, and AUTOMATIC.

EXPLICIT means that only database connections that have been explicitly marked for release by the RELEASE statement are disconnected at commit.

CONDITIONAL means that the database connections that have been marked RELEASE or have no open WITH HOLD cursors are disconnected at commit.

AUTOMATIC means that all database connections are disconnected at commit.

SYNCPOINT <ONEPHASE or TWOPHASE or NONE>
This indicates how to commit or rollback changes among multiple database connections.

ONEPHASE means that no Transaction Manager (TM) is used to perform a two-phase commit. A one-phase commit is used to commit the work done by each database in multiple database transactions.

TWOPHASE means that the TM is required to coordinate two-phase commits among those databases that support this protocol.
NONE means that no TM is used to perform a two-phase commit, and or to enforce single updater, multiple reader. A COMMIT is sent to each participating database. The application is responsible for recovery if any of the commits fail.

MAX_NETBIOS_CONNECTIONS *value*
This specifies the maximum number of concurrent connections that can be made using a NetBios adapter in an application. Maximum value is 254. This parameter must be set before the first NetBios connection is made. Changes subsequent to the first connection are ignored.

• Authorizations

None required

■■■ SET RUN TIME DEGREE

The **SET RUNTIME DEGREE** command sets the maximum runtime degree of parallelism for SQL statements for specified active applications.

UNIX	OS/2	NT
X	X	X

- Syntax

```
SET RUNTIME DEGREE FOR
        < ALL  or ( agent-id,...)>
        [TO degree]
```

- Parameters

    FOR < ALL or (*agent-id,...*)
        This specifies how to apply the degree of parallelism.

        ALL means to apply to all applications.

        agent-id
            This specifies the agent to which the new degree applies. A list of values is obtained using LIST APPLICATIONS.

    TO *degree*
        This specifies the maximum runtime degree of parallelism.

- Authorizations

Authority	Privilege
SYSADM or SYSCTRL	CONTROL

■■■ SET TABLESPACE CONTAINERS

The **SET TABLESPACE CONTAINERS** command is to add, change, or remove table containers for a database that is to be restored.

UNIX	OS/2	NT
X	X	X

● Syntax

```
SET TABLESPACE CONTAINERS tablespace-id
  [ <REPLAY or IGNORE>
    ROLLFORWARD CONTAINER OPERATIONS
  ]
  USING < ( <PATH "container-string">,... )
          or
          ( < <FILE or DEVICE>
              "container-string"
              number-of-pages >,... )
        >
```

● Parameters

FOR *tablespace-id*
This specifies an integer that uniquely represents the tablespace used by the database being restored.

REPLAY ROLLFORWARD CONTAINER OPERATIONS
This specifies that any ALTER TABLESPACE operation issued against this table space since the database was backed up is to be redone during a subsequent roll forward of the database.

IGNORE ROLLFORWARD CONTAINER OPERATIONS
This specifies that ALTER TABLESPACE operations in the log are to be ignored when performing a roll forward.

USING PATH *"container-string"*
For an SMS table space, this identifies one or more containers that will belong to the table space and into which the table space data will be stored. It is an absolute or relative directory name. If the directory name

is not absolute, it is relative to the database directory. The string canno t exceed 240 bytes in length.

USING FILE/DEVICE *"container-string" number-of-pages*
For a DMS table space, this identifies one or more containers that will belong to the table space and into which the table space data will be stored. The container type (either FILE or DEVICE) and its size (in 4K pages) are specified. A mixture of file and device containers can be specified. The string cannot exceed 254 bytes in length.

For a file container, the string must be an absolute or relative file name. If the file name is not absolute, it is relative to the database directory.

For a device container, the string must be a device name. The device must already exist. Device containers are not supported on OS/2.

- Authorizations

Authority	Privilege
SYSADM or DBADM or SYSCTRL or SYSMAINT	CONTROL

■■■■ START DATABASE MANAGER

The **START DATABASE MANAGER** or **DB2START** command starts the DB2 and allocates the necessary resources. You have to issue this command before you can connect to a database, precompile a program, or bind a package to a table or database.

UNIX	OS/2	NT
X	X	X

● Syntax

```
<START <DATABASE MANAGER    or
          DB MANAGER          or
          DBM
          >
          or
          DB2START
  >
      [PROFILE profile]
      [NODENUM nodenum   start-options]
```

```
start-options:

      [ ADDNODE add-node-options   or
      RESTART restart-options     or
      STANDALONE
      ]
```

```
add-node-options:

      [HOSTNAME hostname PORT logical-port [NETNAME netname ]]
```

```
restart-options:

      [HOSTNAME hostname]
      [PORT logical-port]
      [NETNAME netname]
```

● Parameters

PROFILE *profile*
This specifies the name of the profile file to be executed at each node to define the DB2 environment variables. This file is executed before the nodes are started. If this parameter is not specified, the file **db2profile** is executed.

NODENUM *nodenum*
This specifies the node number to be started. If no other options are specified, a normal startup is done at this node.

ADDNODE
This specifies that the new node is added to the **db2nodes.cfg** file of the instance owner with the *hostname* and *logical-port* values. You must ensure that the combination of *hostname* and *logical-port* is unique. With ADDNODE, the following is specified:

HOSTNAME *hostname*
This specifies the host name to be added to the **db2nodes.cfg** file.

PORT *logical-port*
This specifies, with the ADDMODE parameter, the logical port to be added to the **db2nodes.cfg** file. Valid values are from 0 to 999.

NETNAME *netname*
This specifies the network name to be added to the **db2nodes.cfg** file. If not specified, this parameter defaults to the value specified for hostname.

RESTART
This starts the database manager after a failure. Other nodes are still operating, and this node attempts to connect to the others. If neither the host name nor the logical port parameters are specified, the database manager is restarted using the host name and logical port values specified in **db2nodes.cfg**. If either parameter is specified, the new values are sent to the other nodes when a connection is established. The node configuration file is updated with this information. The following can be specified:

HOSTNAME *hostname*
This specifies the host name to be used to override that in the node configuration file.

PORT *logical-port*
This specifies the logical port number to be used to override that in the node configuration file. If not specified, this parameter defaults to the logical port value that corresponds to the node number in the **db2nodes.cfg** file. Valid values are from 0 to 999.

NETNAME *netname*
This specifies the network name to override that specified in the **db2nodes.cfg** file. If not specified, this parameter defaults to the netname value that corresponds to the node number in the **db2nodes.cfg** file.

STANDALONE

This specifies that the node is to be started in stand-alone mode. FCM does not attempt to establish a connection to any other node. This option is used when adding a node.

● Authorizations

Authority	Privilege
SYSADM or SYSCTRL or SYSMAINT	None required

▮▮▮ STOP DATABASE MANAGER

The **STOP DATABASE MANAGER** or **DB2STOP** stops DB2 on a workstation. It also releases all the resources needed by DB2. DB2 cannot be stopped if there is any application program connected to the databases of your workstation.

UNIX	OS/2	NT
X	X	X

● Syntax

```
< STOP <DATABASE MANAGER   or
       DB MANAGER          or
       DBM
    >
      or
   DB2STOP
>
   [PROFILE profile]
   [NODENUM nodenum   or
    DROP NODENUM nodenum   or
    FORCE
    ]
```

● Parameters

PROFILE *profile*
This specifies the name of the profile file which was executed with the DB2START command.

NODENUM *nodenum*
This specifies the node to be stopped. Valid values are from 0 to 999 inclusive, and must be in the **db2nodes.cfg** file. If no node number is specified, all nodes defined in the node configuration file are stopped.

DROP NODENUM *nodenum*
This specifies to drop the node specified by NODENUM from the **db2nodes.cfg** file.

FORCE
This specifies to use the FORCE ALL command when stopping the database manager at each node.

● Authorizations

Authority	Privilege
SYSADM or SYSCTRL or SYSMAINT	None required

▮▮▮ TERMINATE

The **TERMINATE** command explicitly terminates the command line processor's back-end process.

UNIX	OS/2	NT
X	X	X

● Syntax

```
TERMINATE
```

- Parameters

  None required

- Authorizations

  None required

▮▮▮▮ UNCATALOG DATABASE

The **UNCATALOG DATABASE** command deletes an entry from the database directory. This entry, previously entered using the **CATALOG DATABASE** command, is either an indirect or remote database.

UNIX	OS/2	NT
X	X	X

- Syntax

```
UNCATALOG <DATABASE or DB> database
```

- Authorizations

Authority	Privilege
SYSADM	None required

- Parameters

  DATABASE *database*
  This specifies an alias of the database to be uncataloged.

▌▌▌▌ UNCATALOG DCS DATABASE

The **UNCATALOG DCS DATABASE** command is used to delete an entry from the Database Connection Services (DCS) directory. This entry, previously entered using the **CATALOG DCS DATABASE** command, is about a host database that a workstation can access using the DDCS/2 software.

UNIX	OS/2	NT
X	X	X

- Syntax

```
UNCATALOG DCS <DATABASE or DB> database
```

- Parameters

  DATABASE *database*
      This specifies an alias of the database to be uncataloged.

- Authorizations

Authority	Privilege
None required	None required

▌▌▌▌ UNCATALOG NODE

The **UNCATALOG NODE** command is used to delete an entry from the node directory. This entry was previously added to the directory by the following commands:

- CATALOG NODE or CATALOG APPC NODE
- CATALOG APPN NODE
- CATALOG NetBios NODE

UNIX	OS/2	NT
X	X	X

- Syntax

  UNCATALOG NODE *nodename*

- Parameters

  NODE *nodename*
  This specifies the entry being uncataloged.

- Authorizations

Authority	Privilege
SYSADM	None required

▐▐▐▐ UPDATE ADMIN CONFIGURATION

The **UPDATE ADMIN CONFIGURATION** command updates the parameters in the database manager configuration file that apply to the administration server to the system default values. These values are by node type, which is always a server with remote clients. The parameters are:

- AGENT_STATCK_SZ
- AUTHENTICATION
- DFT_ACCOUNT_STR
- DIAGLEVEL
- FILESERVER
- IPX_SOCKET
- NNAME
- NPIPE (NT only)
- OBJECT NAME
- QUERY_HEAP_SZ
- SVCENAME

- SYSADM_GROUP
- TPNAME
- TRUST_ALLCLNTS
- TRUST_CLNTAUTH

UNIX	OS/2	NT
X	X	X

- Syntax

```
UPDATE ADMIN <CONFIGURATION  or
          CONFIG          or
          CFG
        >
        USING config-keyword value
```

- Parameters

USING *config-keyword value*
This specifies the admin configuration parameter to be updated.

- Authorizations

Authority	Privilege
SYSADM	None required

▐▌▐▌ UPDATE COMMAND OPTIONS

The **UPDATE COMMAND OPTIONS** command sets one or more command options during an interactive session. You can also use this command from a batch input file. After the interactive session or the batch file processing is over, the settings revert to the setting before this command is executed.

UNIX	OS/2	NT
X	X	X

- Syntax

```
UPDATE COMMAND OPTIONS USING
   <option  <ON value or OFF>>...
```

- Parameters

  USING *option* <*option* <ON *value* or OFF>>
  This specifies the following option letters:

  a Display SQLCA.
  c Auto-commit SQL statements.
  e Display SQLCODE/SQLSTATE.
  l Log commands in a history file.
  o Display to standard output.
  p Display DB2 interactive prompt.
  r Save output report to a file.
  s Stop execution on command error.
  v Echo current command.
  w Show SQL statement warning messages.
  z Redirect all output to a file.

  ON *value*
  This specifies the required values for some options. For example, for the e option, the value can be c to display the SQLCODE, or s to display the SQLSTATE. For the l, r, and z options, the value represents the name to be used for the history or report file.

  OFF means to turn an option off.

- Authorizations

  None required

■■■■ UPDATE DATABASE CONFIGURATION

The **UPDATE DATABASE CONFIGURATION** command is used to change parameters in the configuration file of a database.

UNIX	OS/2	NT
X	X	X

- Syntax

```
UPDATE DATABASE CONFIGURATION FOR database
    USING <configuration-keyword value>...
```

- Authorizations

Authority	Privilege
SYSADM o SYSCTRL or SYSMAINT	None required

- Parameters

FOR *database*
   This specifies the alias of a database for which the configuration is to be updated.

USING *configuration-keyword*
   This specifies the parameter name for which a *value* is also entered. You can enter one or many pairs of configuration keywords and their associated values. The keywords are:

Keywords	Description
AGENTHEAP	Application agent heap
APPLHEAPSZ	Default application heap
BUFFPAGE	Buffer pool
DBHEAP	Database heap
DBATTR	Database attribute
INDEXREC	When to re-create invalid indexes; possible values are SYSTEM, ACCESS, or RESTART
DLCHKTIME	Time interval
LOCKLIST	Storage for lock list
LOGFILSIZ	Storage for log files

LOGPRIMARY	Number of primary log files
LOGSECOND	Number of secondary log files
MAXAPPLS	Maximum number of application programs connected
MAXFILOP	Maximum number of database files that an application program can have open
MAXLOCKS	Percentage of lock lists a program can use
MAXTOTFILOP	Number of users or database files opened by an application program
NEWLOGPATH	Alternate path to the recovery log files

■■■ UPDATE DATABASE MANAGER CONFIGURATION

The **UPDATE DATABASE MANAGER CONFIGURATION** command is
used to change parameters in the configuration file of DB2.

UNIX	OS/2	NT
X	X	X

- Syntax

```
UPDATE < DATABASE MANAGER or
         DB MANAGER        or
         DBM
     >
     <CONFIGURATION  or
      CONFIG          or
      CFG
     >
     USING <configuration-keyword value>...
```

- Authorizations

Authority	Privilege
SYSADM	None required

- Parameters

  USING *configuration-keyword*
  This specifies the parameter name for which a *value* is also entered. You can enter one or many pairs of configuration keywords and associated values. The keywords are:

Keywords	Description
COMHEAPSZ	Size of the communications heap
NUMRC	Maximum number of remote connections active at one time to or from this workstation
SHEAPTHRES	Amount of memory available for sorts, in 4k-byte pages
INDEXREC	Invalid indexes will be created and will be either ACCESS or RESTART
RQRIOBLK	Storage allocated from communication heap to the I/O block on the database client, in number of segments
RSHEAPSZ	The size of the Remote Data Services heap, in segments
SQLENSEG	Maximum amount of shared storage, in segments
SVRIOBLK	Amount of storage allocated from the communication heap to the I/O block on the database server, in kilobyte segments
NNAME	The workstation name

■■■ UPDATE MONITOR SWITCHES

The **UPDATE MONITOR SWITCHES** command is used to turn one or more database monitor recording switches ON or OFF. When the database manager starts, the settings of the six switches are determined by the database manager configuration parameter *dft_monswitches*.

UNIX	OS/2	NT
X	X	X

- Syntax

```
UPDATE MONITOR SWITCHES
    USING <switch-name <ON or OFF>>...
```

- Parameters

    USING *switch-name*
    This specifies a switch name from the following list:

Name	Description
SORT	Sorting information
LOCK	Lock information
TABLE	Table activity information
BUFFERPOOL	Buffer Pool activity information
UOW	Unit of Work information
STATEMENT SQL	Statement information.

- Authorizations

Authority	Privilege
SYSADM or SYSCTRL or SYSMAINT	None required

▓▓▓ UPDATE RECOVERY HISTORY FILE

The **UPDATE RECOVERY HISTORY FILE** command is used to update the location, device type, or comment for a recovery history file entry.

UNIX	OS/2	NT
X	X	X

● Syntax

```
UPDATE HISTORY
   FOR object-part WITH
   <LOCATION new-location DEVICE TYPE new-device-type
       or
    COMMENT new-comment
   >
```

● Parameters

FOR *object-part*

This specifies the backup or copy image. It is a timestamp with a sequence number from 001 to 999.

LOCATION *new-location*

This specifies the new physical location of a backup. The interpretation of this parameter depends on the device type.

DEVICE TYPE *new-device-type*

This specifies a new device type for storing the backup. The valid types are:

Type	Device
D	Disk
K	Diskette
T	Tape
A	ADSM
U	User exit

COMMENT *new-comment*

This specifies a new comment to describe the entry.

● Authorizations

Authority	Privilege
SYSADM or	None required

DBADM
or
SYSCTRL
or
SYSMAINT

Appdendix A
SQL Communication Area

The **SQLCA**, the SQL communication area, is the memory area that interfaces between your program and DB2. A program that executes an SQL statement (except **DECLARE**, **INCLUDE**, and **WHENEVER**) must include this structure, which is supplied with the precompiler of the language (C, C++, REXX, or COBOL); for example,

```
EXEC SQL INCLUDE SQLCA;
```

                    or

```
EXEC SQL INCLUDE SQLCA END-EXEC
```

The following lists the name of the fields of **SQLCA**, the data type, and a brief description of the data in each field.

Field type	Data type	Description
sqlcaid	CHAR(8)	Contains identifier '**SQLCA**'.
sqlcabc	INTEGER	The length of the **SQLCA** structure.
sqlcode	INTEGER	The return code after executing an SQL statement. If it is zero, the execution is successful. If the return code is a positive value, the statement was executed successfully, but with a warning condition. If it is a negative value, the execution resulted in an error condition.

Field type	Data type	Description
sqlerrml	SMALLINT	The length of sqlerrmc which is in the range 0 to 70.
sqlerrmc	VARCHAR(70)	This field must contain one or more tokens, separated by a hexadecimal value 'FF'. Each token is substituted by variables in the descriptions of error conditions.
sqlerrp	CHAR(8)	The first three characters of this field is 'SQL', followed by the name of the module that returned an error code, if any.
sqlerrd	Array	The array contains six INTEGER elements:
	SQLERRD(1)	Reserved for internal use
	SQLERRD(2)	Reserved for internal use
	SQLERRD(3)	The number of rows affacted by INSERT, UPDATE and DELETE statements
	SQLERRD(4)	Reserved for future use
	SQLERRD(5)	The number of rows updated or deleted
	SQLERRD(6)	Reserved for future use
sqlwarn	Array	It is an array of CHAR(1), each containing a W if there is a warning return code; otherwise it is a blank.
	sqlwarn0	Contains a blank if all other elements of this array contain blanks
	sqlwarn1	Contains W if a truncation occurred when assigning value of a column to a host variable.
	sqlwarn2	Contains W if null values were not given on the argument of a function
	sqlwarn3	Contains W if the number of columns is not the same as the number of host variables
	sqlwarn4	Contains W if a prepared UPDATE or DELETE statement does not have a WHERE clause
	sqlwarn5	Reserved for future use
	sqlwarn6	Contains W if the result of a date calculation was changed to avoid an impossible date
sqlstate	CHAR(5)	The return code of the most recently executed SQL statement.

Appendix B
SQL Descriptor Area

The **SQLDA**, the SQL descriptor area, is required when executing the **SQL DESCRIBE** statement. The **SQLDA** contains variables that are used when executing the **PREPARE, OPEN, FETCH,** and **EXECUTE** statements. If SQLDA is used with a **PREPARE** or **DESCRIBE** statement, then it provides information to your program about a prepared statement. And, if it is used with an **OPEN, EXECUTE,** or **FETCH** statement, it describes the host variables.

Fields	Data Type	Used in PREPARE or DESCRIBE	Used in FETCH, OPEN, or EXECUTE
sqlaid	CHAR(8)	Contains `SQLDA'	Not used
sqldabc	INTEGER		Length of SQLDA
sqln	SMALLINT	Length of SQLDA	Number of occurrences of SQLVAR
sqld	SMALLINT	Number of occurrences of SQLVAR	Number of host variables in SQLVAR

Figure B.1 Description of **SQLDA**.

In a program if a **SQLDA**, which has four variables, is followed by an arbitrary number of occurrences of a five-variable sequence, then collectively this arrangement is called **SQLVAR**. In an **OPEN, FETCH,** or **EXECUTE** statement, each occurrence of **SQLVAR** describes a host variable. However, in the **DESCRIBE** or **PREPARE** statement, each occurrence of **SQLVAR** is for a column of a result table. Figures B.1 and B.2 describe the fields of **SQLDA** and **SQLVAR**.

Fields	Data Type	Used in PREPARE or DESCRIBE	Used in FETCH, OPEN, or EXECUTE
sqltype	SMALLINT	The data type of column	The data type for host variable
sqldlen	SMALLINT	Defines the external length of a value	Defines the external length of a value
sqldata	pointer	0 if the FOR BIT DATA option is used, and if the data type of the of the column is CHAR, VARCHAR, or VARCHAR	The address of the host variable
sqllnd	pointer	0 if the FOR BIT DATA option is used, and if the data type of the of the column is CHAR, VARCHAR, or VARCHAR	The address of an associated indicator variable
sqlname	VARCHAR (30)	Name of the column	Not used

Figure B.2 Description of **SQLVAR**.

Index